THE ELEMENTARY SCHOOL

A Perspective

THE ELEMENTARY SCHOOL

A Perspective

WILLIAM C. WOLF, JR.

Associate Professor and Coordinator of Educational Research
University of Massachusetts

BRADLEY M. LOOMER

Principal, University Elementary School
State University of Iowa

RAND McNALLY & COMPANY • CHICAGO

RAND McNALLY EDUCATION SERIES
B. OTHANEL SMITH, *Advisory Editor*

Broudy and Palmer, *Exemplars of Teaching Method*
Broudy, Smith, and Burnett, *Democracy and Excellence in American Secondary Education*
Burns and Lowe, *The Language Arts in Childhood Education*
Dupuis, *Philosophy of Education in Historical Perspective*
Farwell and Peters, eds., *Guidance Readings for Counselors*
Foshay, ed., *The Rand McNally Handbook of Education*
Haines, *Guiding the Student Teaching Process in Elementary Education*
Kaplan and Steiner, *Musicianship for the Classroom Teacher*
Kimbrough, *Political Power and Educational Decision-Making*
Krumboltz, ed., *Learning and the Educational Process*
Lewenstein, *Teaching Social Studies in Junior and Senior High Schools*
Litwack, Holmes, and O'Hern, *Critical Issues in Student Personnel Work*
Michaelis, *Teaching Units in the Social Sciences*, 3 volumes
Norris, Zeran, and Hatch, *The Information Service in Guidance: Occupational, Educational, Social*, 2nd Edition
Perrodin, ed., *The Student Teacher's Reader*
Peters and Farwell, *Guidance: A Developmental Approach*
Peters, Shertzer, and Van Hoose, *Guidance in Elementary Schools*
Phi Delta Kappa, *Education and the Structure of Knowledge*
Rand McNally Curriculum Series, J. Cecil Parker, ed.
    Ford and Pugno, eds., *The Structure of Knowledge and the Curriculum*
    Wellington and Wellington, *The Underachiever*
Rollins and Unruh, *Introduction to Secondary Education*
Smith, ed., *Aesthetics and Criticism in Art Education*
Smith and Ennis, eds., *Language and Concepts in Education*
Trump and Baynham, *Focus on Change: Guide to Better Schools*
Vassar, ed., *Social History of American Education*, 2 volumes
Wolf and Loomer, *The Elementary School: A Perspective*
Zeran and Riccio, *Organization and Administration of Guidance Services*

Also published by Rand McNally,

    Gage, ed., *Handbook of Research on Teaching*—A Project of the American Educational Research Association

PREFACE

Any attempt to portray the elementary school in print can easily become a monumental undertaking, because the school means many things to many people. It is a cultural meeting place; a purveyor of skills; a cornucopia of knowledge; a flutophone and finger paint; a dodgeball, jump-rope, and jacks; a Parent-Teacher Association and Safety Patrol; and, most important, the future of our country. When all these facets of the school are taken into account, it becomes evident that a textbook about this field will become encyclopedic unless the writers carefully prescribe its parameters. *The Elementary School: A Perspective* is addressed to prospective and in-service teachers who will be or are entrusted with the responsibility of teaching today's children.

The book specifically focuses upon the following topics:

1. The evolving nature of the elementary school's purposes, organization, curriculum, and methodology.
2. The children who attend the school—their characteristics upon entering, during, and upon completing the school experience.
3. The staff that operates the school.

The breadth of these topics reveals one of the book's prime purposes. It is an attempt to portray a "Gestalt" known as the elementary school. Instead of rigorously treating each of these topics under one cover and producing an encyclopedia, the writers have chosen to be selective in extracting data from each of the salient dimensions of the school for inclusion in this book. They have selected data that not only contribute to a person's acquiring a dynamic perspective on the school, but also open the door for intensive study of specific dimensions of the school.

This book is unique is several ways. First, an attempt has been made to use real people in real situations to communicate some basic aspects of the school whenever possible. These individuals are encountered in a number of school situations throughout the book. Second, certain aspects of the Socratic method of inquiry have been used to involve the reader in many of the school situations. Through this involvement, it is believed that the reader will both solve and raise problems relative to the school. Third, the writers offer a perspective, based upon research and experience, on various controversial issues presented. Fourth, when a situation is either particularly controversial or is in need of further clarification, complete statements are reproduced to orient the reader better to situations that he can expect to encounter. And fifth, the changing character of the elementary school has been emphasized, so that the reader can perceive the school's past and present and anticipate the school's future.

Few people would purchase a new drug, a new toothpaste, or a new car if they did not believe, before they committed their funds, that the product was worth purchasing. The same is true of books. A book is only as good as the research and effort that go into it. *The Elementary School: A Perspective* is the outcome of extensive experimentation and field trial. Hundreds of university students, at both the undergraduate and graduate levels, served as guinea pigs for a variety of trial topics and methods of presentation. From these tests, appropriate content and stimulating presentations were selected for this book. Numerous friends and associates shared their views, both verbally and in writing, on the nature of a book that deals with the elementary school. And, of course, the publishers made their significant contributions to improve the quality of the finished product. The best way to recognize these efforts is to read ahead.

W. C. W., Jr.
B. M. L.

TABLE OF CONTENTS

LIST OF FIGURES

Harper—Courtesy Center for School Experimentation, The Ohio State University

Here they are . . . today's children, tomorrow's leaders and followers. When you enter an elementary school classroom as a teacher, these children become your raw materials. They become, in effect, your contribution to the future of mankind. What have you in mind for the future of mankind?

Part One

AN ORIENTATION TO TEACHING
IN AN ELEMENTARY SCHOOL

Chapter One

A PEDAGOGICAL POINT
OF DEPARTURE

Why teach? Even though this question has captured the imagination of learned individuals for centuries, it is unrealistic to believe that a single answer has yet been prescribed. The task is compounded because different individuals derive different satisfactions from teaching. Each person's satisfactions are contingent upon his own desires and ambitions. Therefore, young men and women who contemplate a teaching career need to make their final decision with this in mind.

John H. Fischer, Dean and President-elect of Teachers College, Columbia University, succeeded in capturing the flavor of previous thought on the matter in a nine-paragraph editorial entitled "Why Teach?" which appeared in the *NEA Journal*. While he readily conceded that teaching can be frustrating, he also clarified many of the virtues of the role. "It is the teacher," he wrote, "to whom parents and politicians, businessmen and clergymen turn, time after time, to set straight whatever is wrong with youth or the world. Are children unmindful of their elders' unrealized ambitions? Are the national goals neglected? Is free enterprise endangered? Do we lack the moral strength we ought to have? See the teacher!"[1] In the editorial, Fischer pinpointed a new appreciation of the teacher which is related to an enormous increase in the quantity of physical energy within man's reach. That is, the central element in all man's power, in all his plans for using power, is the educated man.

Today's teacher not only takes on the responsibility for communi-

[1] John H. Fischer, "Why Teach?" *NEA Journal*, 51 (April, 1962), 31. Reprinted with permission.

cating the arts and sciences, the basic skills of our culture, and a whole host of technical competencies to children, but he also takes on a responsibility for orienting children to the ways of the world. If he fails or is only partially successful in his efforts to produce "educated men," he quickly learns that society is not prepared to accept such a performance. Fortunately for all of us, wrote Fischer, the value of education and the urgent need for good teaching are being recognized by growing numbers of able and discerning young people. These people, after cogitating the question, Why teach? have decided to invest their lives in the future of mankind—that is, in the development of educated men.

Once an individual is committed to education, he needs to view the teaching spectrum in order to determine his specific role. Should he pursue general science, English, music, elementary education, physical education, or some other phase of instruction? Or should he specialize in guidance and counseling, psychology, special education, or speech and hearing therapy? This book has been prepared to assist students who decide to teach in the elementary school.

AN OVERVIEW OF TEACHING IN
THE ELEMENTARY SCHOOL

At one large midwestern university, students expressing an interest in becoming classroom teachers are requested to indicate a preference for a major teaching field during their first year of attendance. This practice is typical of numerous American colleges and universities. Many of the students choose elementary education as their major area of study. What motivates them to specify elementary education? Surveys conducted by the writers indicate that students choose elementary education for three prime reasons: First, they feel working with children will be enjoyable; second, they are of the opinion that elementary teaching affords a sense of accomplishment unparalleled in the pedagogical structure; and third, they recognize that elementary teaching provides job security and flexibility. Other reasons offered by prospective teachers include: the nature of tasks involved in teaching, a concept of social service involved, ideal working conditions such as the short teaching day and numerous vacations, the prestige of today's teacher, and accessibility of teacher training facilities. Do any of these reasons account for the reader's decision to enter elementary education?

When a college student indicates elementary education as his major field of study, just what does he mean? Generally, he is stating that he prefers to work with young children, usually between the ages of five and twelve. He also has a preference for teaching children basic aspects of many disciplines rather than detailed aspects of a few subjects, as the typical elementary teacher deals with more than a dozen disciplines each week (e.g., algebra, history, science, health, music, English, etc.). In addition to assuming a responsibility for guiding children's mental development, he makes provisions for their physical, social, and emotional development.

When a student accepts a position as an elementary school teacher, what can he anticipate? Data pertaining to classroom assignments in an elementary school, the people who staff the school, and financial returns for such service have been selected to exemplify what is involved in elementary school teaching. Does the information presented in the following paragraphs confirm or contradict the reader's views on these matters?

INSTRUCTIONAL ASSIGNMENTS

Upon entering the elementary school classroom, the teacher usually assumes instructional responsibilities for one group of children. The group is often characterized by a narrow chronological age range. Even though such a procedure is widely employed in America, other organizational schemes such as departmentalized teaching and nongraded units have recently appeared or reappeared in our schools. Examples of these procedures include the following: (1) A teacher may instruct one classroom group of children whose ages vary from three to six or more years; (2) a teacher may teach one or two disciplines (such as art or science) to a number of classroom groups; (3) a teacher may become a member of a teaching team and share a responsibility for instructing large numbers of children. The nature of the assignment can have an important bearing upon a teacher's style, classroom preparations, daily routine, and in-service education interests.

TEACHING ASSOCIATES

Dedication, imagination, industry, and lightheartedness characterize elementary school teachers as a group. They willingly devote endless hours in and out of their classrooms to tasks like individualizing their reading program, preparing multisensory instructional aids,

5

FIGURE 1

TRENDS IN MEDIANS OF MINIMUM AND OF TOP SCHEDULED SALARIES,
LARGE URBAN SCHOOL SYSTEMS, 1950-51 — 1963-64*

――――― Group I.　Urban school systems 500,000 and over in population
― ― ―　Group II.　Urban school systems 100,000-499,999 in population

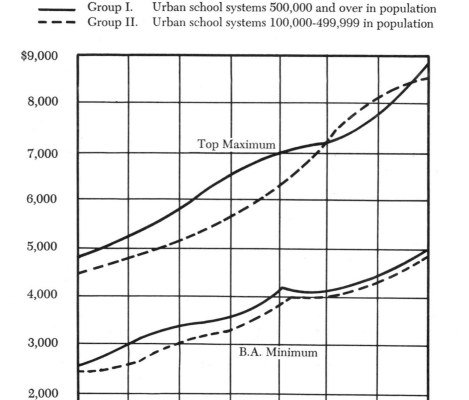

*NEA Staff, "Trends in Salary Schedule Minimums and Maximums in Large School Systems," *NEA Research Bulletin*, 42 (May, 1964), 47. Reprinted with permission.

"boning up" on a new curricular or methodological approach, and so forth. Elementary school teachers are inclined to identify positively with their pupils, and as a result become closely attached to them.

Most students majoring in elementary education in institutions of higher learning are women. The writers of this text can vividly recall being one of two or three males in large undergraduate elementary methods classes. Consequently, more than 80 per cent of today's classroom teachers are women. Data of this nature suggest that few men are attracted to elementary teaching. Margaret Mead has suggested that the shortage of interested prospective male elementary teachers has furthered the imbalance of male and female elementary teachers.[2] She pointed out that our grade schools expect females to set standards in school work, standards of orderliness, accuracy, legibility in handwriting, and proper outlining, with a B following an A and a II following a I. The boys, for the most part, simply remove themselves from this world. They play games, think about cars, follow the major leagues. Meanwhile, the girls forge ahead academically. It is somewhat surprising to note, considering these data, that a sizable percentage of elementary school principals and supervisors are men.

FINANCIAL RETURNS

Most elementary school teachers who budget their incomes are able to live quite comfortably. An exception must be made, however, for individuals who either are accustomed to luxurious living or are the breadwinners of large families. Beginning teachers possessing the bachelor's degree can expect more than $5,000 for a ten-month contract in a large urban area. After 15 to 20 years of employment, these individuals often receive $9,000 to $12,000 for about ten months of teaching. Teachers who select small urban centers, rural school systems, or certain geographical areas in the United States can expect much less financially. (In some instances, the standard of living of a region enables teachers who may earn fewer dollars than their peers in large urban centers actually to enjoy greater purchasing power.) While teaching salaries vary considerably from one community to another, qualified teachers can anticipate at least $125 per week (for twelve months) once they are established in their positions.

Figure 1 depicts trends in salary schedule minimums and maximums in large school systems. As the reader views these data, he must

[2]Margaret Mead, "Are We Squeezing Out Adolescence?" *The PTA Magazine*, 55, No. 1 (September, 1960), 4-6.

decide for himself whether the financial return of teaching is suited to his personal needs.

The data described in this section have been selected to exemplify the elementary school teacher's role. These were not the only data that could have been selected to depict elementary teaching. A brief description of typical building facilities, instructional materials, children's individual differences, or some other topic would have served just as well. Can the reader recall details of the school facilities and instructional materials which he once used, or the instructional techniques utilized by his elementary school teachers? What other aspects of the elementary school seem to stand out in the memory of the reader?

If the reader were asked, first, to identify salient dimensions of elementary education and, second, to organize these topics for systematic study, how would he proceed? By comparing his views with other students' impressions, the reader may obtain more insight into the breadth of his understanding of elementary education.

EDUCATION: A COMMUNITY RESPONSIBILITY

The classified advertisement section of a newspaper and a bulletin board located in the education building of a large university served to disseminate the following notices:

ENGLISH TEACHER. To join the faculty of a high school located in a small but thriving community situated in the southeastern corner of the state. Bachelor's degree and standard certification required. Duties shall include teaching composition and American literature, and advising the Drama Club. Salary open. Send inquiries to Box 303 care of this newspaper.

NOTICE

Appointments are being arranged in the Education Placement Office for prospective June graduates majoring in elementary education and secondary mathematics and science who wish to be interviewed for a teaching position in the Laurian, California Unified School District. Dr. J. M. Eisenhart, Assistant Superintendent, will be on campus on Monday and Tuesday, March 2 and 3, to conduct the interviews. Qualified candidates will be offered a starting salary of $5800.

These notices exemplify one approach used by school officials to recruit teachers for their systems' classrooms. It is one of a number of approaches employed by many local school districts out of necessity, because the demand for qualified teachers has exceeded the supply in recent years. Consequently, education majors who graduate from accredited colleges and universities usually receive a number of overtures for employment. These students can and do consider the assets and liabilities of the communities competing for their services before they sign a contract. This interesting, if not inordinate, pattern of competition results from the organization of education in America.

The responsibility for education in America could have been assumed by the family unit, by a religious sect, by a local, state, or federal governing body, by a political group, by a trade association, or by any number of subgroups existing within our society. This responsibility was delegated to the states by the founding fathers of our country, and the states, in turn, delegated the responsibility for educating children to local governmental units. The local governmental unit, known today as a school district, tended to share geographic boundaries with other local governmental units like towns, cities, townships, and so forth. Thus, "community" and "school district" are treated as if they were reasonable synonyms.

The community is delegated the specific responsibility for organizing, operating, and maintaining a public school system in America. Communities may vary in size from a metropolis exceeding a million people to a crossroads encompassing fewer than a hundred. No matter how large or small the community structure may be, in every case, local persons are elected or appointed to take care of school matters. The caliber of education provided for a community by these chosen representatives is influenced by numerous variables that may or may not be controlled. For example, location, industrial development, or a generous tax levy for schools can markedly affect the extent and quality of education in a given situation. Industrial development and school tax levies can often be controlled by aggressive community leadership. Unfortunately, such leadership cannot transform a desert village into a Miami, Florida, or a small Dakota town into a Chicago suburb. It is for reasons of this nature that a tremendous variance exists among school systems throughout our country. Many systems enjoy the advantage of being able and willing to afford a quality educational structure, while others are of necessity or choice barely meeting the needs of pupils.

Significant variations in the educational opportunities provided by a school district are apparent among as well as within states. This is true even though laws and formulas which aim at equalizing educational opportunities for children and youth have been employed on a broad scale. The location of business and industry in relation to population can influence the nature of a school district within a state. Per capita income and the expenditure of funds for schools can account for variations in the caliber of education among the states.

What might be inferred about educational matters from the data in Figure 2, originally reported in the *NEA Research Bulletin*?

FIGURE 2

PERSONAL INCOME DATA AND CURRENT EXPENDITURES PER PUPIL
IN AVERAGE DAILY ATTENDANCE FOR SEVEN STATES*

	Per-Capita Personal Income 1963	Estimated Current Expenditure for Public Schools per Pupil in ADA, 1964-65	Percent of Increase in Estimated Current Expenditure per Pupil in ADA, 1954-55 to 1964-65
50 States and D.C.	$2,449	$483	
Arkansas	1,607	317	161.6%
Delaware	3,298	536	67.5
Idaho	1,916	332	41.3
Mississippi	1,390	273	101.6
Nevada	3,386	505	71.9
Utah	2,119	407	68.9
Wisconsin	2,368	532	88.0

*NEA Research Division, *NEA Research Bulletin*, 43 (February, 1965), 26. Reprinted with permission. If local governmental units within a state are substituted in place of the listed states, the same variance can be observed.

THE ELEMENTARY TEACHER AND JOHN Q. PUBLIC

Since elementary teachers' salaries have not been outstanding in the past, it is not unreasonable to believe that their rewards may be derived from other factors such as job satisfaction and community support. Teachers in many communities do enjoy this kind of satisfaction and support. Unfortunately, this has not always been true, as many teachers have been exposed to various kinds of criticism and abuse for decades. Fischer pointed out in his editorial that the teacher remains the butt of poor jokes, the object of endless criticism, and the scapegoat for many of society's most widely shared shortcomings. Recent criticism of this sort is surveyed in the following paragraphs.

Education in America has been subjected to particularly extensive and intensive criticism by business, military, professional, and university spokesmen since the Second World War. Their diatribes aroused numerous taxpayers to action—some supporting the critics, others opposing their viewpoints. Controversy of this sort embroiled millions of Americans in the trials and tribulations of education. Since this criticism both directly and indirectly contributed to the present educational "revolution" in America, it is important to give a brief but representative account of public positions which were taken during this period.

THE NATURE OF EDUCATIONAL CRITICISM

Critics tended to direct their attacks toward professional educators, teacher education programs, and the school curriculum. Criticism of professional educators assumed a variety of forms. It varied from a simple statement like Jacques Barzun's observation, "Everyone seems to be dissatisfied with education except those in charge of it,"[3] to a sweeping denunciation from the pen of John Keats or the tongue of Colonel Augustin C. Rudd. Keats noted in his book, *Schools Without Scholars*, that

> If there is a national tendency to sell our children short—and I am convinced there is—I believe the fault lies with those educators who know better How to Teach than What to Teach. Furthermore, I believe the overworked social conscience of these same educators to be partly responsible for a leveling influence in our schools; their fear of establishing, or even admitting of, an intellectual elite has had the effect of scaling the offering down to a level which might lie well below the average ability. I believe another effect of this same conscience leads these educators to a false, overly sentimental concept of the child, and that one result is an emphasis on happiness at the expense of a request for a little hard work.[4]

Rudd, when addressing the Colonel Aaron Ogden Chapter of the Daughters of the American Revolution in April, 1955, stated that

> ... the New Educators have amply proved that they are not interested in improving our traditional system of education—they wish to replace it root and branch with their own *brand*. And in doing so

[3]Jacques Barzun, *Teacher in America* (New York: Doubleday & Company, Inc., 1944), p. 11.

[4]John Keats, *Schools Without Scholars* (Boston: Houghton Mifflin Company, 1958), p. 108. Reprinted with permission.

they change not only the methods of instruction but the curriculum
— in fact, the very purpose of public education itself.[5]

Both Keats and Rudd feared that professional educators did not have
the best interest of our nation in mind.

Probably the most devastating attack upon professional educators
to appear in print was made by Arthur E. Bestor, Jr., while he was
Professor of History at the University of Illinois. He wrote:

> The subversion of American intellectual life is possible be-
> cause the first twelve years of formal schooling . . . have fallen under
> the policy making control of educators who have no real place in—
> who do not respect and are not respected by—the world of science,
> of scholarship, and of the learned professions. . . .
>
> Throughout his entire career the professional educator can
> have only the most fleeting glimpse of the great world of science
> and learning. At worst he may have no contact with it at all . . . his
> professional life is apt to be lived in close association with the
> educational bureaucracy and in isolation, largely self-imposed,
> from the realms of scientific and scholarly research and learning.[6]

Obviously, he concluded that the educators of his day were ill-
equipped to cope with the challenges of the changing world.

These quotations exemplify the opinions of some Americans
about the professional educator. Unfortunately, such comments
served to depict educators as misguided, confused, or stupid individuals who did not have the best interests of education in mind.

Teacher education programs also received their fair share of
criticism. One aspect of this criticism was crystallized by an education
student in the following letter to the editor of a campus newspaper.

> To the Editor:
>
> Most students resent any Education course they have to take
> and complain about them—but not me! I'm taking my first Educa-
> tion course now and I really appreciate it. Why where else could I
> find a better point of comparison? In contrast to my Education
> course, the other courses I have taken up to now seem geared to
> genius level and taught by veritable Einsteins.
>
> No, I don't complain about my Education course, for I am
> grateful for the opportunity to realize the honest worth of my other

[5]Colonel Augustin C. Rudd, "Some Aims in Public Education," *Vital Speeches*, 21
(May, 1955), 1216.

[6]Arthur E. Bestor, Jr., "Aimlessness in Education," *Scientific Monthly*, 75 (August,
1952), 114. Reprinted with permission.

courses and to recognize the intelligence of my other teachers. Of course, when I wear out being grateful and appreciative, I may become a bit bored. Maybe Education teacher will let me bring my teddy bear and an all day sucker to class then. Yes, I'll bet she will. Or, possibly, I could bring my rug and take a nap. That would be fun — fitting too!

Intellectually Insulted

Martin Mayer, a professional writer who studied the schools of America at length, rephrased this idea in the following manner: "Generally speaking, teacher-training programs have divorced in a most artificial manner the study of how to teach a subject from the study of the nature and implications of the material to be taught."[7] Both "Intellectually Insulted" and Mayer expressed a concern that teacher education programs suffered from a severe case of pedagogical myopia.

Charges aimed at education courses by Admiral Hyman G. Rickover also received widespread publicity. The admiral once observed that

> Education courses which count toward certification requirements may be such complicated and difficult matters as how to ventilate a classroom properly, how to run a tape recorder, how to teach the art of listening, group dynamics, "nesting" hand-painted tin cans, and classroom democracy. Courses of this kind are made the criterion of "professional" competence in a teacher. So equipped, he is considered qualified to teacher anything.[8]

In this instance, Rickover selected specific phases of a training program and then generalized from those points to all programs.

Much criticism was directed toward the curriculum of the school. Arthur S. Trace, Jr., a professor of English, compared the American student with his counterpart in Russia. He concluded from this comparison that

> The American school system ... seems during the past thirty years to have come to believe that it is not very important for our students to have a thorough knowledge of ... basic subjects (such as literature, history, foreign language, the basic sciences, mathematics, and geography), but that it is important that they be thoroughly

[7]Martin Mayer, *The Schools* (New York: Harper and Brothers, 1961), p. 422.

[8]Hyman G. Rickover, *Education and Freedom* (New York: E. P. Dutton & Co., Inc., 1959), p. 204. Reprinted with permission.

familiar with the minutiae of community living and that they should above all learn to become adjusted to their environment as they find it. As a result, a great deal of the time our students spend in class in both the grade schools and the high schools is taken up with learning things which have nothing, or virtually nothing, to do with the basic subjects.[9]

A former college teacher and presently a business man, Albert Lynd reinforced this argument.

> A complaint of parents, employers, and college instructors is that ... while neo-pegagogues palaver more and more about the "real needs" of youngsters, the pupils are learning less and less about the arts of word and number, the history and the literature, the science and the esthetics, and the rest of the painfully accumulated culture of this harassed civilization.[10]

Probably the most widespread indictment of the curriculum — that is, the failure of the schools to offer a sound basic education — is captured in the Trace and Lynd quotations.

Rudolf Flesch has attacked the teaching of reading in American elementary schools with vigor. His viewpoint is summed up in one statement written in the book *Why Johnny Can't Read*. "The teaching of reading — all over the United States, in all the schools, in all the textbooks — is totally wrong and flies in the face of all logic and common sense."[11]

The words of Barzun, Keats, Rudd, Bestor, Mayer, Rickover, Trace, Lynd, and Flesch typify the kind of criticism which was aimed at the schools of America after 1945. Each of these individuals attempted to communicate personal dissatisfaction with the operation of the schools through the various news media. Some of them offered alternate courses for the nation's schools to pursue; unfortunately, few were able to make concrete, positive suggestions for change. Hence, much time was spent by critics and educators throughout the forties and fifties in seemingly endless debate over the nature of school objectives and programs, methods of teaching, teacher education, and so forth.

[9]Arthur S. Trace, Jr., *What Ivan Knows That Johnny Doesn't* (New York: Random House, Inc., 1961), p. 182. Reprinted with permission.

[10]Albert Lynd, *Quackery in the Public Schools* (Boston: Little, Brown and Company — Atlantic Monthly Press, 1953), p. 14. Reprinted with permission. Copyright 1950, 1953 by A. Lynd.

[11]Rudolf Flesch, *Why Johnny Can't Read* (New York: Harper and Brothers, 1955), p. 2.

An Overview of Educational Countercriticism

Educators' reactions to the charges expressed by critics varied tremendously. These reactions appeared in the form of an account of the specific contributions made by schools to society; they focused upon analyses of critics' motives; and they were expressed as direct counterattacks. Illustrations of each position are presented as follows:

A recent publication of the Educational Policies Commission is an example of the first kind of reaction. This group of prominent classroom teachers, superintendents, college presidents, and other educational leaders assembled in 1955 to deal with the problems of public education and the future of America. Their joint efforts resulted in a book, appropriately entitled *Public Education and the Future of America*. In this book, they tried to tell the American people the story of public schools — of how they came into being, of how they have contributed to the health of democracy and the American way of life, and of some of the problems they face as they look to the future. Accounts and conclusions reported in this book have been widely read and discussed.

Douglas Rugh analyzed reasons for some of the attacks on the American school in psychological terms. Excerpts from his article in *School and Society* are reported as follows:

> Investigations into the social psychology of motivation ... indicate that these attacks on the American public schools might be explained in part by two dynamic theories of behavior. These are the so-called frustration-aggression theory and the defense mechanism known as projection.
>
> Applying the frustration-aggression theory to this scapegoat situation, we might say that well-intentioned Americans are conscious of the fact that American Democratic ideals are not being realized in our social, economic, and political life. The democratic ideal of respect for the worth of individual personality and the right to self-realization are continually being violated, not only among our school population but for whole adult populations in the minority groups and in the lower classes. These frustrations produce a cumulative tension of guilt in the majority group members who are conscious of these violations. One outlet for such frustrations and guilt feelings is found by aggressively attacking some vulnerable target, not necessarily the cause of these frustrations.
>
> Oddly enough, the American home, American churches, American communities, all of which have considerable influence and responsibility for educating American youth, are apparently by-

15

passed and overlooked by these contemporary critics. Even the local boards of education which have the legal authority and responsibility for public education at the local level have thus far been comparatively immune from these attacks.

... The second theory that might shed some light on the motivation of the critics is the psychoanalytical theory of projection. This in brief states that, when an individual or group has certain socially unacceptable traits, there is a subconscious tendency to project these undesirable traits upon or ascribe them to some other individual or group, the scapegoat, as a means of keeping the self-portrait unblemished and pure.[12]

His argument is quite thought-provoking. For a critic to respond to this kind of analysis is also quite difficult.

Periodically, educators and other scholars are disturbed by criticism to the point where they take up the sword and attack. Joseph Justman of Brooklyn College attacked critics of education in the following manner.

The strength of the opposition lies in its criticism. It aims its shafts well, hitting vulnerable targets in the American school system—slipshodness in maintaining standards, concern with numbers at the expense of quality, dilution of subject matter, pedagogical softness, and the like. To the extent that it exposes weaknesses demanding correction, its influence is salutary. But it is too drastic in condemnation; it employs the devices of the rabble rouser rather than of the professional, and, once its criticism is spent, the weaknesses of its own position stand revealed.

Among other things, American education is accused of being anti-intellectual. Perhaps such a charge, in milder form, is justified. But confronted with the need of submitting an alternative plan of education, the people who make this accusation show themselves to be, if not un-intellectual, at least very tired thinkers. Instead of producing a program of education tailored to present requirements, they dust off the old cliches. We must return to "fundamentals," emphasize "content," discard "fads and frills," and in general cease catering to "mediocrity"—these are slogans, not a responsible attempt to meet educational problems. Which fundamentals, what content? Is education for health a fad or frill? Intellectual mediocrity spells, in statistical terms, more than 100,000,000 Americans who must be educated. What sort of education will be afforded *them*? Underlying these slogans is an old conception of education

[12]Douglas Rugh, "The Scapegoat Value of American Public Education," *School and Society*, 82 (July 14, 1955), 20-22.

aimed primarily at imparting strong academic training to those intellectually privileged to profit from it, a conception not readily made explicit, since to do so might incur public disapproval. If this is the theory of education, both its ends and its means are faulty. A plan of public education should manifest equal concern for all the people, not favor a small segment. And experience has apparently convinced some nations of Western Europe, long the proponents of a rigorous academic training for the elite, that such training falls short of its purpose. Perhaps these critics do offer a democratic theory of education which does not run away from current problems but faces up to them; if so, it is well concealed.[13]

This approach served to salt the wound of controversy.

Many educators preferred to ignore the majority of critics of public education. These individuals recognize that American educators do not have a monopoly on school problems. They are acquainted with scorching denunciations of Russian educational programs which have appeared in that country's education journals. And, they are aware of the serious problems confronting Dutch, Belgian, and English educators. Some even recollect these words:

> The children now love luxury. They have bad manners, and contempt for authority. They show disrespect for their elders and love clatter in place of exercises. They no longer rise when elders enter the room. They contradict their parents, chatter before company, rattle dishes at the table, cross their legs, and tyrannize over their teacher.

This quotation takes on unusual significance, because it was expressed by Socrates approximately 2,400 years ago. Educators who assumed this position preferred to soft-pedal the criticism of the schools, because they believed such criticism centered on the arguments of vituperators who delighted in praising "a superior foreign program of education" or an educational pattern of a bygone era. They refused to enhance a critic's notoriety by recognizing his position.

Hence, educational countercriticism made both positive and negative appearances, it assumed analytical dimensions, or it simply did not emerge.

[13]Joseph Justman, "Wanted: A Philosophy of American Education," *School and Society*, 83 (May 12, 1956), 160. The following publications provide an additional perspective: William Brickman, "Attack and Counterattack in American Education," *School and Society*, 74 (October 27, 1951), 262-269; Harold G. Shane and Wilbur A. Yauch, *Creative School Administration* (New York: Henry Holt & Company, Inc., 1954), pp. 180-192.

THE EFFECTS OF THE CONTROVERSY

While the public debate generated considerable heat on the surface, it had little effect upon school programs, teaching procedures, and, especially, teacher education patterns during the late forties and early fifties. The critics exposed a cancer, but they were unable to prescribe a sensible remedy for it. Educators recognized many deficiencies in school procedures, but they also could argue that children had never been in better hands in the history of our country. One effect of this continuing feud was that millions of people remained abreast of school problems. When a series of minor political, social, and economic setbacks gripped our nation, capable people looked to the school as a prime community institution for confronting basic dimensions of such societal difficulties. These individuals chose to join forces with educators rather than continue to attack educators' accomplishments. Their partnership led to dramatic, startling, and significant changes which have contributed to a pedagogical revolution of sorts in America.

The pedagogical revolution which was initiated in the fifties and which picked up steam in the sixties was characterized by three occurrences: First, scholars from various academic disciplines teamed with educators to initiate the construction of educational programs that might be more responsive to the needs of a rapidly changing world; second, teaching methods which were more amenable to the demands of large classroom groups gained currency; and third, the introduction of multisensory instructional materials provided the necessary support for the reality of tailormade school experiences for children. These developments quite frequently took place in combinations within specified school settings. Teachers and administrators who had the courage to conduct school in a different manner soon were beseiged by their peers for information on the "new education." And the "revolution" was under way.

Many people attribute the massive involvement of academic scholars in school matters to the successful launching of the first Russian space satellite in 1957. Undoubtedly, the shock of the satellite was a potent factor; however, scholarly involvement—especially in the sciences and mathematics—had already been initiated before the Russian spectacle. A group of mathematicians and educators probably pioneered the modern movement at the University of Illinois about six years before Sputnik. Their undertaking was called the University of Illinois Committee on School Mathematics. It triggered other mathematics projects like the Greater Cleveland Mathematics Project, the University of Maryland Mathematics Project, the Syracuse University—Webster College Madison Project, and the School Mathematics Study Group, as well as projects in other disciplines.

Popular projects initiated in the sciences and foreign language include the Physical Science Study Committee, the Biological Sciences Curriculum Study, the Chemical Education Materials Study, and the Modern Language Association-Foreign Language Program. Similar projects have been initiated in the social sciences, in the language arts, and in the fine arts under the auspices of the United States Office of Education, the National Science Foundation, and several private research foundations recently.[14]

One of the most important outcomes of these curriculum projects to date has been the cooperation that developed between the scholar and the educator. Not only did this cooperation have a beneficial effect upon the school itself, but it also enhanced the image of the school immensely.

The second development of this period was long overdue. Almost total teacher dependence upon expository teaching methods was sorely in need of change. This change was initiated by an emphasis upon inductive teaching methods. More and more teachers labored to structure learning situations so that students could assume a major responsibility for conducting their own inquiry into topics at hand. Research reports on motivation, reinforcement, and the learning process also received widespread attention. Teachers, for the first time in the history of pedagogy, began to study empirically their methods of interacting with children.

The third development captured the public fancy much more than either of the others. The sanctity of the basic textbook was violated by the advent of a vast array of new multisensory instructional materials. Teaching machines, programmed materials, language laboratories, and educational television typified materials utilized in the modernized school. These materials enabled teachers to provide realistically for individual differences among students, an accomplishment which always eluded teachers who relied upon the basic textbook.

What effects of the pedagogical controversy might have proven most beneficial, considering today's schools? There is evidence of

---

[14]A more detailed treatment of these developments can be gleaned from John I. Goodlad's *School Curriculum Reform* (New York: The Fund for the Advancement of Education, 1964).

widespread public pride in today's schools. This positive image can be attributed to marked changes that occurred in many school settings which received extensive favorable coverage in the nation's news media. The favorable publicity not only served to inform others, but it also aroused educators and citizens in thousands of communities to re-examine their own practices in terms of the "new" alternatives. A quality-conscious school community which is open minded and receptive to change has emerged from this decade of innovation and evaluation.

The flavor of what occurred during the fifties and of what people can anticipate throughout the sixties is captured in a beautifully written passage by Laura Zirbes in her recent book, *Focus on Values in Elementary Education.*

> Criticism itself is not necessarily damaging, but presumptive criticism which lacks validity, integrity, and concern for values will not improve schools. It needs to be discredited. Educational leadership is reluctant to resort to defensive counter-criticism, but there are other ways of taking a stand and getting the public to identify with the efforts to improve schools. There is a challenge to give citizens direct evidence and concrete news about good things that today's schools are doing — *good* for communities, *good* for children and youth, *good* for staff morale, and *good* for public relations.
>
> There are many adults whose conceptions of elementary schools are based on obsolete imagery and erroneous assumptions. Citizens who support public education should view it realistically. What is old is not *always* worth revering. What is new is not *therefore* to be viewed with skeptical disregard.
>
> Adults who pride themselves on keeping up with improvements in cars, radios, and television often have antiquated conceptions of elementary schools. Citizens whose imagery is anachronistic need to be brought up to date on improvements well worth public appreciation and support.
>
> The very fact that some of the "good things" about today's schools are not generally known, makes them the more newsworthy. It explains why feature writers for newspapers and magazines render a public service when they give their readers vivid glimpses of today's schools in action. Whereas propaganda, scandal, and controversy may make the headlines oftener, the vividly informative news stories have a cumulative impact on the public mind, and they do something to challenge the unwarranted high regard for some of the sloganized stereotypes which block the way to improved curricular practices in today's schools. School people them-

selves would do well to liquidate unfounded rumors, misjudgments, and misrepresentations that too often pass for fact.[15]

Zirbes' view is widely supported by individuals responsible for today's schools.

This section has depicted characteristic criticisms once directed toward educators, educators' reactions to the criticisms, and changes which have taken place in our schools as an indirect or direct result of the controversy. Can the reader envision himself as a part of this sometimes confusing, sometimes frustrating, and sometimes exhilarating process? The writers extend a hearty welcome to those who respond in the affirmative and encourage them to read ahead.

QUESTIONS FOR DISCUSSION

Mary Anderson is beginning her first year of teaching in a medium-sized midwestern town. She received an orientation to the schools, businesses, and patrons during the week before the opening of school in September.

Experiences were provided to make Mary feel a part of the community and identify with the educational purpose of the school system. Mary was invited to the citizens' homes so she would be better acquainted with the mores of the community. She also received a number of orientation lectures from some of the curriculum leaders in the system.

After completing this orientation phase, Mary had a number of questions she felt worthy of more thought. Do you feel that Mary was correct when she identified the following questions as remaining unanswered?

1. Why is it important for a teacher to know the community, its businesses, and people?
2. Are the public groups she met with influential in giving directions to school programs?
3. What can Mary do if she doesn't agree with certain aspects of the social studies curriculum?
4. What role does Mary play in helping citizens understand how they can help in the educative process?
5. Does Mary have a philosophy of education, or is she in the process of building one?

[15]Laura Zirbes, *Focus on Values in Elementary Education* (New York: G. P. Putnam's Sons, 1960), pp. 2-3. Reprinted with permission.

ADDITIONAL REFERENCES

Brookover, Wilbur B., and Gottlieb, David, *A Sociology of Education*. New York: American Book Company, 1964. 488 pp.

Broudy, Harry S., *Building a Philosophy of Education*, 2nd ed. Englewood Cliffs, N.J.: Prentice-Hall, Inc., 1961. 410 pp.

Bruner, Jerome, *Process of Education*. Cambridge, Mass.: Harvard University Press, 1960. 97 pp.

Kelley, Earl C., *Education for What Is Real*. New York: Harper and Brothers, 1947. 114 pp.

Woodring, Paul, *Let's Talk Sense about Our Schools*. New York: McGraw-Hill Book Company, Inc., 1953. 215 pp.

Chapter Two

TEACHER EDUCATION
AND THE COMMUNITY SETTING

Even though some individuals openly criticize teacher education programs, it is not unreasonable to believe that teachers are now entering professional service better prepared than ever before. While these teachers seem less certain of educational absolutes than their predecessors, they seem more inclined toward self-analysis and experimentation in the classroom. They are more curious about the nature of curricula, methods of teaching, and the learning process.

In order to convey the essence of a contemporary teacher's role in the classroom, an attempt is made in this and subsequent chapters to involve the reader vicariously in the experiences of a representative teacher who instructs in a suburban community. Through this involvement, the authors hope to make relevant topics more meaningful and thought-provoking. This chapter serves to introduce the teacher and the school setting and sets the stage for selected probes into salient dimensions of elementary education.

Finally, this chapter describes patterns of teacher preparation. Knowledge of alternative patterns will not only enhance the reader's perspective of topics introduced in Parts Two and Four of the book, but it will also permit him to examine critically his own professional education course sequence.

JOAN RITTER AND THE TOWN OF JACKSON

THE SCHOOL DISTRICT

Many people residing in Jackson, an expanding suburban community, are employed in commercial and industrial enterprises in the mother city. The residents of Jackson view education as a vital factor in the lives of their children. Townspeople enthusiastically patronize school concerts and plays, athletic contests, and PTA organizations. They attend school board meetings in large numbers, they participate actively in the election of local school board members, and they usually provide financial support for the school system—when it is requested—in the form of an increased tax levy or a bond issue. The people of Jackson are willing to support a better-than-average school system because they value education highly.

The townspeople's enthusiasm for education attracts more prospective teachers than the best recruiter the school district could employ. Contrary to the national trend, Jackson has experienced a teacher deluge rather than a teacher shortage in recent years. Applicants include both beginning and in-service teachers. As a result, hiring officials are able to be quite selective in their choice of teachers for the school system.

Teachers in Jackson enjoy many advantages over co-workers in neighboring school districts. Their salaries are substantially higher than the state average; buildings are relatively new and well kept; extensive teaching materials are available; teachers participate in formulating school policies that affect their classroom activities; and teachers are given time away from the classroom to attend professional meetings during the school year. Teacher morale could not be at a higher level than it is in Jackson.

These job conditions plus the vigorous support of the community have practically eliminated the problem of recruiting teachers for the Jackson schools. Jackson's enviable position of getting its choice of the available teaching supply is shared by districts paying higher-than-average salaries or large districts that can afford to employ personnel for recruiting purposes. School districts that face serious annual teacher shortages almost invariably do not pay competitive salaries, do not provide adequate working facilities, or do not enjoy much community support. "Success begets success" appropriately depicts Jackson's circumstances.

This description of an imaginary expanding suburban community adjacent to a sizable metropolis serves as a point of departure for a variety of pedagogical analyses in this book. Even though this community is atypical in terms of its ability to support a better-than-average school system, it can function effectively as a study model. School matters treated in terms of this school system are characteristic of many others. Problems that arise in the course of expediting these school matters are also shared by many school systems. The reader is advised to keep these points in mind.

NEW TEACHERS IN THE DISTRICT

Joan Ritter, a newly appointed teacher in the district, is introduced as a representative classroom practitioner. It is the authors' hope that the reader will be able to follow the practices and experiences of Miss Ritter in particular, and a number of educators in general, through many of the important phases of teaching treated in the book.

After teaching in a rural community for two years, Miss Ritter decided to transfer to Jackson. Her classroom assignment happened to be in the newest of four elementary schools in the school district. During Teacher Orientation Day at her school, she met many professional associates and toured the building for the first time. On the tour, she met Anita Yost and Stella Marks, two first-year teachers who also were assigned to the school. Even though Miss Ritter had taught elementary-aged children for two years, as a newcomer to the community she had much in common with Anita and Stella. Similar interests and circumstances contributed to the rapid development of their friendship.

None of the girls grew up in Jackson. Miss Ritter was raised in an industrial community in the northern part of the state, while Miss Yost and Miss Marks both grew up on farms not far from Jackson. These girls followed an established pattern of job selection. (A number of surveys conducted by one of the authors revealed that nearly two-thirds of all prospective teachers sign their first contracts to teach in communities other than their home community. It is interesting to note that more than 25 per cent accept their first position in another state.) Anita and Stella selected a community in their home state, while Joan moved from one community to another in her home state.

While Joan, Anita, and Stella may have much in common socially, their respective preparations for teaching certainly varied. Joan obtained her undergraduate degree from the state university. This was her choice because she felt its program provided an extensive liberal education as well as an intensive professional preparation. Anita selected a teachers' college near home for her training because the program enabled her to satisfy state certification requirements in both elementary and secondary education and provided many opportunities for classroom observation and participation. Stella had no intention of teaching when she entered an outstanding liberal arts college. She pursued studies in the humanities until her final year, when she decided to enter teaching. Consequently, she was barely able to schedule the education courses necessary to meet minimum state certification requirements for elementary teaching during her last year of study. Each girl brought a unique set of credentials to Jackson.

PATTERNS OF TEACHER PREPARATION

The reader may wonder why hiring officials recommend individuals with such varied credentials for employment in the Jackson schools. A stringent hiring policy, based upon the undergraduate experience, seems appropriate for a district with more applicants than available positions. Such a policy exists, but it is not rooted to the individual's undergraduate experience. Hiring officials recognize that teacher training programs vary markedly. Some educators, for example, believe that extensive professional preparation is essential. However, these educators often cannot agree upon the specific preparation needed. Other educators argue that a liberal education is prerequisite to becoming an effective classroom teacher. Diplomatic educators try to incorporate elements from each positon in their training programs. Can the reader describe variations in the structure of contemporary teacher education programs? How might these variations influence the classroom performance of the practitioner or the supply of teachers for today's classrooms?

Several program schemes are readily recognized. One plan eliminates so-called professional education courses from the undergraduate experience. Education courses are concentrated into a graduate-level undertaking which ranges from summer study to a year-round program. A Master of Education degree is often awarded to individuals who pursue such a course of action.

Another plan builds a sequence of professional education courses into the undergraduate program during the junior and senior years. Under this arrangement, students schedule professional education courses along with general education, subject specialization, and elective courses. A program of this sort usually leads to a Bachelor of Science degree.

A third plan enables students to schedule professional education courses throughout the undergraduate experience along with required university, subject specialization, and elective courses. The hours allocated to educational inquiry usually increase yearly over a four- or five-year span. Both alternatives may lead to a B.S. degree, although the five-year program often leads to a Master of Education degree.

In Europe, secondary schools and technical institutes (somewhat like the normal schools which once flourished in the United States) provide facilities for intensive teacher education experiences. As a result, relatively few "lower school" teachers possess the equivalent of a university education.

Obviously, there are different conceptions of the essence of effective teacher education programs. Educators and officials in institutions of higher learning are confronted with the task of exploring available alternatives before deciding upon the scope and sequence of such programs. Some day, they may be assisted in their choice by the availability of information that describes the strengths and weaknesses of each plan. Unfortunately, educators have much to learn about evaluating teacher education programs before helpful descriptive data are obtained.

PROFESSIONAL EDUCATION PROGRAMS

Teacher education is still in its infancy in America, and this accounts for some of the variations in present practice. Many colleges of education do not prescribe entrance requirements, as do the medical, dental, or legal professions. A student possessing adequate grades can enter a typical teacher education program. Course requirements for prospective elementary school teachers may and do vary from one institution of higher education to another. The fact that elementary education is such a broad concept has made it difficult for educators to specify, in concrete terms, exactly what should be included in the prescribed program.

There are educators, for example, who believe that the program should stress a knowledge of methodology and child development. Such a program includes a series of "Teaching of XXX" courses, one or more courses stressing child development, and several courses in educational philosophy and psychology. Others argue that a comprehensive liberal education is the best preparation for teaching. Individuals supporting this viewpoint tend to criticize education courses as being beneath the dignity of a college or university. Hence, their education programs are likely to include only those courses which are required for state certification.

Individuals advocating a liberal education as the most effective way to prepare a teacher support their position with varied arguments. An exchange of letters pertaining to the art of teaching, published in Mortimer Adler's *Great Ideas from the Great Books,* sheds a beam of light upon the nature of their thinking. These letters are reproduced for careful analysis.

Dear Dr. Adler,

We all remember teachers who have had a great affect on us in school or in college. But we find it hard to put our finger on just what it was that they transmitted to us and how they did it. All the talk on education today does not seem to shed any light on the art of teaching. What is it that goes on in the relation between teacher and student? What does the teacher do, and what happens to the student?

W. G.

Dear W. G.,

Socrates gives us a basic insight into the nature of teaching when he compares the art of teaching to the ancient craft of the midwife. Just as the midwife assists the body to give birth to new life, so the teacher assists the mind to deliver itself of ideas, knowledge, and understanding. The essential notion here is that teaching is a humble, helping art. The teacher does not produce knowledge or stuff ideas into an empty, passive mind. It is the learner, not the teacher, who is the active producer of knowledge and ideas.

The ancients distinguish the skills of the physician and the farmer from those of the shoemaker and the house builder. Aristotle calls medicine and agriculture cooperative arts, because they work with nature to achieve results that nature is able to produce by itself. Shoes and houses would not exist unless men produced them; but the living body attains health without the intervention of doctors, and plants and animals grow without the aid of farmers. The skilled physician or farmer simply makes health or growth more certain and regular.

Teaching, like farming and healing, is a cooperative art which helps nature do what it can do itself—though not as well—without it. We have all learned many things without the aid of a teacher. Some exceptional individuals have acquired wide learning and deep insight with very little formal schooling. But for most of us the process of learning is made more certain and less painful when we have a teacher's help. His methodical guidance makes our learning —and it is still ours—easier and more effective.

One basic aspect of teaching is not found in the other two cooperative arts that work with organic nature. Teaching always involves a relation between the mind of one person and the mind of another. The teacher is not merely a talking book, an animated phonograph record, broadcast to an unknown audience. He enters into a dialogue with his student. This dialogue goes far beyond mere "talk", for a good deal of what is taught is transmitted almost unconsciously in the personal interchange between teacher and student. We might get by with encyclopedias, phonograph records, and TV broadcasts if it were not for this intangible element, which is present in every good teacher-student relation.

This is a two-way relation. The teacher gives, and the student receives aid and guidance. The student is a "disciple"; that is, he accepts and follows the discipline prescribed by the teacher for the development of his mind. This is not a passive submission to arbitrary authority. It is an active appropriation by the student of the directions indicated by the teacher. The good student uses his teacher just as a child uses his parents, as a means of attaining maturity and independence. The recalcitrant student, who spurns a teacher's help, is wasteful and self destructive.

Speaking simply and in the broadest sense, the teacher shows the student how to discern, evaluate, judge, and recognize the truth. He does not impose a fixed content of ideas and doctrines that the student must learn by rote. He teaches the student how to learn and think for himself. He encourages rather than suppresses a critical and intelligent response.

The student's response and growth is the only reward suitable for such a labor of love. Teaching, the highest of the ministerial or cooperative arts, is devoted to the good of others. It is an act of supreme generosity. St. Augustine calls it the greatest act of charity.

M. Adler[1]

This view holds that the ability to show students how to "discern, evaluate, judge, and recognize the truth" is an art. If it is an art, then learned individuals are in the best position to "make learning more certain and less painful" for children. Adler's view is an alternative to the popular belief that individuals who have specialized in pedagogical method are best qualified to teacher the "truth."

[1]Mortimer J. Adler, *Great Ideas from the Great Books* (New York: Washington Square Press, Inc., 1961), pp. 115-117. Reprinted with permission.

Professional education programs usually are completed within the framework of the four-year undergraduate experience. Consequently, general college or university requirements usually affect the number of course hours available for the experience. Educators responsible for the program have the task of identifying and selecting crucial aspects from the above-mentioned possibilities for their sequence of courses.

It becomes apparent that a professional education program frequently reflects a point of view on teaching. If few methodology courses are perceived in a program, individuals responsible for the program in all probability view teaching primarily as an art. If numerous methodology courses are incorporated in a program, responsible individuals in all probability view teaching primarily as a science.

TEACHING: AN ART OR A SCIENCE?

Few educators would deny the fact that some individuals teach unusually well even though they have never been exposed to teacher training courses. These individuals somehow have acquired extraordinary teaching capabilities. Unfortunately, there are too few of these people to fill the typical school district's teaching vacancies. Dependence upon a supply of untrained but enlightened individuals for classroom teaching positions seems unfeasible.

Most educators would agree that effective teaching procedures are known, and that individuals can acquire these skills. It is for this reason that many institutions of higher learning were established solely to train teachers for America's schools, many universities and colleges established departments of education, and many state departments began to prescribe certification requirements for teaching. While educators are in agreement on the matter of communicating teaching skills, much controversy centers on how to communicate the most effective procedures and what should be the extent of the experience.

Teacher education may come of age when membership in the profession is controlled more effectively, when essential ingredients for a program are identified and utilized, and when individual progress throughout the program is measured in a realistic manner. At that time, hiring officials in Jackson and other communities will view an applicant's undergraduate preparation for teaching more carefully than is the case today.

An Opportunity for Appraisal

In many instances, the reader of this book is on the threshold of a teacher education program. By this time, he has probably been exposed to such comments as, "Those who can, do; those who can't, teach," or "Courses in education consist of about 10 per cent solid substance and 90 per cent mixed wind and humbug," or "Material covered in education courses bears little resemblance to on-the-job conditions." These comments should motivate the reader to obtain a copy of his college catalogue and examine the required courses in the education sequence. Do the course titles indicate that the student will be exposed to profitable training experiences? Does the campus grapevine suggest that the various instructors implement the course descriptions? Do students who complete the program have difficulty obtaining teaching positions? Every student of education needs to answer each of these questions to his satisfaction.

The reader is undoubtedly able to recall numerous personal experiences as a child in an elementary school. He may have visited an elementary school recently. Very likely, he possesses many ideas about teaching in the elementary schools which are based upon experiences of this sort. If the reader desires to assess his personal sensitivity to the ramifications of teaching in the elementary school, he might attempt to conceptualize a training program designed to produce competent elementary school teachers. Then, he might compare his concept of a program with the sequence of courses prescribed by his college of education. Students who perceive the structure of a teacher training program and its underlying implications are in a better position to react to critics of the program.

THE NATURE OF THIS BOOK

At this point, the reader should possess some knowledge of the nature of elementary education, and he certainly ought to be aware of some basic aspects of the process of change in education. It will be to his advantage to keep the perspective and the process in mind as he examines the various spheres of teaching in the elementary school which are detailed throughout this book. As he is exposed, chapter by chapter, to contemporary practices in elementary education, the criticisms and countercriticisms already encountered assume meaningful dimensions. It is probable that other controversial circumstances may emerge from the exposure. Controversy arouses emotions. According to available research, emotionally loaded situations stimulate an active learning set; hence, the prospective teacher ought to benefit from a clearer understanding of the process of education.

This book is not intended to be an expository account of the American elementary school. Instead, the writers offer a perspective on education which focuses upon salient features of the school in our society.

The theme of this book is based upon a fictitious teacher in a fictitious school system. This theme weaves its way both directly and indirectly through each section. Even though Miss Ritter and the Jackson School System are fictional, they reflect real people, real places, and real situations across the United States.

The reader is introduced to teaching in the elementary school in a unique and functional manner. He is able to follow selected practices and experiences of one teacher in particular and a number of teachers in general through many of the important phases of teaching. He is challenged by problem situations to become personally involved in a variety of real school experiences. The student who is exposed to these experiences should acquire sufficient knowledge to raise penetrating and thought-provoking questions about elementary education. If such behavior occurs, it is not unreasonable to believe that the student's professional course sequence will become a vital and enriching experience.

Since nonscientific experience and experimentation have been prime factors in shaping the elementary school in our society, an empirical rather than a scientific research-oriented approach is necessarily employed throughout this book to orient the reader to elementary education.

QUESTIONS FOR DISCUSSION

Midville and Rocktown are two communities within the same state. They are approximately equal in population, but Rocktown is situated much closer to a large metropolitan city. The total school population of the Midville Community School is 7,000, while that of Rocktown approaches the 10,000 figure. The average salary of an elementary teacher in Midville is $5,400, while $6,400 is the average in Rocktown. Special teachers in art, music, and physical education are utilized in Rocktown, whereas none are found in Midville.

With the above information how would you react to the following questions?

1. Why does one community have special teachers in art, music, and physical education?
2. What basic facts are discernible that would attract teachers to the two communities?
3. How should the prospective teacher decide upon a community for future professional employment?
4. Are students in the two communities receiving "like education" or "different education?" Explain.
5. List the specific advantages of teaching in the two communities.

ADDITIONAL REFERENCES

Eye, Glen G., and Lane, Willard, *The New Teacher Comes to School.* New York: Harper and Brothers, 1956. 376 pp.

Lieberman, Myron, *Education as a Profession.* Englewood Cliffs, N.J.: Prentice-Hall, Inc., 1956. 540 pp.

Ryans, David G., *Characteristics of Teachers.* Washington, D.C.: American Council on Education, 1900. 416 pp.

SUMMARY: PART ONE

Chapters One and Two are analogous to the steel beams in a multi-story building. Just as the steel girders serve as the structure for the building, these chapters serve as a frame of reference for the remainder of the book.

A bird's-eye view of selected aspects of the elementary school situation, of the community responsibility for education, and of the elementary school teacher in contemporary society, was provided initially. Then, selected activities of a fictitious classroom practitioner in a fictitious suburban community were described. These educational models serve to exemplify present pedagogical practices or to provide a departure point for topics presented in forthcoming chapters. A survey of patterns of teacher preparation completed the frame of reference for a study of salient dimensions of elementary education.

Part Two

BASIC DIMENSIONS
OF THE ELEMENTARY SCHOOL

Chapter Three

PORTRAIT OF AN ELEMENTARY SCHOOL CLASSROOM

William Sydney Porter observed, "No calamity so touches the common heart of humanity as does the straying of a little child. Their feet are so uncertain and feeble; the ways are so steep and strange." In this chapter, the child's "uncertain and feeble" steps are traced through the "steep and strange" ways of Miss Ritter's elementary school classroom. Specifically, four aspects of the child's school experience with Miss Ritter are explored on the following pages. A description of the child's classroom environment precedes a discussion of data-gathering and record-keeping in the school, Miss Ritter's instructional program, and daily activities in Miss Ritter's classroom.

The content of this chapter is not intended as "the" answer to pedagogical problems confronting educators in today's elementary school. Rather, an attempt has been made to portray one set of solutions — whether proper or improper — to pedagogical problems. The solutions portrayed often mirror widespread contemporary practices in elementary schools. In several instances, the solutions reflect either outstanding or severely limited educational insight. The content of this chapter has been organized to orient the reader to a tangible, structured elementary school operation.

After studying sections of this text and other selected educational literature, through discussions with school officials and education instructors and by comparing procedures and practices utilized in operating elementary schools known to him, the reader ought to be able to assess intelligently the procedure and practices described in this chapter.

FIGURE 3

MISS RITTER'S CLASSROOM ARRANGEMENT

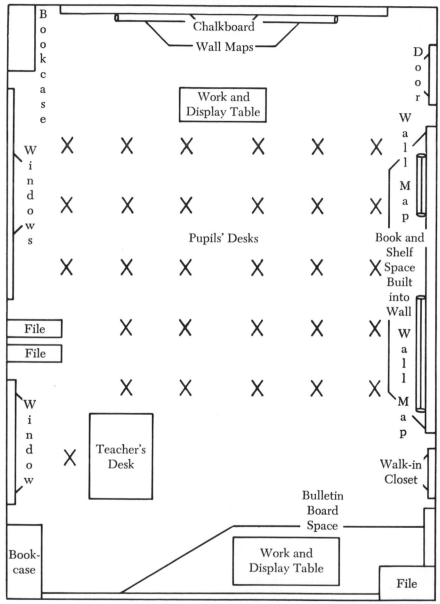

MISS RITTER'S CLASSROOM FACILITIES

Miss Ritter takes fullest advantage of her classroom, which is slightly smaller than average. She is able to find room within the 28-by-36 foot room for 28 pupils' desks and 1 teacher's desk, 2 work or display tables, 3 file cabinets, 2 bookcases (in addition to extensive built-in book storage facilities), 4 scroll-mounted wall maps, and an extensive bulletin-board display area. Her room arrangement is depicted in Figure 3. Since the pupils' desks are movable, she is able to rearrange them to suit her daily needs.

Materials accumulated by Miss Ritter, plus materials available in her new classroom, amount to an impressive array of accessible instructional resources. Each child is provided with a dictionary and text materials in the following curricular areas: reading, language skills, arithmetic, spelling, music, social science, and general science. These texts are housed in each child's desk. In addition, from 6 to 20 copies each of four alternate reading series, two alternate general science series, and two alternate social science series are available as reference sources. Most of these books are older texts previously used in the classroom. Other hardback books include a complete encyclopedia, nearly 100 primary social science sources, and more than 220 children's literature sources. Many paperbacks and pamphlets are available for instructional purposes. These materials range from a primary to an adult reading level. Two factors have contributed to the wealth of hardback and paperback materials available in Miss Ritter's classroom: first, her industry, and second, a school policy favoring classroom libraries rather than one central library.

Other materials in her classroom include an extensive picture file, numerous flat maps, a globe, a variety of general science equipment, and a variety of instructional tapes. Audio-visual equipment is provided for the entire school in a multipurpose room.

Twenty-eight children plan to make this classroom their second home for approximately 180 school days.

DATA-GATHERING AND RECORD-KEEPING

BEFORE THE FIRST DAY OF CLASS

Miss Ritter knows a great deal about the 28 children who are enrolled in her fourth grade before she actually meets the group. She acquires this information by consulting each child's past school record before the first day of class. In her school, a biographical survey of each child's mental, physical, social, and emotional growth and development is assembled in a cumulative folder which follows the child throughout his school experience. Primary-level teachers provide the data made available to Miss Ritter via the cumulative folder. In turn,

FIGURE 4

HALF OF THE COVER OF THE CUMULATIVE FOLDER USED BY MISS RITTER

NAME _____ SEX _____ DATE & PLACE OF BIRTH _____

ADDRESS _____ PHONE _____

MOTHER'S NAME __ OCCUPATION __ EDUCATION __ BIRTH __ LIVING? ____

FATHER'S NAME __ OCCUPATION __ EDUCATION __ BIRTH __ LIVING? ____

SIBLINGS _____ THEIR AGES _____

OTHER INFORMATION _____

Grade	Name of Test	Date Administered	Results

she will contribute additional information throughout the school year for the benefit of other teachers who will guide the children's school experiences in the future. The folder serves as a longitudinal record of the child's school progress.

The cover of the cumulative folder contains family data, intelligence and achievement test data, and health records. Half of the the folder cover used in Miss Ritter's school is portrayed in Figure 4. On the basis of data recorded on the cover, she is able to acquire considerable information pertaining to a child's family background and school progress. As a result of an examination of all 28 cumulative folders, Miss Ritter may be able to generalize about her group in the following manner:

1. Twenty-four of the 28 children in the group live at home with both parents.
2. The intelligence quotients of 17 of the 28 children exceed 100.
3. Six of the 28 children in the group do not have siblings.

These generalizations provide the teacher with advance insight into the nature of her group. What other descriptive statements, based upon data included on the cover of the 28 mythical cumulative record folders, can the reader add to Miss Ritter's list?

Test profiles are often filed in the cumulative folder for reference purposes. Samples of the pupils' work, teachers' statements describing the child's social and emotional progress, health records and profiles, and other miscellaneous information (sociometric data, parent conference notes, etc.) are also included within the cumulative folder. This information not only provides Miss Ritter with additional insight into a child's mental, physical, and academic progress, but it also sensitizes her to a child's social and emotional development in school. Data of this nature contribute to and significantly extend the above-mentioned descriptive statements of the group.

Each cumulative folder serves to introduce an individual to Miss Ritter. Twenty-eight cumulative folders afford her an opportunity to derive a series of descriptive generalizations which serve to introduce the group to her. On the basis of her perceptions of the children in the group and of the group itself, Miss Ritter is able to structure a stimulating learning environment that involves all children in worthwhile classroom activity starting with the first day of school.

Throughout the School Year

Survey tests are administered to 28 fourth-grade children during the first week of school. Miss Ritter files a copy of each child's test performance in spelling, arithmetic, composition, and handwriting in his cumulative folder. Since the same tests are administered near the end of the school year, by comparing the test results she can perceive each child's progress in the four skill areas. Late in January, a standardized achievement test is administered to the children as another phase of the school's testing program. Test results are reported in a pupil profile which is based upon performance in vocabulary, reading comprehension, language, work study, and arithmetic. A profile is filed in each child's cumulative folder. In addition, Miss Ritter files two reports of her impressions of each child's social and emotional behavior throughout the school year in the permanent record folder. She also contributes achievement data and behavioral observations to the record during the year. Data about the intelligence, achievement, physical health, and behavior of each child in her group provide Miss Ritter with an extensive sampling of knowledge. The value of such data is gauged in terms of their application in the school environment.

MISS RITTER'S INSTRUCTIONAL PROGRAM

A large midwestern university currently employs more than 2,000 instructors to teach 111 areas of knowledge ranging from accounting to zoology. Each instructor is responsible for structuring and teaching his area of specialization to interested students. Miss Ritter assumes the responsibility for structuring and teaching all aspects of her instructional program except music, art, and physical education. Unlike the typical instructor who has trained for and who lectures in an explicit field of inquiry, she, as an elementary school teacher, is confronted with life itself as the frame of reference for developing a program. Since her program is restricted to six hours per day for 180 school days each year, Miss Ritter must overcome two problems before a single child enters the classroom. First, she must identify the areas of knowledge which will constitute her instructional program. Second, she must prescribe the approximate amount of time needed per day or week to teach these various areas of knowledge.

A Frame of Reference

Actually, Miss Ritter does not assume a great deal of responsibility for determining the specific areas of knowledge which constitute her instructional program. The state legislature, state departments of education, local boards of education, teacher training institutions, school officials, curriculum guides, and a whole host of economic, political, and sociological factors influence, in varying degrees, the nature of the program. For example, in one midwestern state, children study state history before the completion of their fifth year in school, because the legislative body of the state enacted a law to that effect.

Required elementary school instruction prescribed in the educational code of a far western state encompasses the following:

> (Section 10302 of the Education Code) The course of study in the elementary schools shall include instruction in the following prescribed branches in the several grades in which each is required pursuant to this article: (a) reading, (b) writing, (c) spelling, (d) language study, (e) arithmetic, (f) geography, (g) history of the United States and of California, (h) civics including a study of the Declaration of Independence and of the Constitution of the United States, (i) music, (j) art, (k) training for healthful living, (l) morals and manners, and such other studies not to exceed three as may be prescribed by the board of education of the city, county, or city and county; provided, however, that whenever any part of "training for healthful living" conflicts with the religious beliefs of the parent or guardian of any pupil, then on written request of the parent or guardian the pupil may be excused from the part of the training which conflicts with such religious beliefs.

> (Section 10303) A minimum of fifty per cent of each school week shall be devoted to reading, writing, language study, spelling, arithmetic, and civics in grade one to six, inclusive, and a minimum of 600 minutes of each school week shall be devoted to such subjects in grades seven and eight.[1]

Most state lawmaking bodies have at one time or another enacted legislation pertaining to education.

Public opinion also exerts considerable influence upon the elementary school curriculum. Recently, public school officials and individuals in teacher training institutions have been able to direct public awareness of the need for better-trained scientists, mathematicians, and linguists into expanded curricular offerings in these areas at the elementary school level. On the other hand, the school board of Twin Lakes, Wisconsin, voted in the fall of 1961 to reintroduce a modern version of the McGuffey Readers in the elementary school, because these readers "... emphasize the teaching of fundamentals and good, wholesome Americanism." These school practices focus upon the unpredictable impact of public opinion upon an elementary school program.

[1] California Education Code (Sacramento: State Department of Education).

Many school systems provide entering teachers with a curriculum guide which describes the system's educational program. Curriculum guides usually outline the instructional program of the school system and briefly elaborate upon content to be taught within each curricular area. These guides are often prepared by joint committees of teachers, supervisors, and school administrators in a school system. A beginning teacher may or may not be requested to adhere religiously to the instructional pattern of the guide.

Thus, Miss Ritter must examine state and local curricular mandates, she must investigate professional literature pertaining to a "balanced" curriculum, and she must take into account local educational needs and expectations, in order to identify spheres of knowledge which will constitute her instructional program.

TIME ALLOCATIONS

After Miss Ritter identifies the realm of content for her instructional program, she must arrange daily and weekly time allotments in order to teach all aspects of the program. She is faced with problems like: (1) How much time is required by fourth-grade children to learn prescribed arithmetic concepts and skills? (2) Can handwriting best be taught in conjunction with other curricular areas or as a separate body of content? (3) Should recess be considered as a part of the physical education time allocation? Her attempt to solve these problems will be based upon what she and other educators have discovered through the years. If she attempts to resolve such problems by consulting the publications of more informed educators, she is apt to be thwarted. Experimental evidence on specifically how much daily or weekly time is required to teach a prescribed area of knowledge to children is sparse. As Henry Otto pointed out in the *Encyclopedia of Educational Research:*

> The scientific determination of time allotments is fraught with many difficulties — disagreements as to objectives and content of courses, variations in methods of teaching, variation in the needs and abilities of pupils, and constantly changing theories of education. Generally speaking, existing time allotments have been established with little or no reference to the findings of researches in educational psychology, curriculum, and method.[2]

[2]Henry J. Otto, "Time Allotments," in Walter S. Monroe, ed., *Encyclopedia of Educational Research* (Rev. ed.; New York: The Macmillan Company, 1950), p. 379. Reprinted with permission.

44

He concluded that most changes in time-allotment practices in the elementary school during the past fifty years were influenced by opinion and expanded curricular offerings.

Since Miss Ritter is unlikely to uncover a scientifically oriented time-allotment plan in the professional literature, she must seek elsewhere for assistance. One seemingly worthwhile source is plans utilized by fourth-grade teachers in other elementary schools. An extensive survey of fourth-grade time-allotment practices would provide Miss Ritter with a frame of reference for solving her specific

FIGURE 5

TIME ALLOTMENTS FOR SUBJECTS PRESCRIBED FOR
FOURTH GRADES IN LONG BEACH, CALIFORNIA*

Subject	Minutes Per Week	
	Minimum	Maximum
Arithmetic	250	300
Art	—	—
Health and Dental Health	30	40
Music	75	100
Language Arts		
(Oral and Written Expression and Handwriting)	200	250
Physical Education	100	100
Reading	300	350
Safety	—	—
Science	60	60
Social Studies	300	350
Spelling	100	125

NOTE: Art, safety, science, and health may be taught as separate subjects or in conjunction with other curricular areas.

*Long Beach Unified School District, Long Beach, California, "Time Allotment and Outline of the Curriculum for the Elementary Grades" (September, 1962), p. 87. Reprinted with permission.

problems. As an example, weekly plans for fourth grades in the Long Beach, California, Unified School District are presented in Figure 5. This plan can be implemented by using either of the following suggested daily schedules outlined in the Long Beach curriculum guide. Time-allotment plans in Northampton, Pennsylvania; Winnetka, Illinois; Pecos, Texas; and Macon, Georgia would certainly differ from the Long Beach pattern reported above. Time-allotment patterns and daily schedules employed in American elementary schools are many and varied.

The plan depicted in Figure 7 represents the areas of knowledge which constitute Miss Ritter's instructional program and the approximate time allocations prescribed for implementing these areas during a school week. The structure of the plan encompasses both state and local mandates and Miss Ritter's personal beliefs and preferences. No one, for example, required her to teach reading and arithmetic in the

FIGURE 6
TWO SUGGESTED DAILY SCHEDULES FOR FOURTH GRADE*

Schedule I

Time	Subject	Minutes per Day
9:00 – 10:10	Flag Salute; Social Studies	70
10:10 – 10:30	Music	20
10:30 – 10:40	Recess	10
10:40 – 11:00	Physical Education	20
11:00 – 11:50	Language Arts, Oral and Written Expression, Handwriting	50
11:50 – 12:10	Spelling	20
12:10 – 1:00	Noon	50
1:00 – 2:00	Reading	60
2:00 – 2:10	Recess	10
2:10 – 3:10	Arithmetic	60

Schedule III

Time	Subject	Minutes per Day
9:00 – 10:10	Flag Salute; Reading	70
10:10 – 10:30	Music	20
10:30 – 10:40	Recess	10
10:40 – 11:00	Physical Education	20
11:00 – 11:50	Arithmetic	50
11:50 – 12:10	Spelling	20
12:10 – 1:00	Noon	50
1:00 – 2:10	Social Studies	70
2:10 – 2:20	Recess	10
2:20 – 3:10	Language Arts, Oral and Written Expression, Handwriting	50

*Long Beach Unified School District, Long Beach, California, "Time Allotment and Outline of the Curriculum for the Elementary Grades" (September, 1962), p. 58. Reprinted with permission.

FIGURE 7

A Diagram of Miss Ritter's Instructional Program

Time / Day	9:00-9:15	9:15-9:45	9:45-10:15	10:15-10:35	10:35-11:00	11:00-11:30	11:30-12:00	12:00-1:00	1:00-1:30	1:30-2:10	2:10-2:50	2:50-3:00
Monday	Orientation Activities and Independent Activities			Spelling	Recess	Vocal Music		Social Science and General Science Unit Study		Physical Education	Language Skills	Dismissal Preparation
Tuesday		Reading Skills	Arithmetic Skills	Recess	Independent Study				Art		Library and Math Club	
Wednesday				Spelling	Recess	Vocal Music	Lunch			Physical Education	Language Skills	
Thursday				Recess	Instrumental Music				Art		Student Council	
Friday				Spelling	Recess	Vocal Music				Physical Education	Language Skills	

forenoon session. No one demanded that she establish a room council and an independent study hour. Therefore, she evolved a program that "met the requirements" and also incorporated elements which she deemed desirable. Time allocations are kept flexible so that she is able to capitalize upon penetrating or unexpectedly fruitful learning experiences.

If the reader tabulates the weekly time allocations for each area included in Miss Ritter's instructional plan, he can obtain an interesting perspective by comparing her plan with the Long Beach plan in Figure 5.

Ordinarily, the amount of time devoted to the various curricular areas differs in terms of the children's maturity. Beginning pupils

FIGURE 8

TIME ALLOCATIONS FOR THE ELEMENTARY SCHOOL
PRESCRIBED IN A STATE COURSE OF STUDY*

Areas of Experience	General Percentage of Time by Weeks	
	Primary	Intermediate
Opening Routines	4	4
Language Arts (Reading)	25	14
Language Arts (Phases other than Reading)	9	13
Free Play Activities	8	8
Health & Physical Education	8	8
Arithmetic	7	11
Experiences in the Social Living Areas (Social, Natural, & Physical Sciences)	14	17
Aesthetics and Creative Experiences	10	10
Lunch Period Activities	15	15

*The Elementary Course of Study, Bulletin 233-B (Harrisburg: Pennsylvania Department of Public Instruction, 1959), pp. 42-43. Reprinted with permission.

spend considerable time studying the skills aspects of the curriculum, such as reading, writing, and arithmetic. Children in their fourth, fifth, and sixth school years, on the other hand, devote much time to the study of the social, natural, and physical sciences. Suggested time allotments for the primary and intermediate grade levels, reported in the elementary course of study for the state of Pennsylvania, provide for differences in the children's maturity. The time allocations reported in Figure 8 are reasonably typical of contemporary practices in the elementary school.

DAILY CLASSROOM ACTIVITIES

Many teacher training institutions incorporate student participation in actual classroom situations as part of a prescribed program. Student participation may vary from observing a classroom teacher for a short time to an intensive student teaching experience. Participation affords a prospective teacher the opportunity to apply his educational theory either directly or vicariously in an actual classroom situation. Also, theoretical instruction seems to be more effectively communicated when a student is able to relate the instruction to real classroom situations. While this textbook cannot duplicate actual classroom observation, it can report an account of classroom activities involving a group of fourth-grade children. Therefore, a description of learning experiences for a typical school day (Monday) in Miss Ritter's room is included in this section.

In directing classroom activities, Miss Ritter adheres to certain learning guides which are valued by her pedagogical associates. The most important of these guides, which serve as the basis for her instructional program, are briefly described as follows:

1. *Content Defined.* The content to receive major emphasis in each grade is defined. The exactness of this definition is more marked in the upper than in the lower grades. Teachers are able to make detailed plans and collect materials to be used before the time of teaching. Deviation from assigned content is advised when the circumstances, such as current interest or vital concern, will assure definite advantages. In no case, however, should there be duplication of content already assigned to another grade. In addition to the content which is to receive major emphasis, specific skills to be taught—such as use of the dictionary in fourth grade—are assigned to each grade.

2. *Child Responsibility in Learning.* The teacher makes a conscious effort to lead the children to assume responsibility for learning the things they are being taught. In the content subjects, this is accomplished in a large measure by so directing the work that children raise problems for which they find answers. In the skill subjects, leading children to assume a responsibility for learning is achieved by acquainting them with personal deficiencies and by prescribing ways to eliminate deficiencies.

3. *Genuine Problems.* Problems children attack in school are genuine, not make believe. The examples that follow illustrate this point: (1) Why do we sometimes see only half the moon, while at other times we see it all? (2) What important things about Brazil's coffee industry should sixth graders know? (3) What materials did the pioneers use in building their homes?

4. *Ways to Study.* Acquainting children with the best ways to study or to work is one of the major goals of instruction in each grade. Since schoolwork is the major undertaking of elementary school-aged children, it seems logical that the best ways of studying should be taught to children.

5. *Individual Differences.* Effort is made to adjust instruction to the ability of the individual in a class. However, at times children of varying ability can work profitably on the same content.

6. *Use of Recall.* Since the practice of recall is one of the best known ways to retard forgetting, this process is used frequently in instruction. Summaries, reconsideration of original questions, reference to material previously studied, test questions, and the like are some of the common ways of using recall.

Can the reader identify specific manifestations of these principles of learning in the following descriptive sampling of Miss Ritter's instructional program? Are inconsistencies between principle and practice apparent to the reader?

ORIENTATION

Children ordinarily enter the classroom between 8:45 and 9:00 o'clock. Each day they find problems or puzzles presented on the chalkboard. Many children enter the room, take their seats, and attempt to solve the problem or puzzle presented by the teacher. Other children prefer to read or engage in conversation with a close school friend. A few moments past nine, the teacher directs attention toward the problem or puzzle presented. A short discussion aimed at solving it follows. After the group has successfully dealt with the situation, the children pledge allegiance to the flag of the United States and sing one or two songs. Occasionally, Miss Ritter reads to the children for a few moments before the reading skills lesson.

READING SKILLS

At times, all 28 children pursue a common activity during the reading skills period, but for the most part they are divided into subgroups structured to expedite specific learning tasks. Between five and ten children usually are grouped together for remedial and diagnostic purposes, while the remaining children are organized into a second group to receive instruction in prescribed reading lessons. A lesson focusing upon the interpretation of reading material is described as an example of instruction directed toward the entire group.

"Occasionally a tape recorder is used for oral reading purposes," said the teacher as an introduction to the lesson. "By means of taping read passages," she continued, "we hope to improve our oral reading ability. Let's listen to the tape recording we made during last Friday's reading class. Listen carefully to the way each child reads his passage."

One child had read a passage pertaining to a recent presidential election. She evidently had practiced reading the passage, as her presentation was excellent. Next, a boy read a passage completely unfamiliar to him until that moment. He stumbled through the reading. Periodically the recording was stopped so that children in the class could evaluate the readings. The children concluded that certain conditions such as good expression, familiarity with the topic, personal interest, and so forth, must be met when reading a passage orally.

Then a question arose as to whether punctuation was an important factor to be reckoned with when reading orally. To clarify this point, the teacher conducted an experiment. She distributed a dittoed paper, containing a paragraph lacking punctuation of any kind, to each child in the class. Several children were asked to read the paragraph orally. After a few children stumbled through the paragraph, the group surmised that punctuation was an important aspect of oral reading.

A second paper was then distributed to the children. It incorporated passages indicating fear, anger, disgust, disappointment, grief, joy, and suspense. Various children were selected to interpret orally the passages presented on the paper. These interpretations were evaluated by the group. The group concluded that printed passages must be examined carefully in order to convey the proper feeling orally in each instance.

The teacher culminated the lesson by distributing a third

paper which challenged the children to read aloud on their own a series of selected passages describing different emotional states.

ARITHMETIC SKILLS

Many aspects of the teacher's arithmetic skills lessons are tailor-made to the individual differences apparent within the group. At a given moment, five or six children may be pursuing an arithmetic problem. Again, introductory lessons, specific arithmetical applications, summary lessons, and so forth, may involve all children for a specified time.

In the following description of an arithmetic lesson, the teacher attempted to clarify the importance of proof in arithmetic.

The teacher distributed to each child one of three sets of selected arithmetic problems of varying difficulty. She asked the children to solve the problems and prove via diagrams, drawings, or what have you, that each solution was accurate. The problems were practical applications involving skills various individuals and subgroups had been studying. Thus, while the children worked as a cohesive entity, individuals with varying capabilities were challenged by the learning situation.

As the children worked at their seats, the teacher circulated among them. Occasionally, she requested a child to put his solution and proof for a specific problem on the chalkboard. After most children had completed the assigned task, the teacher directed their attention to the board solutions. On the board were a series of solutions and proofs for a number of the problems distributed. The arithmetic proofs were based upon circles, balls, graphs, a type of drawn footrule, ones and tens groupings, and number charts.

A class discussion of the principal aspects of the lesson terminated the arithmetic skills class.

SPELLING

Spelling instruction is based upon two prime concepts: First, words to be spelled are selected on the basis of their social utility; and second, a test-study-test-study-test method of teaching is employed. Monday's spelling lesson customarily follows this pattern:

1. The teacher pronounces each word to be spelled.
2. The children repeat each pronunciation.
3. Then, the teacher pronounces each word, uses it in a sen-

tence, and pronounces it a second time. This time, the children attempt to write out each word.

4. After the spelling list has been dictated, the teacher spells out each word correctly and the children check their own efforts.
5. The lesson is concluded after each child has identified misspelled words requiring attention before the next spelling test.

RECESS

Miss Ritter's 25-minute recess period is usually devoted to free play. However, she frequently organizes and participates in a variety of group games. A child may or may not desire to participate in these group ventures. Recess provides a change of pace for the instructional program.

VOCAL MUSIC

Since a special teacher provides vocal music instruction, Miss Ritter is free to remain in the classroom as a participant, to plan other instructional activities, or to take a break in the teacher's lounge.

LUNCH

Lunch facilities are provided in the school's cafeteria.

UNIT WORK

Each school year Miss Ritter guides fourth-grade pupils through a series of selected social, natural, and physical science units of instruction. These units are selected by the teacher on the basis of (1) their cruciality, (2) the availability of materials pertaining to the topic, and (3) the suitability of the topic in terms of the children's previous experiences. Unit instruction in Miss Ritter's room is a cooperative process. She identifies and broadly structures each unit to be studied. The unit is an excellent vehicle for individualizing instruction in the classroom. Tremendous pupil variations in concept formation are feasible within the framework of such a common learning experience. Some children invariably pursue a given problem at great length. Others may barely grasp its surface implications. An effective unit experience serves to increase individual differences among children.

The entire time allocation for unit study is usually devoted to either social science or general science topics for a given interval. These time intervals may vary from one to five or six weeks, depending upon the complexity of the topic. Approximately two-thirds of the available unit study time is devoted to the social sciences. A sample lesson from an on-going social science unit study is portrayed as follows:

The children utilized the first portion of the lesson to complete an oral summary of information pertaining to "Tools and Utensils" and "Raw Materials." These topics were part of a unit study focusing upon people living in the Arctic cold lands. After the group presented and summarized information obtained on the two topics, the teacher suggested an interesting follow-up.

Before the study of artifacts and raw materials, various children in the group attempted to anticipate possible solutions to the specific problems at hand. Their responses were recorded on tape. The teacher thus suggested to the group a comparative analysis of hypotheses stated prior to the actual study and knowledge derived as a result of considerable study. After each child's hypothesis was replayed, the teacher stopped the recorder and probed into similarities and differences between the hypothesis stated and the information gathered. The teacher used this discussion as one means of sensitizing children to the role of a hypothesis in a study situation, and to the necessity of utilizing data uncovered to verify or reject stated hypotheses.

Of course, the children were not specifically introduced to the word, *hypothesis*, in this lesson. Nor were they especially aware of the scientific nature of their inquiry. They were, however, acquainted with one very elementary mode of scientific inquiry, plus some specific information relating to raw materials and artifacts utilized by people living in the Arctic cold lands.

Physical Education

Again, a special teacher directs the children's activities. Miss Ritter uses the time to prepare instructional materials.

Language Skills

Even though reading and spelling fall within the realm of language skills, they are treated separately in Miss Ritter's instructional program. The language skills aspect of the program includes writing, listening, speaking, and grammar. Generally, Miss Ritter structures a lifelike lesson or series of lessons focusing upon the need for a particular language skill. She then guides the children to identify the nature of the problem confronted and to investigate ways of resolving the problem situation. Rules and regulations characteristic of the English language are derived as one outcome of this study procedure. Occasionally, she presents specific lessons or a series of lessons to reinforce or clarify a previously studied skill. The language skills lessons are structured to take into account differing needs and abilities of children in the group.

The following example of a language skills lesson is the third in a sequence focusing upon the development of pupil perception. These lessons expose children to experiences that require either written or oral exposition. The expository reports of the children are compared with the actual experience in each case. As a result of these experiences, the children are able to assess critically their own sensitivity to events occurring in the world around them.

The teacher initiated the lesson as follows, "Today we are going to conduct another language experiment. In a moment you will view a short motion picture about an unusual camping experience. As you watch the film, make believe you are playing the part of the camper." After the film presentation, the teacher asked each child to record on paper his conception of the events taking place in the film.

As the children carried out the assignment, the teacher circulated among them. She selected several children who completed the assignment quickly to copy their work on the chalkboard while the other children worked. After most of the children had completed the assignment, the teacher derived a composite description based upon the pupils' perceptions of the film. The accuracy of this composite description was determined by comparing it to a second viewing of the film.

A teacher-led discussion of reasons for differences existing between the pupils' composite description of the film and the actual film served to conclude the lesson.

DISMISSAL

At this time, children gather their possessions, dress for the outdoors, and depart from the classroom. Time is provided for an orderly departure at the final bell.

A one-day sample from Miss Ritter's instructional program is presented to raise questions and issues rather than answer them specifically. Certain aspects of her instruction take on considerable meaning in the light of problems listed below.

1. Try to list alternate procedures which Miss Ritter may resort to when planned instruction either exceeds or falls short of the prescribed time allocation for the lesson.
2. In what ways can Miss Ritter deal with children who either complete prescribed tasks quickly or seldom complete them? Should each child be expected to complete each assignment?
3. Review the sampled lessons from Miss Ritter's instructional program to note specific materials and equipment employed in her classroom. When does the classroom teacher find time to prepare for the school day?
4. The statement, "An effective unit experience serves to increase individual differences among children," was made in conjunction with the description of unit work in Miss Ritter's classroom. Is increasing individual differences a valid objective for an instructional program?
5. Should art and music experiences be integrated with other areas of the instructional program?
6. Is the child's education enhanced by special music, art, and physical education teachers in the elementary school? Could science and mathematics specialists guide the learning experiences of children more effectively than Miss Ritter?
7. Miss Ritter incorporates a classroom student council, an independent study period, and a combined library-mathematics club period in her instructional program. What does she hope to accomplish by including these areas within her instructional program?

This list of questions can be extended almost infinitely. The seven questions listed are examples of those the reader needs to raise in order to comprehend the implications of Miss Ritter's instructional program. Numerous suggestions and solutions to such problems can be uncovered throughout the remainder of this book.

QUESTIONS FOR DISCUSSION

1. Miss Ritter bases spelling instruction upon two prime concepts: First, words to be spelled are selected on the basis of their social utility; and second, a test-study-test-study-test method of teaching is employed. Mr. Paige, a fourth-grade teacher in another school

district, employs similar teaching methods, but he derives word lists from the weekly topics treated in his classroom. Mrs. Peta, a fifth-grade teacher in still another school district, uses neither word lists nor prescribed spelling test periods. Instead, she has attempted to tailor spelling experiences to the needs of her children. No two children follow the same sequence or scope of experiences.

Discuss the advantages and disadvantages of these approaches to teaching spelling to elementary school children. Which approach, if any, would you deem superior to the others? Why?

2. During her lesson on arithmetic proof, Miss Ritter asked the children to use diagrams, drawings, or other visual means to verify the accuracy of each solution. Since the children probably invested considerable time and effort in the diagrams and drawings, is it possible that the mathematical point of the lesson might be missed? How would you evaluate methods like this in general when they are utilized to "make mathematics more meaningful" for children?

ADDITIONAL REFERENCES

See the lists at the ends of Chapters Four, Five, Six, and Seven, pages 81-82, 125, 157-158.

PURPOSES OF EDUCATION
IN THE ELEMENTARY SCHOOL

In order to understand what is meant by the purpose of education in the elementary school, let us consider an analogy. Let us assume that we are concerned, not with elementary education, but with the development of the Junior Chamber of Commerce movement.[1] More specifically, we wish to understand how the purposes of an organization or institution are defined.

The first Jaycee type of group, called the Young Men's Progressive Civic Association, emerged in 1915 from a St. Louis dancing federation. Interest in this group, which brashly insisted that young men should play an important role in civic affairs, grew swiftly. By 1918, it was known as the Junior Chamber of Commerce. Two years later, after a caucus of other young men's associations in the country, the name was expanded to the United States Junior Chamber of Commerce.

The Junior Chamber's growth was not spectacular in the early years. A solid foundation was poured, however, and a growth boom began in the late 1930's. During the Second World War, the organization not only survived, it established the world Jaycee group known as Junior Chamber International. Today, the United States Jaycees boast more than 4,100 chapters and over 200,000 members. Jaycee groups are also found in about 90 other nations.

The basic motivation for the development of this organization is captured in the words of Jaycee founder Henry Giessenbier, Jr., "That

[1]Historical data have been obtained from the United States Junior Chamber of Commerce periodical, *Future,* 24, No. 3 (March, 1962), 11 and 41.

America might feel the energy of its young men ....." This idea was further crystallized with the adoption in 1947 of an official Jaycee Creed, which captures the spirit and sets forth the purposes of the Jaycee movement. Today, activities undertaken by local chapters are designed to implement the purposes stated in the Creed, which was revised in 1951.

The United States Junior Chamber of Commerce is the outcome of a felt need of a group of perceptive young men. It prospered because many young Americans shared this need to become actively involved in civic affairs.

Now, what does this discussion contribute to our knowledge of the purpose of education in the elementary school? The facts contribute nothing; however, the process is of paramount importance. The institution known as the elementary school also owes its existence to felt needs. Furthermore, numerous attempts have been made over the years to translate this need into a statement of purposes for the elementary school in our society's educational structure. It is the purpose of this chapter to examine needs and purposes that have influenced elementary education in America.

SOME SOCIAL AND PHILOSOPHIC PRESSES UPON THE ELEMENTARY SCHOOL

The common school owes its existence to the needs of the common people. Just as a felt need led to the Jaycee movement, social needs contributed to the creation and maintenance of the common school. These needs are reported in the following paragraphs, and they are then related to the political philosophy of our social order.

The American elementary school as we know it did not emerge from a scholastic vacuum. Rather, early colonists brought to this country a heritage of hundreds of years of experience with a common school. While no one is certain of the origin of the elementary school in Western society, historians have traced the common school idea to the vernacular schools of the Middle Ages. These schools served the needs of the burghers, the expanding social class of the time. Functional skills like reading the mother tongue, writing, and simple arithmetic were needed by the burghers to conduct their commercial business, and the vernacular schools were established to meet this need.

The common school idea received considerable impetus from

FIGURE 9

VARIOUS TYPES OF SCHOOLS WHICH PREDOMINATED IN THE DEVELOPMENT OF
AMERICA'S EDUCATIONAL SYSTEMS

Period Before	School Pattern
Washington's inauguration	Dame School Reading and Writing School English Grammar School Latin Grammar School Academy College
The Civil War	Dame School or other Primary Unit Graded Elementary School Reading and Writing School English Grammar School Latin Grammar School Academy High School College Postgraduate Study
The Twentieth Century	Preschool Unit Graded Elementary School Academy High School Higher Education Postgraduate Study
The 1960's	Preschool Unit 6 or 8 Grade Elementary School Junior High School Senior High School Postgraduate Study

three subsequent developments in Europe.[2] First, the invention of printing made many books available. Second, leaders of the successful Protestant Reformation believed that everyone should be able to read religious texts, especially the Bible. Third, a new social philosophy, which dignified the common man and made him seem worth educating for other than religious and commercial purposes, attracted attention in the eighteenth century. These three developments expedited the growth of the common school in Europe.

This notion of a common school was carried to America by the Puritans, Huguenots, Quakers, Dutch, and other dissenters who shared a common belief in the value of education. Hence, early educational needs in America centered on teaching literacy to perpetuate the word of God and teaching skills necessary to engage in commerce.

The American Revolution of 1776 was fought in the belief that all men have inalienable rights, such as life, liberty, and the pursuit of happiness, and that governments exist for the welfare of man. This successful revolution resulted in a new role for the common school in America. Colonial leaders realized that the future of the new nation depended upon a rational citizenry. It was for this reason that Jefferson and others argued for free public education responsive to the needs of the common man.

The seeds of education planted by the Colonial leaders produced an abundant harvest in the nineteenth century. The common schools offered children a broad range of study that included physical training, citizenship training, vocational training, and cultural inculcation at the turn of this century. Various types of school patterns utilized in the course of our national growth are shown in Figure 9. Societal needs formed by emerging nationalism, an industrial revolution, and a complex federal government markedly altered the nature of the elementary school in America. Not only have physical training, vocational training, and cultural inculcation continued to be emphasized in elementary schools along with intellectual development in the twentieth century, but social adjustment has become one of the major goals of the modern elementary school. The intricacies of contemporary life have probably contributed to this development.

Social needs have changed the common school in America from a purveyor of the basic skills needed to read the Bible and engage in

[2]Edwin H. Reeder, in Walter S. Monroe, ed., *Encyclopedia of Educational Research* (Rev. ed.; New York: The Macmillan Company, 1950), pp. 354-355.

commerce to a complex educational institution designed to meet the needs of an even more complex social order. There is a direct relationship between society and the educational task. The more complex the society is in general, the greater the tendency for a complex educational system. The opposite of this also holds true. One problem today's educator must solve relates to which needs must be taken into account during the elementary school years.

In 1947, the President's Commission on Education set forth a challenge to educators.

> Education is an institution of every civilized society, but the purposes of education are not the same in all societies. An educational system finds its guiding principles and ultimate goals in the aims and philosophy of the social order in which it functions. The two predominant types of society in the world today are the democratic and the authoritarian, and the social role of education is very different in the two systems.
>
> American society is a democracy: that is, its folkways and institutions, its arts and sciences and religions, are based on the principle of equal freedom and equal rights for all its members, regardless of race, faith, sex, occupation, or economic status. The law of the land, providing equal justice for the poor as well as the rich, for the weak as well as the strong, is one instrument by which a democratic society establishes, maintains, and protects this equality among different persons and groups. The other instrument is education, which, as all the leaders in the making of democracy have pointed out again and again, is necessary to give effect to the equality prescribed by law.[3]

The challenge to educators lies in formulating and implementing "guiding principles and ultimate goals" of education that are consistent with the aims and philosophy of our social order.

Since the philosophy desired is to be democratic, educators are charged with the responsibility for translating this ideal into a tangible, functional educational plan. Once such a plan is conceived, a statement of the purposes of education in the elementary school can be derived. The elementary school's existence as an institution is contingent upon the degree to which its uniqueness can be spelled out in the statement. Is this a reasonable charge? It is difficult to address such a question, since no consistent philosophy of education

[3]The President's Commission on Education, *Higher Education for American Democracy*, 6 vols. (Washington, D.C.: U.S. Government Printing Office, 1947), I, 5.

has as yet served as a frame of reference for determining the objectives of education in the American elementary school.

Caswell and Foshay illuminate the crux of this dilemma in their book, *Education in the Elementary School*. They note that

> The central problem... which the elementary school worker should face is to discover how children of elementary school age develop the attitudes and abilities that make for the effective citizen, homemaker, and worker in a democratic society such as we have and are seeking to preserve and improve.... Such understandings are necessary if a direction known to be good and desirable, rather than an uncertain drifting on the basis of tradition, is to be achieved in the program of the elementary school.[4]

In recent years, researchers representing a number of disciplines have provided a wealth of information relating to how children are assimilated into our culture. The time seems appropriate to compile such data, analyze it critically, and then utilize it as a vital ingredient in the process of formulating a statement of purposes of education for the elementary school.

Sir William Osler observed in the *Montreal Medical Journal* that "the philosophies of one age have become the absurdities of the next, and the foolishness of yesterday has become the wisdom of tomorrow." Today's discerning educators are confronted with the problem of discriminating between philosophic foolishness and philosophic wisdom as they attempt to solve their pedagogical problems. Which philosophic base can best serve educators who attempt to implement the ideas expressed by Caswell and Foshay? Is it conceivable that a single philosophic base can meet the needs of elementary education in America? These are vital questions that demand concise answers. They have been raised because the writers believe prospective teachers ought to be aware of this dimension of education.

PHILOSOPHICAL FOUNDATIONS: THEIR POTENTIAL INFLUENCE

When the Jaycees adopted their Creed in 1947, they gave official recognition to a statement of beliefs that clearly prescribed the nature of their organization. Numerous attempts have been made by educa-

[4]Hollis L. Caswell and A. Wellesley Foshay, *Education in the Elementary School* (2nd ed.; New York: American Book Company, 1950), pp. 81-82. Reprinted with permission. (A third edition is also available.)

tors in recent years to duplicate this accomplishment for the elementary school. Several of these are detailed later in the chapter. Unfortunately, no one has succeeded in setting forth purposes of education for the elementary school that have widespread appeal. Since purposes of this sort are based upon a point of view of life, of knowing, of value, and so forth, the writers have attempted to convey the potential influence of philosophic points of view on the problem of defining purposes.

A review of categories of education that have emerged in the course of history will serve as a point of departure. Educational thought to date has been categorized by scholars according to points of view, "schools," or positions. These categories usually share some common presuppositions, and there is considerable overlapping. For our purposes, educational thought is viewed in terms of five philosophic schools — Realism, Idealism, Experimentalism, Neo-Thomism, and Existentialism.

All of these philosophic schools seek answers to (1) What is real? (2) What is good? (3) What is true? They differ on the nature of (1) self, (2) mind, (3) knowledge, (4) value theory, and (5) metaphysics. As the reader studies the brief summary of each position, he should pay special attention to factors that could contribute to the problem of prescribing purposes for the elementary school.

REALISM

Realists view the universe as being composed of entities existing in themselves and independent of any knowledge of their existence. They believe that these entities can be known by the human mind as they are in themselves, and that such knowledge can provide bases for the guidance of individual and social action. Realism was first explicitly detailed by Plato and then developed by Aristotle. It persisted century after century because many prominent scholars accepted and supported its salient dimensions. Niccolo Machiavelli, Johann Friedrich Herbart, Herbert Spencer, and Bertrand Russell are some of these scholars.

Common sense as a study approach is indicative of realism. It is a way to truth so long as the human faculties are able to acquire accurate, reliable data. To discern truth about things as they really are and to extend and integrate truth are important aims of education as the Realist sees things. He wants to acquire knowledge that is theoretically justified. He seeks faithful knowledge about the actual world.

IDEALISM

While Idealism seems to be declining in stature, it still exerts an important influence on varied modes of thought. Broadly, any view emphasizing mind, soul, or spirit represents Idealism. Specifically, Idealists view all reality as the essence of spirit, they recognize ideas as the essential factors of knowledge, and they pursue ideals as ultimate objects. Gottfried von Leibnitz, Immanuel Kant, G. W. F. Hegel, and Ralph Waldo Emerson espoused this point of view.

Kantian Idealists believed that the human mind can never know things in themselves as they really are, but only as they are warped by the cognitive process. Hegelian Idealists extended this belief to the point where they denied any purely physical existence. Pure thought developed into even richer, higher, and freer forms epitomized their world. All that can be known about the world, according to their view, are ideas of it.

An Idealist's view of education would encompass: (1) knowing oneself and his environment; (2) recognizing one's dependence upon his complex environment; (3) recognizing that knowledge is the product of one's attempts to interpret experiences in their relation to one another; (4) being aware of an orderly "objective reality" that is sought and that must be known for one to live well; and (5) viewing values as a part of reality.[5] Man's life is good, says the Idealist, in proportion to the success of his search for value dimensions of reality and his resultant responses to the reality which is uncovered.

EXPERIMENTALISM

Scientific progress during the Enlightenment probably contributed significantly to the evolution of Experimentalism (it is also referred to as "Instrumentalism" and "Pragmatism"). This progress, combined with the choas and stagnation of the philosophy of the era, contributed to a change in the conception of philosophy that can be traced to David Hume. He argued that bases existed for doubting validity of any of the so-called eternal truths or laws of nature which philosophers had been discovering.[6]

This doubt served as a harbinger of a point of view that regarded

[5]Theodore M. Greene, "A Liberal Christian Idealist Philosophy of Education," *Modern Philosophies of Education* (Chicago: The University of Chicago Press, 1955), pp. 99-105.

[6]Daniel J. Bronstein, *et al.*, eds., *Basic Problems of Philosophy* (Englewood Cliffs, N.J.: Prentice-Hall, Inc., 1955), p. 541.

ideas only as consequences in experience, that recognized experience as social in origin and purpose, and that apprehended life by studying experimentally uniformities within experience. Experimentalism focuses upon a description of knowledge as experience — which is both an organism and an environment. Hence, truth is put on an operational basis. Self-evident truths are rejected, and in their place are offered experiences accepted only after verification.

Advocates of this point of view include Friedrich Nietzsche, William James, and John Dewey. Dewey's views have commanded considerable attention in the twentieth century, because they set forth the foundation of the so-called Progressive Education movement in America. Later in this chapter, pedagogical implications of Dewey's Experimentalism are treated more extensively.

NEO-THOMISM

Neo-Thomism is a view that subordinates philosophy to theology in that conclusions to be reached by philosophy are determined in advance. A philosopher may utilize methods of rational inquiry to derive conclusions, so long as his conclusions do not interfere with the established truths of theology. It is held that these truths, which are received by faith through revelation, cannot be contradicted by a truth of philosophy obtained by reason, since both kinds of truth have a common denominator, namely God.[7]

The Neo-Thomist believes the knower has the capacity for knowing the object of his studies — that is, to know being. The process of knowing is one wherein percepts are reduced to concepts. Since knowledge is guaranteed by God, the Neo-Thomist is able to attain an infallible knowledge of truth. Jacques Maritain is one of the most prolific proponents of this point of view.

The ultimate role of education in the Neo-Thomist plan is to equip youth with the tools needed to understand that which brings to him intimations of immortality. This involves a liberal education based upon religion. Studies of truth, beauty, and goodness lead to the Creator of it all. Therefore, the hereafter rather than the here is of paramount importance.

EXISTENTIALISM

Soren Kierkegaard, Martin Heidegger, Jean Paul Sartre, and a number of other contemporary philosophers have put forth a theory

[7]*Ibid.*, p. 544.

that stresses self as the ultimate reality and its inner struggle as the basic fact of existence. Knowledge is viewed as sensations as they exist in one's consciousness, and it is assessed according to its biological value when unaffected by prejudice, emotions, and volitions. Biological "characters" like "being," "equal," "similar," "perceived," and "represented" have no truth value. Nothing may be truly known as an object of reason; reality must be encountered in experience by man to be known.

Existentialism is viewed without a metaphysical dimension; it is antihypothetical; and it offers only a surface account of psychological realities. It centers on the individual in a situation in which he finds himself. The unfolding of the individual within his environment of time and place represents the end sought by Existentialists.

Since it is the existence of man that is important, education must stress all that bears upon such existence. Existentialists regard as salient aspects of education a teacher, a pupil, and a curriculum. The interaction of these raw materials enables man to know himself in his own time and place.

One is apt to comment that all this is fine, but what difference does it make to a prospective elementary school teacher? William Drake stated that each of the above-mentioned philosophies demands a different type of school, implying differences in school administration, methods of teaching, curricular materials, courses of study, methods and means of support, and differences in the purposes and functions of education. "The fact that . . . these philosophies [are] finding active expression in our schools," he wrote, "tends to confuse both the public and the teacher."[8] Essentially, the likenesses and differences revolve around what education is for and how it is to be accomplished. Involved are such questions as, What should be the basic content in elementary schools? What approach should be utilized in the instruction of children? and What is the essential goal of pedagogy? These are examples of questions that bring different responses from advocates of the different educational philosophies.

A number of prolific thinkers have devoted much time to the problem of educating children during the past several centuries. The educational ideas of Jean-Jacques Rousseau, Johann Pestalozzi, Friedrich Froebel, Johann Friedrich Herbart, Maria Montessori, and Ralph Waldo Emerson, just to mention a few, are recorded for poster-

[8] William E. Drake, *The American School in Transition* (Englewood Cliffs, N.J.: Prentice-Hall, Inc., 1955), p. 564.

ity. These ideas cannot be treated fairly in a book of this nature. Instead, the writers have decided to amplify the position of one thinker — John Dewey, America's most famous twentieth-century educational philosopher — by reporting excerpts of his educational views.

Dewey's ideas reflect Experimentalism, one of the five schools of philosophy mentioned previously. Once introduced, his point of view is contrasted with several contemporary positions based upon different philosophical premises. The writers believe that this exposure is sufficient to make the reader aware of reasons why the purposes of education in the American elementary school are not as clearly prescribed as the purposes of the Jaycees.

In 1897 Dewey wrote an educational credo that sets forth his vision of the nature of education. "Article 1 — What Education Is" from Dewey's "My Pedagogic Creed," is reproduced to convey the true impact of this man's belief.

ARTICLE 1 — WHAT EDUCATION IS[9]

I believe that all education proceeds by the participation of the individual in the social consciousness of the race. This process begins unconsciously almost at birth, and is continually shaping the individual's powers, saturating his consciousness, forming his habits, training his ideas, and arousing his feelings and emotions. Through this unconscious education the individual gradually comes to share in the intellectual and moral resources which humanity has succeeded in getting together. He becomes an inheritor of the funded capital of civilization. The most formal and technical education in the world cannot safely depart from this general process. It can only organize it or differentiate it in some particular direction.

I believe that the only true education comes through the stimulation of the child's powers by the demands of the social situations in which he finds himself. Through these demands he is stimulated to act as a member of a unity, to emerge from his original narrowness of action and feeling, and to conceive of himself from the standpoint of the welfare of the group to which he belongs. Through the responses which others make to his activities he comes to know what these mean in social terms. The value which they have is reflected back into them. For instance, through the response which is made to the child's instinctive babblings the child comes to know what those babblings mean; they are transformed into

[9]John Dewey, "My Pedagogic Creed," *The School Journal,* 54 (January 16, 1897), 77-80.

articulate language and thus the child is introduced into the con-
solidated wealth of ideas and emotions which are now summed up
in language.

I believe that this educational process has two sides — one
psychological and one sociological; and that neither can be subordinated to the other or neglected without evil results following. Of
these two sides, the psychological is the basis. The child's own
instincts and powers furnish the material and give the starting point
for all education. Save as the efforts of the educator connect with
some activity which the child is carrying on of his own initiative
independent of the educator, education becomes reduced to a
pressure from without. It may, indeed, give certain external results,
but cannot truly be called educative. Without insight into the
psychological structure and activities of the individual, the educative process will, therefore, be haphazard and arbitrary. If it
chances to coincide with the child's activity it will get a leverage; if
it does not, it will result in friction, or disintegration, or arrest of the
child nature.

I believe that knowledge of social conditions, of the present
state of civilization, is necessary in order properly to interpret the
child's powers. The child has his own instincts and tendencies, but
we do not know what these mean until we can translate them into
their social equivalents. We must be able to carry them back into a
social past and see them as the inheritance of previous race activities. We must also be able to project them into the future to see what
their outcome and end will be. In the illustration just used, it is the
ability to see in the child's babblings the promise and potency of a
future social intercourse and conversation which enables one to
deal in the proper way with that instinct.

I believe that the psychological and social sides are organically
related and that education cannot be regarded as a compromise
between the two, or a superimposition of one upon the other. We
are told that the psychological definition of education is barren and
formal — that it gives us only the idea of a development of all the
mental powers without giving us any idea of the use to which these
powers are put. On the other hand, it is urged that the social
definition of education, as getting adjusted to civilization, makes of
it a forced and external process, and results in subordinating the
freedom of the individual to a preconceived social and political
status.

I believe that each of these objections is true when urged
against one side isolated from the other. In order to know what a
power really is we must know what its end, use, or function is; and
this we cannot know save as we conceive of the individual as active

in social relationships. But, on the other hand, the only possible adjustment which we can give to the child under existing conditions, is that which arises through putting him in complete possession of all his powers. With the advent of democracy and modern industrial conditions, it is impossible to foretell definitely just what civilization will be twenty years from now. Hence it is impossible to prepare the child for any precise set of conditions. To prepare him for the future life means to give him command of himself; it means so to train him that he will have the full and ready use of all his capacities; that his eye and ear and hand may be tools ready to command, that his judgment may be capable of grasping the conditions under which it has to work, and the executive forces be trained to act economically and efficiently. It is impossible to reach this sort of adjustment save as constant regard is had to the individual's own powers, tastes, and interests — say, that is, as education is continually converted into psychological terms.

In sum, I believe that the individual who is to be educated is a social individual and that society is an organic union of individuals. If we eliminate the social factor from the child we are left only with an abstraction; if we eliminate the individual factor from society, we are left only with an inert and lifeless mass. Education, therefore, must begin with a psychological insight into the child's capacities, interests, and habits. It must be controlled at every point by reference to these same considerations. These powers, interests, and habits must be continually interpreted — we must know what they mean. They must be translated into terms of their social equivalents — into terms of what they are capable of in the way of social service.

Subsequent articles from "My Pedagogic Creed" amplify Dewey's view of the school, the subject matter of education, the nature of method, and social progress. Dewey's name has been associated over the years with the expression, "learn by doing." Other widely quoted ideas that are expressed in his creed are: (1) the school is not a prelude to life, it is life; (2) democracy must be lived *in* the school; (3) the curriculum is not a series of set studies; rather, it is based upon the interests of the children; and (4) the social and aesthetic aspects of the curriculum are more crucial than the basic skills aspects. When the reader reflects upon the fact that these ideas were being implemented in Dewey's elementary school at the University of Chicago before the turn of the twentieth century, he can better understand the pioneering nature of Dewey's beliefs.

The popularity of Dewey's educational ideas in the twentieth century tends to veil the fact that other eminent American philosophers have some notions about the process of education. A number of contemporary philosophers represent the philosophical Realist viewpoint. These individuals accept Aristotle's belief that certain permanent values exist in the universe, applicable to human life in all times and all places. Since this knowledge is necessary to perpetuate humanity, they hold that educators must assume the responsibility for helping society's youth to discover these values. Consequently, their bases of education seriously conflict with Dewey's Experimentalistic beliefs.

William C. Bagley viewed the process of education as a philosophical Realist. He believed that education must be society-centered rather than child-centered. Bagley opposed Dewey's ideas of individual freedom, interest, and discipline. He argued that the individual must be taught in school to conform to the demands of group life, since it is only through his relations with others that he can achieve true self-realization. By conformity he meant old-fashioned discipline, the subordination of individual liberties, and a structured curriculum. Bagley stated that the aim of education is social efficiency. Robert Hutchins and Mortimer Adler also share the Aristotelian belief that truth is absolute. They argue that the great books of the past reveal the truth, so it is the responsibility of the schools to perpetuate this heritage of wisdom.

Dewey's Experimentalism and Realism are only two of the five recognizable philosophic categories that influence the aims of education currently. These multiple philosophic bases of education compound the difficulties of arriving at a clear-cut statement of the purposes of education in elementary education. It is for this reason that many diverse statements of the purposes of education have been formulated in the twentieth century. Only an inspired optimist can envision a unifying educational creed similar to the Jaycee Creed emerging from a gathering of elementary educators in the near future. Until that event takes place, the reader is advised to heed Havelock Ellis' warning that a man must not swallow more beliefs than he can digest.

The fact that there is much disagreement is an indication of the magnitude of contemporary thought about purposes. One should not disregard the efforts of these countless individuals just because disagreement exists; rather, one should hope that their labor will eventually provide the direction that is desired. Effective utilization of brainpower to provide a meaningful frame of reference and clear-cut purposes for elementary education must be the hope of tomorrow.

IMPLEMENTING NEEDS AND PHILOSOPHIES

Various groups of educators gather together from time to time to crystallize in written statements what the elementary school is trying to do. Each statement usually reflects a philosophical point of view, and it takes into account specified social needs. These efforts have been markedly accelerated in recent decades of the twentieth century, as educators have become acutely aware of the importance of the child's early school experiences. Beardsley Ruml noted that it takes only a period of about a dozen years to implant a basic culture in the mind of man—the period between the age of two and the age of fourteen. If this is a valid contention, elementary educators certainly ought to be held responsible for the product of their school.

Several written statements of a philosophy of education have been reproduced below for analysis. One represents the efforts of a national commission; two represent the efforts of urban school systems. As the reader examines each of these statements, he should keep in mind two questions: First, what individual and social needs are taken into account? and second, Does the statement reveal a particular viewpoint? These statements represent attempts on the part of a group of educators to provide a general framework for directing the education of youth.

The Educational Policies Commission, a group of educational leaders invited annually by the National Education Association to join together to attack a major educational problem, published in 1938 an intensive statement of the general purposes of education for America. Four major groups of objectives were identified. The gist of this statement is reported as follows:

I. THE OBJECTIVES OF SELF-REALIZATION[10]

The Inquiring Mind. The educated person has an appetite for learning.

Speech. The educated person can speak the mother tongue clearly.

[10]Educational Policies Commission, National Education Association, *The Purposes of Education in American Democracy* (Washington, D.C.: The Association, 1938), pp. 50, 72, 90, and 108. Reprinted with permission.

Reading. The educated person reads the mother tongue efficiently.

Writing. The educated person writes the mother tongue effectively.

Number. The educated person solves his problems of counting and calculating.

Sight and Hearing. The educated person is skilled in listening and observing.

Health Knowledge. The educated person understands the basic facts concerning health and disease.

Health Habits. The educated person protects his own health and that of his dependents.

Public Health. The educated person works to improve the health of the community.

Recreation. The educated person is participant and spectator in many sports and other pastimes.

Intellectual Interests. The educated person has mental resources for the use of leisure.

Esthetic Interests. The educated person appreciates beauty.

Character. The educated person gives responsible direction to his own life.

II. The Objectives of Human Relationships

Respect for Humanity. The educated person puts human relationships first.

Friendships. The educated person enjoys a rich, sincere, and varied social life.

Cooperation. The educated person can work and play with others.

Courtesy. The educated person observes the amenities of social behavior.

Appreciation of the Home. The educated person appreciates the family as a social institution.

Conservation of the Home. The educated person conserves family ideals.

Homemaking. The educated person is skilled in homemaking.

Democracy in the Home. The educated person maintains democratic family relationships.

III. The Objectives of Economic Efficiency

Work. The educated producer knows the satisfaction of good workmanship.

Occupational Information. The educated producer understands the requirements and opportunities for various jobs.

Occupational Choice. The educated producer has selected his occupation.

Occupational Efficiency. The educated producer succeeds in his chosen vocation.

Occupational Adjustment. The educated producer maintains and improves his efficiency.

Occupational Appreciation. The educated producer appreciates the social value of his work.

Personal Economics. The educated consumer plans the economics of his own life.

Consumer Judgment. The educated consumer develops standards for guiding his expenditures.

Efficiency in Buying. The educated consumer is an informed and skillful buyer.

Consumer Protection. The educated consumer takes appropriate measures to safeguard his interests.

IV. The Objectives of Civic Responsibility

Social Justice. The educated citizen is sensitive to the disparities of human circumstance.

Social Activity. The educated citizen acts to correct unsatisfactory conditions.

Social Understanding. The educated citizen seeks to understand social structures and social processes.

Critical Judgment. The educated citizen has defenses against propaganda.

Tolerance. The educated citizen respects honest differences of opinion.

Conservation. The educated citizen has a regard for the nation's resources.

Social Applications of Science. The educated citizen measures scientific advance by its contribution to the general welfare.

World Citizenship. The educated citzen is a cooperating member of the world community.

Law Observance. The educated citizen respects the law.

Economic Literacy. The educated citizen is economically literate.

Political Citizenship. The educated citizen accepts his civic duties.

Devotion of Democracy. The educated citizen acts upon an unswerving loyalty to democratic ideals.

This statement represents one of the best twentieth-century efforts to clarify the purposes of education in America. Even though critics have pointed out a number of limitations of the statement, the Educational Policies Commission report has received the strong endorsement of laymen and educators throughout the country.[11]

Many public school systems have prepared detailed statements of their educational point of view in recent decades. These statements vary in length from a few paragraphs to hundreds of pages. A point of view that is unique to the local school situation is usually spelled out in the statement. The statements of Columbus and Euclid, Ohio, are presented below for examination:

COLUMBUS PUBLIC SCHOOLS, COLUMBUS, OHIO[12]

We believe that the Columbus Public Schools should provide opportunities in wholesome surroundings for the child to. . . .
Develop his capacities to the fullest through. . . .
    Growth in self-reliance
    Continuous quest for information
    Ability to formulate principles for action
    Utilization of outlets for creativeness
    Ability to evaluate ideas and objects critically
    Development of pride in good workmanship
    Wise use of leisure
Develop acceptable social patterns through. . . .
    Respect for likeness and differences among people
    Awareness of one's responsibility to others
    Recognition of the rights of others
    Desire to help others
    Growth in good manners and principles of good conduct
    Enjoyment of varied social experiences
    Appreciation for the contributions made by creative artists
    Ability to adjust to problems of a changing world
    Development of a respect for the dignity of work
Develop faith in the American Way of Life and good citizenship through. . . .
    Awareness of the increasing interdependence of people
    Growth in skills needed for participation in democratic processes

[11]The San Diego, California, Public Schools attempted to implement the EPC statement in their elementary school curriculum guide. For further information, see *Curriculum Guide: The Elementary Program* (San Diego: City Schools, 1960).

[12]Columbus, Ohio, Public Schools, *Agreements Booklet,* mimeographed statement distributed by Columbus, Ohio, Public Schools. Reprinted with permission.

Realization of the privileges and responsibilities of a
citizen
Desire to correct unsatisfactory conditions
Understanding and respecting rules and regulations
Concern for spiritual and moral values
Intelligent use of individual and community resources

EUCLID PUBLIC SCHOOLS, EUCLID, OHIO[13]

Statement of Beliefs

We believe that:
1. the curriculum consists of the total environment that the school creates in order to stimulate and guide the wholesome growth and development of children.
2. every child attending our schools should have a curriculum suited to his abilities, interests, and needs.
3. the schools must therefore continuously study the individual child, maintain a cumulative record of his development, and use these findings in creating his educational program. A fundamental of public-school education is the recognition of the individual worth of each child.
4. the varied needs and abilities of children require differing standards of achievement, but every child ought to achieve according to standards appropriate for him.
5. children learn by participating in and responding to a challenging comprehensive environment.
6. the curriculum should largely consist of problem-solving situations which are both on the level of children's understanding and typical of fundamental problems in human life.
7. solving these problems requires both the use of personal experiences and the thoughtful appraisal of our heritage.
8. the curriculum should make pupils sensitive to individual and social problems, and develop a desire and ability to find solutions which are satisfactory yet subject to revision.
9. the curriculum should be rich in experiences that develop the appreciations, understandings, skills, abilities, and habits needed in living together in a democracy.

[13]Euclid Public Schools, *Teaching Guide: Grade 2*, Curriculum Bulletin 3 (Euclid, Ohio: Board of Education, 1954). Reprinted with permission.

10. the curriculum should promote good health and safety habits.
11. the curriculum should foster the effective use of language as a tool of thought and means of communication.
12. all aspects of the curriculum should be concerned with improving emotional health, emphasizing such factors as regard for individual worth, self-respect, security, affection, recognition, and self-reliance.
13. the curriculum should always give adequate attention to the fundamentals in relation to their social setting. Among these are reading, writing, speaking, listening, arithmetic, scientific methods in solving problems, and effective membership in groups.
14. effective group membership develops qualities necessary for successful democratic participation as followers and as leaders.
15. pupils should develop the desire and ability to assume the responsibilities and duties of democratic citizenship as well as to appreciate the corresponding rights and privileges.
16. the curriculum should develop from the immediate known interests of children and this motivation should be used to extend the breadth of intellectual curiosity which will stimulate physical, moral, and intellectual growth of every child.
17. all experiences affect emotional and physical health, ethical and spiritual values, skills, habits, appreciations, and understandings.
18. the schools should develop the attitudes, skills, etc., which contribute to a worthy use of leisure — a use which fosters individual creative powers and participation in wholesome forms of social recreation.
19. the curriculum should provide abundant opportunities for pupils to analyze their needs, to propose, to plan, to participate actively, and to evaluate experiences.
20. the curriculum should contribute to a respect for the successful participation in family living.
21. the schools should co-operate with the home, church, and other worthy social agencies which influence child growth and development. The school should not usurp the functions of other agencies but should assume responsibility for supplementing other efforts in order that the child's well rounded development may be assured.

22. the curriculum should assure the development of the moral values necessary for democratic citizenship. In developing these values pupils will become aware of the conflicts and contradictions in their society and will be guided and assisted in resolving them, thus developing personal standards of values for themselves.
23. the curriculum should assist pupils to develop worthy attitudes toward work and the world of work leading to intelligent vocational choice. Pupils should experience often the genuine satisfactions resulting from ambition and sustained effort to achieve according to their abilities.
24. pupils should more and more value their American heritage, learn the meaning of democracy by living it, and appraise their experiences in terms of their contributions to democratic living. Pupils should appreciate the contributions of the rest of the world to our American way of life and our role in world citizenship.
25. our American heritage is based upon a recognition of the worth of each individual citizen and upon the freedom of that individual in American society. It is, therefore, a responsibility of the public school to develop a strong pride in the American heritage of freedom and to provide experiences in citizenship which will strengthen this ideal in the child's adult life.

In what respect are these two plans similar? How do they differ? Are the plans internally consistent? The pursuit of this kind of information is valuable in that it contributes to the reader's perspective of educational direction at the local level.

There are numerous objectives that may be pursued by an individual as well as by a community. These objectives reflect the values held by the individual and the community, and they are based upon a philosophic point of view that may or may not be consciously realized. It is the function of the educational system to implement goals defined by the community and made articulate by the professional educators. Just as the citizens of Columbus and Euclid, Ohio, set forth a charge to be implemented by their professional educators, the citizens of the town of Jackson have prescribed a philosophy of education. Their point of view served as a frame of reference for the following institutional objectives defined by Jackson's professional staff:

1. To develop an appreciation and understanding of the nature of knowledge, the structure of the disciplines, and the aesthetic values of the arts;

2. To develop socio-civic sensitivity and responsibility, sound emotional attitudes, and good health habits;
3. To employ communication and computation skills meaningfully;
4. To develop understanding and facility to apply the processes of inquiry;
5. To research ideas and concepts using a wide range of resources and materials;
6. To develop a sense of responsibility for one's education.

Data presented in Chapter Three reveal some salient dimensions of Miss Ritter's interpretation of the above charge. Underlying her practice is a belief that every child who enters school has a right to expect a well-planned program of fundamental education. She implements this belief with a program of instruction that (1) provides for children's individual differences, (2) acquaints children with proven study patterns, and (3) utilizes genuine and meaningful problems. Her ideas and practices are further amplified in subsequent chapters.

On the basis of what you now know about Miss Ritter, would you say that her views and classroom ractices are compatible with the point of view set forth by the Jackson School District? That is, do illustrations of Miss Ritter's classroom instruction presented in Chapter Three reveal any clues to how she "develops an appreciation and understanding of the nature of knowledge," or how good health habits are taught, or how she develops facility in the processes of inquiry? Is the basis of her spelling instruction consistent with the third and sixth objectives identified by the professional staff of the Jackson School District? How would her "independent study," "student council," and "library and mathematics club" periods relate to the statement of objectives?

Is it possible to identify the philosophic orientation of either Miss Ritter or the town of Jackson on the basis of information presented thus far? That is, does the Jackson point of view or the practice of Miss Ritter reflect a belief in an "objective reality" that is sought and that must be known for one to live well; a belief that an infallible knowledge of truth can be attained; a belief that reality must be encountered in experience by man to be known; a belief that focuses upon ideas only as consequences in experience, and puts truth on an operational basis; or a belief that the human mind can know reality which exists independent of any knowledge of its existence? If you are unable to make such a distinction, what additional information would be required to do so?

QUESTIONS FOR DISCUSSION

1. Jennifer Jensen boasts that she never experiences any difficulty in controlling the 31 children in her sixth-grade classroom. She attributes her good fortune to a classroom routine which is prescribed early in the school year. The routine is based upon children's adherence to set times and procedures throughout the school day. For example, (1) instructional materials are distributed and collected in the same way; (2) spelling, reading, and arithmetic lesson plans are carefully patterned from the same mold each week; (3) the children line up for recess, lunch, and dismissal in a prescribed manner; and (4) all study is initiated and directed by the teacher. A child who fails to get the teacher's permission to sharpen his pencil, go to the drinking fountain, or go to the restroom can expect to be punished by Mrs. Jensen.

Are these children receiving the kinds of educational experiences that will enable them, as adults, to participate actively in a democratic society? Does Mrs. Jensen employ teaching methods consistent with the values cherished in a democratic society? Is she able to meet the challenge set forth in the 1957 report of the President's Commission?

2. Centertown is in the process of evaluating its school system. Schools have always been considered an important community asset, and the citizenry is extremely proud of their contributions. The present undertaking, which involves the professional staff as well as laymen, is aimed at assessing where the schools are and where they ought to be heading.

How would you respond to the following questions pertaining to this undertaking?

a. How could the various philosophical viewpoints expressed in the chapter be utilized to create better understanding among the different sections of the public?

b. Do needs and purposes vary from one level of education to another, i.e., from elementary to secondary to higher education?

c. What role does each of the following play in formulating purposes of education: teacher, pupil, parent, and other citizens?

d. Is it possible to evaluate a school system that does not subscribe to a clear-cut philosophy of education?

3. The following statement was reported by John Goodlad in a fall, 1962, issue of *Theory Into Practice:*

> Schooling is a rather wasteful business. The ends to be achieved are vaguely stated, and dimly understood. The selection

of means is a haphazard, trial and error business. The process is akin to shooting at flies with a shotgun without knowing whether we are supposed to kill flies, snakes or sparrows. Worse, this is what we do so often; too many people have come to assume flies to be the target and a shotgun to be the most effective means to their end.[14]

Are you in sympathy with his belief that schooling is a wasteful business? How might educators better define "targets" on which their "weapons" might be trained?

4. According to S. A. Courtis; evidence shows conclusively that learning is a maturation process like growth in height and weight. He believes that teachers can influence learning to the same extent that they can influence growth in height and weight. Consequently, teaching, teachers, and schools of learning as we know them must be abolished. New and revolutionary insititutions must be invented and put in place of schools to provide for education in our society.

a. What kind of evidence might Courtis be able to offer in defense of his position?

b. Why do you believe his viewpoint has not had a pronounced impact upon contemporary education?

c. If you tried to invent a new social institution that would be charged with a responsibility for education, what form might it assume?

ADDITIONAL REFERENCES

American Educational Research Association, "Philosophical and Social Framework of Education," *Review of Educational Research,* 34 (February, 1964). 113 pp.

Brameld, Theodore, *Philosophies of Education in Cultural Perspective.* New York: Dryden Press, 1955. 446 pp.

Broudy, Harry S., *Building a Philosophy of Education.* 2nd ed. Englewood Cliffs, N.J.: Prentice-Hall, Inc., 1961. 410 pp.

Brubacher, John S., Chairman, *Philosophies of Education,* Forty-First Yearbook of the National Society for the Study of Education, Part I. Chicago: The University of Chicago Press, 1942. 321 pp.

Brubacher, John S., Chairman, *Modern Philosophies of Education,* Fifty-Fourth Yearbook of the National Society for the Study of Education, Part I. Chicago: The University of Chicago Press, 1955. 374 pp.

Drake, William E., *The American School in Transition.* Englewood Cliffs, N.J.: Prentice-Hall, Inc., 1955. 624 pp.

[14]John I. Goodlad, "The Organizing Center in Curriculum Theory and Practice," *Theory Into Practice,* 1, No. 4 (October, 1962), 220.

Durant, William J., *The Story of Philosophy.* New York: Simon and Schuster, Inc., 1953. 404 pp.

Educational Leadership. The theme of the May, 1963, issue is "Pressures and Concerns"; the theme of the October, 1964, issue is "Commitment: To What and Why?"

Lindvall, C. M., ed., *Defining Educational Objectives.* Pittsburgh: The University of Pittsburgh Press, 1964. 83 pp.

Mayer, Frederick, *A History of Educational Thought.* Columbus, Ohio: Charles E. Merrill Books, Inc., 1960. 494 pp.

Mayer, Frederick, *Philosophy of Education for Our Time.* New York: The Odyssey Press, Inc., 1958. 245 pp.

Morris, Van Cleve, *Philosophy and the American School.* Boston: Houghton Mifflin Company, 1961. 492 pp.

National Education Association Staff, *Schools For the Sixties,* A Report of the NEA Project on Instruction. New York: McGraw-Hill Book Company, Inc., 1963. 146 pp.

Price, Kingsley, *Education and Philosophical Thought.* Boston: Allyn and Bacon, Inc., 1962. 511 pp.

Smith, B. Othanel, and Ennis, Robert H., eds., *Language and Concepts In Education.* Chicago: Rand McNally & Company, 1961. 221 pp.

Chapter Five

PATTERNS OF ORGANIZING
THE ELEMENTARY SCHOOL

The school in which Miss Ritter teaches is the newest of four elementary schools in Jackson. Three years ago, when the building was opened to students for the first time, the western edge of Jackson's corporation limits bordered the school's playground. One could view spacious fields and wooded tracts to the south and west of the school grounds. Today, the school grounds are entirely encircled by single family ranch-style homes. Considerable home-building in the area has changed the nature of the school environment drastically during the past three years. As the community expanded westward, annexations moved the corporation limits well beyond the school grounds. The school's student population literally exploded as a result of the community's rapid expansion.

Miss Ritter's classroom is one of 13 spacious classrooms in the building. Besides these, the structure includes a large gym-cafeteria, a music room, an art room, a multipurpose room (used as a visual-aids presentation and storage area by the school staff), a small infirmary, a small teachers' lounge, and a suite of offices which house the principal and his staff. Professional and community leaders of the school system originally believed the building would meet the educational needs of children residing in the western area of Jackson for many years. Yet, merely three years after the school's doors were opened to children for the first time, school officials recognized that the building's pupil capacity limit was close at hand. The problem of keeping pace with a rapidly expanding pupil enrollment has been

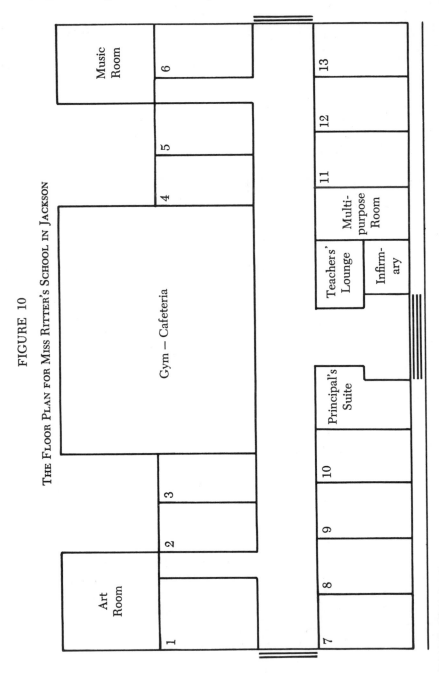

FIGURE 10

THE FLOOR PLAN FOR MISS RITTER'S SCHOOL IN JACKSON

and continues to be shared by many school districts in recent years in the United States.

Pupil enrollment increased from 210 children during the first year of operation to 370 children three years later. The average class size was approximately 21 pupils throughout the school's maiden year. Three years later, this average figure had increased to nearly 29 pupils per classroom. A breakdown of enrollment data for the school reveals considerable variation, as shown in Figure 11.

Someone in every school district must assume the responsibility for classifying the children who will be entering school into available classroom space. This responsibility may be assumed by a committee of teachers, a head teacher, a building principal, or the executive head of a school district. At the elementary level, the building principal usually accepts this type of responsibility. The reader may better comprehend the nature of current grouping practices in the elementary school—and at the same time become sensitized to one problem which elementary school administrators encounter yearly—by attempting to classify the 370 enrolled pupils within the framework of the building portrayed in Figure 10. Try to group the 370 children into the school's 13 available classrooms before reading ahead.

FIGURE 11
CURRENT PUPIL ENROLLMENT IN MISS RITTER'S SCHOOL

Average Chronological Age	Number of Pupils
5	43
6	57
7	62
8	49
9	52
10	54
11	53
Total Enrollment	370

CONTEMPORARY ORGANIZATIONAL PRACTICES

There is no single correct pattern for classifying children in an elementary school. Numerous factors contribute to the pattern finally agreed upon in a given school district, and this pattern may differ from plans evolved in neighboring school districts. The children's chronological ages, mental capabilities, peer relations, sex, and social class may or may not affect the nature of the plan. Also, actual classroom space contributes to the pupil capacity of a given room. Thus, pupil data may or may not be carefully gathered by school officials prior to classifying children enrolled in a district into available school space.

HARRY MEYERS' PLAN

Harry Meyers, principal of Miss Ritter's school, tries to divide the children into two grade-level groups on the basis of sex balance. He attempts to balance the number of boys and girls in each room. Each group, with the exception of the kindergarten, is then assigned to a classroom in the building. Since each kindergarten group attends school only half of the day, both groups share the same room. Thus, one room in the building is shared by two kindergarten groups, while each of the remaining 12 groups of children is assigned to one of the remaining 12 classrooms. Most elementary school principals probably adhere to this pattern in order to classify 370 pupils into 13 available classrooms.

CELIA PORTER'S PLAN

Celia Porter, an elementary school principal in a suburban school district southeast of Jackson, bases her classification plan upon mental maturity test data, reading readiness data (for the lower grades), and teachers' judgments about pupil progress in school. She needs to gather many data as a basis for two classroom groups at each grade level in the school (not counting kindergarten). Her school district attempts to organize children into grade-level groups on the basis of their ability to learn. The organizational pattern reflects the belief that children can be taught more effectively when they are classified according to their ability.

The system's leaders also believe that a single teacher cannot treat all aspects of the curriculum effectively, so each elementary school teacher in the system specializes in one or two phases of the curriculum. Therefore, a pupil in this system is classified according to his ability and is instructed by teaching specialists.

ELEANOR STARLING'S PLAN

The classification plan developed by Eleanor Starling, an elementary school principal in a third community, differs markedly from the other two patterns described. Her district recently substituted a nongraded organizational pattern for the traditional graded concept at the elementary school level. Hence, instead of grouping children into grades one, two, three, and so forth, Miss Starling organizes classroom groups on the basis of primary units and intermediate units. Each primary classroom unit includes children six, seven, and eight years old, whereas each intermediate classroom unit includes children approximately nine, ten, and eleven years old. The only variable controlled by Miss Starling relates to balancing the number of six-, seven-, and eight-year-olds, and nine-, ten-, and eleven-year-olds in each classroom group. Miss Starling's district has experimented with a variety of grouping patterns in recent years in order to determine an optimum pattern for the community.

The classification plans developed by Harry Meyers, Celia Porter, and Eleanor Starling are certainly varied. Yet, they do not begin to exhaust the diverse patterns currently used by educators in elementary schools. Thousands of children attend schools in which both heterogeneous and homogeneous grouping is practiced at the elementary level. In certain instances, these children are selected at random (heterogeneously) for classroom groups during the first two or three years of school. They are then classified in the third or fourth year on the basis of their previous school record (one form of homogeneous grouping). Another pattern combines random grouping for some aspects of the school day (that is, physical education, music, art, and spelling) and ability grouping for prescribed skills and content areas of the curriculum (that is, reading, arithmetic, general science, and so forth). Many school districts across the nation have taken an active part in determining the most desirable pupil classification pattern for their community's children.

Over the years, a legion of educators have reported school experimentation and expressed personal opinions pertaining to this problem. These ideas are given historical perspective in the following section of this chapter. Then, in the final section, the above-mentioned organizational patterns are examined in terms of variable pupil enrollment and contemporary technological and administrative innovations.

ORGANIZATIONAL PRACTICES IN RETROSPECT

"It is the function of the school, among other things, to accept and enroll the child, to classify and assign him to a teacher group, to take stock of his growth, and to regulate his progress month by month and year by year. In discharging these functions, the school either profits or suffers from the kind of administrative machinery that exists to govern each child's advancement."[1] Examples sketched in the first section of this chapter indicate considerable variation in classification plans currently applied within elementary schools. The graded school patterns mentioned reflect certain theories of education quite contrary to the nongraded pattern which was described briefly. Yet, a logical case could readily be constructed in defense of each pattern. The prime purpose of this section is to report antecedent events relating to contemporary classification practices, so that the reader may profit from a time perspective when examining these practices.

Four phases in the development of classification practices in America are sketched in the following paragraphs. Classification patterns employed in elementary (or lower) schools (1) before the inauguration of our first president, (2) before the Civil War, (3) before the turn of the twentieth century, and (4) before the 1960's are described. If the reader recollects salient aspects of his elementary and secondary school social science instruction, he may be able to parallel the evolution of these patterns with America's growth during the past three and one-half centuries.

CLASSIFICATION PATTERNS BEFORE THE INAUGURATION OF OUR FIRST PRESIDENT

Instruction assumed sizable proportions during the seventeenth and eighteenth centuries. Individuals were able to earn a living by tutoring children of wealthy families or by establishing "hatcheck" schools (school was in session wherever the teacher placed his hat). The "classroom" consisted of the teacher's environment at a given moment. Student attendance varied from one to eight, ten, or twelve children, depending upon local circumstances. Some tutors were hired by the local citizenry to conduct neighborhood schools, usually attended by small groups of boys. Community citizens' committees eventually discovered that some "educated" women living in the community could conduct a school at home with some degree of success. Young boys and some older girls attended these schools in order to acquire certain skills requisite for admittance to the existing secondary schools of the time or to learn how to read the Bible. Both the "dames" and the traveling teachers generally offered a narrow,

[1]John I. Goodlad and Robert H. Anderson, *The Nongraded Elementary School* (New York: Harcourt, Brace & Company, 1959), p. 61. Reprinted with permission.

structured program of study. Since these teachers worked with small groups of children, classification problems were nonexistent.

Various circumstances accounted for the development of private schools, parochial schools, and charity schools in many communities during this era. Usually, pupil enrollment was small, and instruction was carried on in a single room. A number of reading and writing schools flourished in the New England area during the seventeenth and eighteenth centuries. These schools are recognized as the forerunner of "departmentalization" in the United States. Instruction in reading and writing was directed by different schoolmasters in separate rooms (often in separate buildings). Children usually attended each of these schools for half of the day. The establishment of departmentalized reading and writing schools reflects one of the earliest recorded elementary school classification ventures in America.

Classification Patterns Before the Civil War

It is almost impossible to identify one date or one event which singles the beginning of the American public elementary school characteristic of the twentieth century. As William Drake pointed out:

> In considering its establishment, the elementary schools of Colonial Massachusetts must be taken into consideration, along with the early apprenticeship practices. It must be remembered, however, that such schools were limited to a two-year period of instruction, were moral discipline-centered, and had a curriculum so narrow that it could all be put into a single small volume. Also, due consideration must be given to eighteenth century educational thought, for it was out of such thought that much of the high idealism back of the nineteenth century elementary school found its origin. Probably, the infant school should be considered as marking the beginning of the primary department of the modern elementary school, for the infant school was marked by a prime consideration for the welfare of the young child through a spirit of love rather than through harsh corporal punishment.[2]

The elementary schools of colonial Massachusetts, early apprenticeship practices, eighteenth-century educational thought, and the infant school in all probability influenced the establishment of the American public elementary school. However, many years elapsed before the

[2]William E. Drake, *The American School in Transition* (Englewood Cliffs, N.J.: Prentice-Hall, Inc., 1955), p. 226. Reprinted with permission.

one-room institution of the early nineteenth century evolved into the graded structure characteristic of our time.

Many patterns of elementary school organization were tested during the early decades of the nineteenth century. Drake reported the beginning of a graded elementary school as early as 1818:

> At this time, children were being admitted into the English grammar school in Boston from the primary school. These schools were being taught by one teacher in a one-room school building. The primary school was organized into six classes, beginning with the learning of the ABC's and providing elementary instruction in reading and writing. By 1823, the English grammar school was divided vertically into reading and writing schools, with the reading school being further divided into four classes. This general pattern continued to prevail until 1848, with a tendency toward grading as new buildings were constructed. These new buildings contained more but smaller classrooms. The tendency was toward a room for each grade and a grade for each year between six and fourteen years. The nine-year elementary school was the characteristic pattern for New England, and the eight year school was for the rest of the country.[3]

Increased enrollment in the English grammar school and the development of a specialized curriculum provided a framework for the first graded elementary school in America.

The Lancastrian school idea, pioneered in England, proved to be extremely popular in many American communities during the second and third decades of the nineteenth century. One teacher, working with several assistants, was able to offer instruction to innumerable children. This low-cost pattern of education spread among urban centers very rapidly. School facilities ordinarily included one large room with several adjacent recitation rooms.

The English grammar school in Boston and the Lancastrian school movement both contributed to our knowledge of classifying children. They also markedly influenced the creation of the first planned graded elementary school in the United States. This school was opened in Boston under the direction of John D. Philbrick in 1848. Children were classified into self-contained grade levels roughly corresponding to their chronological age. The impact of Philbrick's school upon urban education during the following years is described by Henry Otto as follows:

[3]*Ibid.*, pp. 226-227. Reprinted with permission.

The advantages of the graded organization were soon recognized, and many of the large halls of departmental schools were partitioned so as to form a number of smaller classrooms. Although school administrators readily recognized the feasibility of the graded plan, the difficulty of adjusting the old buildings to the new organization prevented many cities from effecting the graded organization as a city-wide practice. The complete reorganization of the elementary schools of a district could be brought about only as the older buildings were remodeled or new buildings erected. Consequently, the extension of graded schools was slow at first, but within 12 or 15 years after the establishment of the Quincy Grammar School of Boston nearly every city or town had adopted the plan, at least in the newer buildings.[4]

As W. I. Shearer noted, the schools had evolved from no system to nothing but system by 1870.[5] Even though Shearer's statement is somewhat exaggerated, it does take into account the rapid development of classification patterns in the elementary school. The basis for today's graded structure and the Lancastrian "team-teaching" concept was formulated during this era.

CLASSIFICATION PATTERNS BEFORE THE TWENTIETH CENTURY

Shearer's statement more accurately portrays urban than rural school practices in the United States. After a graded pattern was adopted within an urban area, educators in the system began experimenting with alternate methods of classifying children in school. Early study efforts focused upon children's passage through the grades of the elementary school. Educators experimented with grade-level content, grade-level expectations, and promotion periods during the school year. As a result, school progress began to influence the nature of existing classification patterns.

A small group of educators who were thoroughly disenchanted with the "lockstep" nature of the graded elementary school began experimenting with curriculum structures and teaching methods utilized in the school. The experimentation undertaken by these men influenced the classification of children significantly in later decades. Preston Search at Pueblo, Colorado, and Frederic Burk at Santa Barbara, and later San Francisco, California, both sought to individu-

[4]Henry J. Otto, *Elementary-School Organization and Administration*, p. 13. Copyright 1954 by Appleton-Century-Crofts, Inc. Reprinted with permission.

[5]W. J. Shearer, *The Grading of Schools* (New York: H. P. Smith Publishing Company, 1899), p. 21.

alize the elementary school program. Their attempts to provide for some degree of individualization in the selection of a school program, and for a system of individual progress through the school, met with a measure of success. More important, their experiments inspired other educators to advance the frontiers of knowledge considerably during the early decades of the twentieth century.

During the latter part of the nineteenth century, a number of educators in urban school systems across the country initiated experiments to determine the feasibility of ability grouping in the elementary school. They sought to develop a classification system based upon children's ability to learn in school. The impact of their efforts was pronounced during the 1930's in the United States.

A casual reader of elementary school history can easily misinterpret the impact of classification experimentation upon schools during the late nineteenth century. Educational literature available at the time devoted much space to this experimentation. Recent educational publications, reporting historical events of this time, usually describe the urban school classification patterns at length. While these experiments did serve as the basis for many twentieth-century practices, their impact upon nineteenth-century schools was limited, because most of the pupils attending elementary schools at that time lived in rural areas. These children were not affected by the experimentation, as their schools usually were one-room, single-teacher institutions. Population shifts to urban centers in the United States after 1900 stimulated extensive experimentation to discover an effective plan for enrolling and classifying the rapidly increasing number of children in these areas.

Classification Patterns Before the 1960's

Even though numerous attempts were made in the twentieth century to replace the lockstep method of instruction at the elementary school level with more individualized patterns of instruction, the net result of these ventures has not been very impressive thus far. A vast majority of children currently attending American elementary schools are being taught from the same mold. Progress has probably been retarded by the controversial nature of certain classification experiments conducted during the early decades of this century, and by the fact that many desirable outcomes of these experiments were not applicable in small school situations. An accumulation of distasteful experimental side-effects, poor experimental designs, and a serious lack of objective data necessary to evaluate experimental patterns resulted in midcentury elementary school leaders who were quite skeptical of "new fads." These school leaders preferred to retain existing patterns until sufficient data were gathered to warrant change. Hence, the late 1940's and early 1950's may historically be referred to as the "sit-tight" era.

What type of experimentation resulted in a midcentury attitude which can be effectively portrayed by the slightly altered cliche, "Don't just do something, stand there"? Figure 12 depicts an over-

FIGURE 12

VARIATIONS FROM THE USUAL TYPE OF
ELEMENTARY SCHOOL ORGANIZATION, 1862-1932*

Plan or Practice	Person Associated with Its Establishment	Date of Establishment
St. Louis	W. T. Harris	1862
Pueblo	P. W. Search	1888
Cambridge	Francis Cogswell	1893
Elizabeth, New Jersey	W. J. Shearer	1895
Portland, Oregon	Frank Figler	1897
Batavia	John Kennedy	1898
North Denver	J. H. Van Sickle	1898
Santa Barbara Concentric	Frederic Burk	1898
Platoon	W. A. Wirt	1900
Burk's Individual	Frederic Burk	1913
Dalton	Helen Parkhurst	1919
Winnetka	C. W. Washburne	1919
Detroit X-Y-Z grouping	C. S. Berry	1919
Cooperative Group	J. F. Hosic	1930

*Henry J. Otto, *Elementary-School Organization and Administration*, p. 24. Copyright 1954 by Appleton-Century-Crofts, Inc. Reprinted with permission. For a complete historical account of these plans, see Henry J. Otto, "Historical Sketches of Administration Innovations," *Educational Administration and Supervision*, 20 (March, 1934), 161-172.

view of significant variations from the usual type of elementary school organization between 1862 and 1932. Generally, these plans focused upon the individual child's learning capabilities.

A number of the above-mentioned organizational plans enabled children to study prescribed content at their own rate of speed. As a result, children were classified on the basis of progress rather than chronological age. Educators trying to administer multiple-track courses of study, unit progress plans, ungraded classrooms, and quarterly or midyear promotions undoubtedly experienced innumerable woes. Administrative inconvenience very likely curtailed the impact of these plans upon schools of their time.

While there are a variety of plans currently employed to classify children in an elementary school, most school systems employ one or a combination of three particular plans. These are the nongraded school plan, the departmentalized plan, and the self-contained classroom plan. The nongraded school plan is primarily experimental at present, whereas both of the others are well established. As the reader studies the description of each of these plans, he should try to determine which one (if any) best depicts Miss Ritter's classroom situation (see Chapter Three).

NONGRADED CLASSES

Educators from all parts of the United States have streamed into the little Michigan village of Carson City recently to observe the manifestations of an experiment with a "nongraded" school organization. Carson City is one of numerous school districts currently experimenting with nongraded classes to determine an optimum method of adjusting teaching and administrative procedures to meet individual differences among children. Those responsible for initiating experimentation with nongraded approaches generally hold the conviction that the graded structure of elementary education has outlived its usefulness and should be abandoned.

Warren Hamilton and Walter Rehwoldt adhere to this conviction and have contributed significantly to the development of a multigrade plan at Torrance, California. They questioned whether "... we threw out the baby with the bathwater when we brought American education out of the little red schoolhouse, and then discarded the practice of having pupils from several grades in the same classroom?"[6] The Torrance plan is based on the premise that a child does not always advance at the same speed in all subjects; hence, children in school must be taught as individuals and not as groups.

The Torrance multigrade program was initiated in the Walteria school during the 1955-1956 school year for the purpose of determining the effect of alternated classroom units—containing pupils from

[6]Warren Hamilton and Walter Rehwoldt, "By Their Differences They Learn," *The National Elementary Principal*, 37 (December, 1957), 27.

three grade levels with an age range of three or more years—upon pupil growth and learning. These units were established for the primary and intermediate levels of the elementary school. Each unit contains approximately 33 children—11 first, second, and third graders, or 11 fourth, fifth, and sixth graders. At times, these children are grouped homogeneously (when studying prescribed skill areas), but generally classroom units are heterogeneously structured. In any event, the instructional program is extensively individualized.

Extensive experimentation with nongraded elementary schools has attracted considerable attention within the past six to eight years. The pioneering efforts of the Milwaukee public school system with an ungraded primary unit in the early 1940's have caught the imagination of many educators. Today, experimentation with ungraded classrooms is under way in school systems of many states. While this lively interest heartened Robert Anderson and John Goodlad, two active contemporary proponents of the nongraded elementary school concept, they confess to deep concern over the superficiality and inadequacy of much that is being done in the name of nongrading. They consider the following characteristics essential to the organization of a nongraded school:

1. "The nongraded school provides for the continuous, unbroken, upward progression of all pupils, the slowest and the most able."

2. "The nongraded school provides for the irregular upward progression that is characteristic of almost every child."

3. "The nongraded school provides several alternative vertical classroom placements for every child at any time, no one of which denotes nonpromotion of skipping."[7]

These characteristics must be adopted before a graded system can become nongraded in fact if not in name.

The reader may obtain additional specific information relating to these patterns by consulting the following references:

1. R. H. Anderson and J. I. Goodlad, "Self-Appraisal in Nongraded Schools: A Survey of Findings and Perceptions," *The Elementary School Journal*, 62 (February, 1962), 261-269.

2. Robert F. Carbone, "A Comparison of Graded and Non-Graded Elementary Schools," *The Elementary School Journal*, 62 (November, 1961), 82-88.

3. D. M. Eldred and M. Hillson, "The Nongraded School and

[7]John I. Goodlad and Robert H. Anderson, *The Nongraded Elementary School* (2nd ed.; New York: Harcourt, Brace & Company, 1963), pp. 219-220.

Mental Health," *The Elementary School Journal,* 63 (January, 1963), 218-222.

4. J. I. Goodlad and R. A. Anderson, "Educational Practices in Nongraded Schools: A Survey of Perceptions," *The Elementary School Journal,* 63 (October, 1962), 33-40.
5. Harold G. Shane, "Grouping in the Elementary School," *The Phi Delta Kappan,* 41 (April, 1960), 313-319.
6. Carleton W. Washburne, "Adjusting the Program to the Child," *Educational Leadership,* 11 (December, 1953), 138-147.

A Departmentalized Plan

Departmentalized patterns of instruction were revitalized during the early years of the twentieth century. One plan was put into effect in the upper grades of New York's elementary schools. Another, known as the Platoon School, evolved in several midwestern communities. Both plans required specialized instructors to teach only one or two subjects to different groups of children throughout the school day. A more effective presentation of the expanding curriculum seemed to motivate the New York City plan, whereas more efficient utilization of school plant inspired the platoon type of classification pattern. Most departmentalized programs in recent years have developed in graded schools which often classify pupils according to their learning capabilities.

Data reported in the journals of several prominent professional organizations during the 1940's and early 1950's revealed that departmentalization seemed to be experiencing another of its downward trends. This trend was suddenly reversed after the mid-1950's with the introduction of "team teaching" into the American elementary school. A study involving the use of teaching aides (frequently housewives) at Bay City, Michigan, is viewed as the instigator of extensive and intensive team-teaching experimentation in several New England and midwestern communities. Children attending schools involved in this type of research are usually classified within a large chronological age or multiage group for instructional purposes. A team of teachers provides large-group, small-group, and individualized learning experiences within this structure. While there is no typical instructional team, Lambert describes a team that might be assigned to a class of about 125 children ranging in age from five to eight years.

> At its head is the team chairman — an outstanding and experienced teacher, who, let us say, is especially strong in the fields of language

arts and social studies. He is assisted by two other fully licensed teachers: one has had several years of experience and some special preparation in the teaching of primary math and science, while the other, who has just received his credentials, is especially interested in arts and crafts. There are also two teaching interns who are completing their college or university preparation, and an instructional secretary, perhaps a mother, who serves as a part-time teachers' aide. The salaries of these last three staff members added together come to less than that of two fully qualified teachers. Since the team chairman receives an increased salary in recognition of his special responsibilities, the cost of the whole team is approximately the same as that of the teachers who would have been assigned to the same number of children under the present system.[8]

A variety of classification patterns have evolved within the framework of this structure for a number of reasons. One problem encountered in establishing these patterns is of a financial nature. Since the pattern is financed by the taxpayer, he must be sold on its potential. Many successful sales efforts are apparent in the New England area. The potential impact of team-teaching experimentation upon tomorrow's elementary school organization is explored in a later part of this chapter.

Additional information pertaining to departmentalization within the elementary school may be derived by consulting the Shane, Otto, and Washburne sources cited on pages 93 and 96.

THE SELF-CONTAINED CLASSROOM PLAN

The ageless self-contained classroom concept has been given considerable stature during this era. The earliest manifestations of the self-contained idea undoubtedly can be traced to the tutor, who assumed the responsibility for teaching his ward or wards all knowledge of importance. Later, after one-room schools were established, a single teacher assumed the responsibility for educating children who attended the school. The establishment of a graded plan of instruction during the midnineteenth century reinforced the self-contained classroom concept. Throughout the eighteenth century and parts of the nineteenth century, departmentalized organizational plans threatened to replace the all-knowing single teacher of elementary school-aged children. Departmentalized plans actually replaced many self-contained classroom plans in the twentieth century.

The serious challenge to the self-contained classroom concept

[8]Philip Lambert, "Team Teaching for the Elementary School," *Educational Leadership*, 18 (November, 1960), 86. Reprinted with permission.

School Buildings. The elementary school structure has assumed many forms during the past 150 years. These changes have been attributed to pedagogical, social, and technological progress. How can the structure of the school influence an educational program? Is it logical to conclude that the quality of a school program is related to the amount of money invested in the school building?

Harper—Courtesy Center for School Experimentation, The Ohio State University

Wolf — Courtesy Earl Township School District, Berks County, Pa.

Courtesy Carl Purcell, NEA

School Facilities. Varied facilities can be observed in many contemporary elementary schools. Six illustrations of such facilities are shown. It is unlikely that all of these would be found in a single elementary school. Now, imagine yourself as a classroom teacher. Which of these facilities would you consider essential to an educational program? Then, imagine yourself as a taxpayer in a community. Which of these might appear to be "frills" or luxuries in an educational program?

Courtesy Carl Purcell, NEA

Courtesy H. Armstrong Roberts

Courtesy H. Armstrong Roberts

Courtesy Carl Purcell, NEA

102

Harper—Courtesy Center for School Experimentation, The Ohio State University

Harper—Courtesy Center for School Experimentation, The Ohio State University

103

Wolf—Courtesy University Elementary School, State University of Iowa

Classroom Interiors. Classroom interiors have changed considerably during the past century, as portrayed in the photographs. How might the type and arrangement of furniture, the available bulletin board space, and the sources of light and heat affect the teacher and the children in the classroom?

Wolf—Courtesy Center for School Experimentation, The Ohio State University

Wolf—Courtesy Earl Township School District, Berks County, Pa.

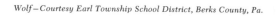

106

Courtesy Carl Purcell, NEA

Playground Facilities. School playground facilities vary substantially both in area and equipment. Yet, the authors have learned from surveys they have conducted that students and teachers, when asked to describe "typical" elementary school playground facilities, invariably include swings, slides, and seesaws similar to those depicted in the upper lefthand photograph. Why have these particular pieces of playground equipment become so stereotyped in the minds of prospective and in-service elementary school teachers? Also, what contribution does such equipment make to the education of children?

107

posed by a plan with numerous recognizable limitations inspired many educators to assess intensively the pros and cons of the self-contained classroom pattern during this century. Information acquired as an outcome of such study resulted in a new suit of clothing for the single teacher per classroom structure. Undoubtedly, increased emphasis upon the importance of human relations in teaching during the 1920's and 1930's influenced the style of the new self-contained classroom idea. Educators ultimately succeeded in crystallizing a classification scheme, known as the self-contained classroom unit, which purportedly provided an effective all-round education experience for children in the elementary school. This plan, without question, has been the most widespread elementary school practice of our pedagogical era. Several seemingly successful organizational experiments which have been conducted at the elementary level recently serve notice that the self-contained unit may be in for another severe test in the years ahead.

The following sources are recommended for those readers who intend to pursue the self-contained classroom concept more intensively.

1. Alice Miel, "The Self-Contained Classroom: An Assessment," *Teachers College Record,* 59 (February, 1958), 282-291.
2. Rosella Roff, "Grouping and Individualizing in the Elementary Classroom," *Educational Leadership,* 15 (December, 1957), 171.
3. Rodney Tillman, "Self-Contained Classroom: Where Do We Stand?" *Educational Leadership,* 19 (November, 1960), 82-84.
4. Edith R. Snyder, ed., *The Self-Contained Classroom* (Washington, D.C.: Association for Supervision and Curriculum Development [NEA], 1960).

Throughout the twentieth century, extensive experimentation has been conducted to determine an effective, administratively feasible plan for classifying children in the elementary school. Various individualization patterns have evolved, and a number of departmentalized patterns have been tested, but for the most part these developments have not altered the traditional nature of the self-contained classroom. Unusually widespread public school experimentation at the present time strongly suggests that many elementary school leaders are dissatisfied with existing organizational structures for enrolling and classifying children within the elementary school.

INFLUENCES OF ENROLLMENT UPON
SCHOOL ORGANIZATION

Pertinent aspects of current elementary school organization and classification practices — graded and nongraded school structures, homogeneous and heterogeneous classroom groups, and self-contained and departmentalized classroom units — were touched upon by example in the first part of this chapter. These practices were given a historical perspective in the second part, so that the reader could better comprehend the diverse nature of our present elementary school structure. The prime theme developed within the third part of this chapter pertains to the nature of problems encountered when a school's pupil enrollment varies.

Three different methods of classifying 370 children within an elementary school were described earlier in this chapter. Two plans resulted in the establishment of a pair of groups for the kindergarten through sixth grade, respectively, whereas a third plan employed multiaged primary and intermediate classroom units. In order to assess the impact of an increase in enrollment upon these classification methods, the data in Figure 11 have been extended for analytical purposes. Extensive home-building in the school neighborhood resulted in a significant increase in projected pupil enrollment for the forthcoming school year. Data reported in Figure 13 indicate the enrollment increase by chronological age levels.

Since 370 children already tax the existing physical facilities of the building (see Figure 10), an enrollment increase of 53 pupils creates serious problems for an administrator — especially when the

FIGURE 13

PRESENT AND PROJECTED ENROLLMENT DATA FOR MISS RITTER'S SCHOOL

Chronological Age	Pupils Currently Enrolled	Next Year's Anticipated Enrollment
5	43	56
6	57	70
7	62	74
8	49	77
9	52	47
10	54	48
11	53	51
Total	370	423

expanded attendance is concentrated within a narrow age range. Several courses of action are open to an administrator who must house 423 children within a building designed for a maximum enrollment of approximately 390 pupils. Can the reader anticipate possible solutions to the problem encountered by Harry Meyers, Celia Porter, and Eleanor Starling? By jotting down proposals that seem feasible and then comparing them with patterns described in the following paragraphs, the reader can assess his awareness of practices currently employed in elementary schools to provide for rapidly increasing pupil enrollment.

Probably the most apparent solution to the problem of increased enrollment is to expand the physical facilities of the building. Unfortunately, this process is frequently cumbersome and time-consuming. An executive officer must justify the need for expanding the school's facilities before the local board of education. If the school board approves the proposal, the next step involves financing the classroom construction. Assuming that no problems are encountered at this point, actual construction can be undertaken. Ordinarily, this process is too slow to provide for an unexpected enrollment expansion. Several school districts which faced a problem of basing school construction plans upon unstable population growth data resorted to mobile classrooms to resolve their dilemma—inexpensive, flexible building materials which could easily be assembled or dismantled and reused were employed to meet temporary enrollment peaks and declines. These temporary facilities adequately housed pupils and at the same time enabled school officials to provide quickly for unexpected population shifts within the district.

Other measures are necessary in order to house 53 additional children within the existing building structure. Fifty-three children approximate two classroom units, so the administrator's task narrows to either spreading the children throughout the 13 classrooms in use or to providing space within the building for two additional classroom units. The former alternative is unfeasible, as the expanded enrollment is concentrated among a few age levels. Hence, the latter alternative appears to be the most profitable course of action. Special-purpose rooms are often converted into temporary classroom quarters during a peak enrollment period. Or large classrooms are partitioned into two smaller classrooms in certain instances. Since two rooms must be prepared for the entering children, the school staff is forced to decide upon the facilities to be converted. The staff in this case decided to convert the special-purpose room and the art room into classrooms.

Once additional classroom space has been provided, the administrator is confronted with the task of classifying children enrolled within the school's expanded facilities. Harry Meyers and Celia Porter in all likelihood would designate one of the newly converted classrooms as a third first-grade unit and the other as a split second- and third-grade unit. A split class arrangement is often employed as an undesirable but essential stopgap measure until more effective long-range plans materialize. Eleanor Starling could easily absorb 53 additional pupils by forming two multiaged primary units, thus increasing the number of primary units in her school from six to eight (not counting the kindergarten). Another approach utilized within some school systems involves transporting designated groups of children attending overcrowded schools to other, less-crowded building facilities in the district.

The practice of converting special-purpose rooms into classrooms, and the practice of building additional classrooms onto an existing school structure are frequently used by school leaders to provide for minor enrollment variations. Major enrollment variations within a school district necessitate more drastic action. These variations often occur in rapidly expanding residential sections of a school district, in transition areas of a community (for example, residential neighborhoods), and as a direct outgrowth of predictable and unpredictable sociological and economic influences (that is, the addition or loss of a major income source in a community). Some school districts institute two half-day sessions as one means of coping with unexpectedly large pupil enrollment. A building's maximum pupil capacity is doubled by such an administrative procedure. Other school districts have been known to lease emergency classroom facilities in churches and community buildings to meet their pressing need for space. School districts can temporarily resolve increased or decreased enrollment problems in some instances by redefining attendance boundaries around buildings in the system. Usually, the method employed to alleviate major enrollment variations is dependent upon numerous local circumstances.

Contemporary administrative practices utilized by numerous school districts to alleviate pupil enrollment variations have been reported in this section for two reasons: first, to acquaint prospective teachers with the nature of these patterns; and second, to provide prospective teachers with one means of evaluating future job opportunities critically. Additional perspective can be obtained by consulting the following references.

1. Virgil Herrick, *et. al., The Elementary School* (Englewood Cliffs, N.J.: Prentice-Hall, Inc., 1956), Chapter 13.
2. Henry J. Otto, "Grouping Pupils for Maximum Achievement," *School Review,* 67 (Winter, 1959), 387-395.
3. C. R. Spain, H. D. Drummond, and J. I. Goodlad, *Educational Leadership and the Elementary School Principal* (New York: Rinehart and Company, 1956).
4. *What Price Double Sessions?* (Washington, D.C.: National School Boards Association, 1959.)
5. H. F. Spitzer, "Class Size and Pupil Achievement in Elementary Schools," *The Elementary School Journal,* 55 (October, 1954), 82-86.

INFLUENCES UPON TOMORROW'S ORGANIZATIONAL PATTERNS

A number of educators are presently carrying on research designed to assess the potential impact upon elementary education of two recent technological developments, educational television and teaching machines. Extensive experimentation has also appreciably advanced the frontiers of our knowledge of team teaching and nongraded organizational patterns in recent years. Controversial as well as promising aspects of each of these undertakings have contributed to their present widespread popularity and adaptation (often for experimental purposes) in American schools. Therefore, an effort has been made in the following paragraphs to explore the potential influence of technological developments, team-teaching schemes, and nongraded schemes upon elementary school organization and classification practices during the coming decades. While these certainly do not exhaust the range of innovations influencing current pedagogical practices, they serve as an excellent example of recent developments which could materially alter the structure of the elementary school in our country.

TECHNOLOGY IN EDUCATION

The embodiment of the ethos of our age may best be found in the automation processes and gimmicks exemplified by the vending

112

machines (gum, soft drinks, newspapers, or pocket combs), the washing machines (clothes, dishes, even automobiles), and, on a more grandiose scale, the IBM installations. All these automatic devices save time and labor—and, of course, money.

Perhaps it is inevitable with the inroads made by the projector, record player, tape and wire recorder, TV screen, and teaching machine that the classroom of the future will take on more and more the efficient and economical appearance of an educational automat. If so, what is likely to be gained and what is likely to be lost to the young learner through the fast-growing trend toward this type of self-teaching process?

Three personal incidents, in one way or another, have accentuated the "teaching machine" or automation issue for me in recent weeks.

Motoring from Boston to New York City recently, I drove down the new Connecticut Pike—a multi-laned highway studded with toll stations. As I approached the first toll gate the big decision "correct change this-a-way and all others that-a-way" was forced upon me. Armed with the "right change" I fed the automatic register and as my coins clinked in, a most impersonal sign blinked out a mechanical "Thank You." After two of these "Thank you's," I found myself driving through the stiles manned with humans rather than machines. Somehow I felt less lonely and more a part of a live universe hearing a human voice say, "Thank you"—even though in perfunctory fashion—and seeing a human hand take my change.

Walking across a well-known eastern university campus not long ago, I glanced in on a classroom (perhaps better described as a learning laboratory) and noted a number of students closeted in separate cubicles. They were all wearing earphones and were apparently listening to tapes. But there was no sign of a mentor around. If students are present, need there be a mentor nearby?

On returning home one evening, I was greeted by my daughter, Jane, now in the fifth grade and in her second year of TV French: "Bon soir, Papa! Je m'appelle Jeanne." "Merci," I answered, "mais tu parles comme une jeune fille Francaise." She had learned all her conversational French from a TV screen.

How depersonalized can the classroom be and what are the effects—immediate and long term, good and bad—of seeding the classroom with mechanical aids that enable or even insure effective self-instruction and learning?[9]

[9]William C. Kvaraceus, "Future Classroom—An Educational Automat?" *Educational Leadership*, 18 (February, 1961), 288-289. Reprinted with permission.

Rapidly materializing problems and issues pertaining to the utilization of pioneering technological developments in American classrooms have undoubtedly contributed to the initiation of innumerable research probes in our schools. These experiments are usually designed to evaluate the impact of technical devices upon learning in a classroom setting, or to determine a technical device's role within a learning situation. School leaders who incorporate televised or programmed lessons within the instructional setting today must operate on a hit or miss basis until sufficient experimental evidence is obtained. Eventually, experimental evidence will prescribe the framework for employing today's technological developments in a learning situation. The reader may obtain a flicker of insight into the possible influences of current technological developments upon tomorrow's elementary school organization by examining the following descriptions of programmed instruction, educational television, and computers.

1. Programmed Instruction. The teaching machine idea was inspired by S. L. Pressey of The Ohio State University soon after the conclusion of the First World War. While Dr. Pressey's arguments in favor of teaching machines for classroom purposes were sound, teaching machines did not receive widespread attention until a few years ago. Much of the surge of interest in teaching machines during the past several years can be attributed to the work of Harvard University psychologist B. F. Skinner. Dr. Skinner has championed the belief that teaching machines effectively individualize and reinforce content which children must learn.

What is a teaching machine? According to James Finn, "a teaching machine or auto-instructional device is a piece of apparatus designed to be operated by an individual student."[10] These machines and devices are available in a wide range of technical sophistication (and cost). Possibly the reader was introduced to the game of bridge via a $3.50 teaching machine called Autobridge. Or perhaps the reader's first view of an auto-instructional device was a thousand-dollar gadget manufactured for school use. In any event, Finn has pointed out that all machines and devices have the following characteristics in common:

[10]James D. Finn, "Auto-Instructional Devices," *NEA Journal*, 49 (November, 1960), 41. Reprinted with permission.

1. The student is presented with a question or problem by some form of display on the machine.
2. The student is required to respond overtly—that is, he must do something about the problem such as writing an answer or pushing a button to indicate an answer.
3. The student is informed, one way or another, as to whether his answer is right or wrong and, in some cases, why he is right or wrong.
4. Often an account is kept of the response to each item—not for testing purposes, as, for example, when the machine has a provision to repeat items that have been previously missed.

He also stated that the actual vehicle is subordinate to the "program," which is the heart of the auto-instructional concept.[11]

Devices and machines have been used to teach preschool children to discriminate patterns and shapes, elementary school children spelling and arithmetic, and secondary school students math, science, and foreign languages. Generally, these programmed lessons have been presented to existing classroom groups. Instead of a teacher-directed situation, each student adjusted the programmed lessons to his own rate of learning. For example, a group of second-grade children were taught spelling in the following manner.

> The teaching materials are fed past a double window in the machine. The student writes his responses directly on the teaching materials through the open window. Then he pushes a lever that moves his answer under a transparent piece of plastic. Now he can still see it but can no longer change it. Simultaneously, the correct answer is exposed.[12]

Early experimental results suggest that children can learn certain content effectively when it is presented by a teaching machine.

Auto-instructional techniques have become widely used because they seem able to accomplish certain objectives more expeditiously than either existing instructional aids or a teacher in a classroom with many students. Leslie Briggs noted two reasons for the popularity of programmed instruction: First, the machines appear to keep students working attentively—probably because of their monitoring, informing, and motivating characteristics; and second, the material pre-

[11]*Ibid.*
[12]A. A. Lumsdaine, "Teaching Machines and Auto-Instructional Programs," *Educational Leadership*, 18 (February, 1961), 275. Reprinted with permission.

sented is much more carefully and laboriously developed than are most forms of educational media now in common use.[13] A teaching machine is designed to introduce controlled communication, and for this reason it is becoming a potential fixture in the educational system.

Since auto-instruction is tutorial instruction, a single classroom teacher may be able effectively to direct certain individualized learning experiences for large numbers of children. In fact, it may only be through intelligent use of programmed instruction that some of the administrative problems of the ungraded school and other similar ventures can be rectified. Schramm sees programmed instruction administering the coup de grace to the old dragon of progress-by-yearly-lockstep in the closed classroom.[14]

2. Educational Television. The president of a leading American electronics corporation, during a recent address on educational television, expressed the belief that a single teacher can instruct 100,000 students at one time on a national educational network. He also observed that "the ablest teachers will be better paid and will do a better job for more pupils in less time, at less cost than ever in the past." These statements certainly reflect the optimism shared by many of our country's business and professional leaders with regard to the impact educational television will have on our schools. The reader is invited to examine critically data presented in the following paragraphs as one means of determining whether these visions will eventually become a reality in American schools.

Educational television is a broad classification frequently applied to television programming developed for individual or group instructional purposes. To date, commercial frequencies, ultra-high frequencies, and closed-circuit networks have been utilized for educational television. While 275 channels have been authorized for educational purposes, only 60 channels—40 VHF outlets and 20 in the UHF portion of the spectrum—have been used thus far. "Continental Classroom" and "Sunrise Semester" are examples of programming on commercial frequencies. Commercial programming has not been extensively exploited, because prime viewing time is at a premium. The number of hours UHF channels actually transmit each day varies

[13]Leslie Briggs, "The Probable Role of Teaching Machines in Classroom Practice," *Theory Into Practice*, 1 (February, 1962), 54.

[14]Jack Edling, *et al., Four Case Studies of Programmed Instruction* (New York: The Fund for the Advancement of Education, 1964), p. 112.

considerably due to their budget limitations and local acceptance of the medium. Much programming for elementary-level pupils on UHF channels has been directed toward science and math, foreign language, and fine arts instruction. Closed-circuit facilities are currently in operation in schools on a city, county, and state-wide basis. South Carolina recently established the country's first state-wide closed-circuit television project. Closed-circuit television programming does not differ markedly from UHF station program patterns.

How can a televised lesson influence a group of children in the elementary school? The following account has been extracted from a report of an elementary school administrator to her superior, a state superintendent of schools.

> When the time comes for the TV lesson, the children gather in groups of ten to fifteen (in auditorium classes, the range may be from fifty to sixty), peering at the home-size 21-inch TV sets. They sit, without moving or speaking, while the small, black-and-white image of a "Master Teacher" goes into action. The teacher does all the work.
>
> Occasionally, the boys and girls repeat certain words or phrases in unison at her request; occasionally, they write down dictated items of information. But for the most part, they look and listen — or think their own thoughts. The TV teacher asks questions — and answers them herself. No interruptions are possible. The captive audience is passive.
>
> Bored, bright children, ahead of the lesson being given, may read the "School Edition" of TV GUIDE, which looks just like its commercial counterpart. A puzzled small boy raises his hand, then hopelessly lets it drop as the "Master-Teacher" sweeps on. Unable to ask questions at the proper time, the less gifted children fail to understand, fall behind, and waste the period. The TV lesson is geared to a mythical "average" in which Johnny and Mary are lost.[15]

This account vividly portrays a serious misuse of educational television for instructional purposes. Abuses like this one occur frequently, because much ETV programming presented in elementary schools has been poorly planned, presented, and evaluated.

Educational television has been able to make a contribution to classroom instruction in spite of the above-mentioned abuses of the medium. Its effectiveness seems to be influenced by its role in

[15]M. G. Dawson, "Is Something Wrong with the ETV Picture?" *NEA Journal*, 50 (May, 1961), 44. Reprinted with permission.

relation to the teacher in the classroom. Educational television has been used in classrooms as an enrichment vehicle and for direct teaching. The former application is not apt to alter the nature of the present school structure. The latter has aroused considerable controversy.

A major ETV research breakthrough could markedly alter the nature of the school arrangement. As an example, tomorrow's elementary school may consist of several large viewing rooms with numerous smaller study rooms, or it may house a viewing chamber in every classroom. Organizational patterns may or may not be influenced by a significant ETV development. Some pedagogical seers can envision large multiaged classroom groups receiving major portions of their instruction via television. The classroom teacher is relieved of most instructional responsibilities with such a framework. These seers may ultimately be recognized for their farsightedness. However, history has buried many similar prophets who made comparable predictions for the textbook, the filmstrip, and the motion picture.

3. Computers. In 1671, Gottfried von Leibnitz observed, "It is unworthy of excellent men to lose hours like slaves in the labor of calculation which could safely be relegated to anyone else if machines were used." He and Blaise Pascal each developed a mechanical calculator during the seventeenth century in the hope of conserving man's mental energies. These inventions were followed by Charles Babbage's Difference Engine, a machine designed to compute by successive differences and then print out the results in the form of tables, in the early nineteenth century; by the Harvard Mark I, an electromechanical machine that processed data automatically, completed in 1944; by ENIAC, the first completely electronic computer, completed in 1946; by the mathematician John von Neumann's work on the idea of the stored program; and by numerous inventions and developments since 1950 that contributed to machine efficiency, capacity, miniaturization, and sophistication. Today, thousands of computers are serving mankind in sundry areas of inquiry and application.

The machine age, or if you prefer, the age of information processing, has become a vital part of society so rapidly that few individuals realize the implications of recent events. James R. Oliver described the great strides made as follows:

Just before 1940 ... ten-digit numbers could be multiplied together in a time somewhat in excess of one second. At the present time, however, we find that it is not too difficult to find a computer which can perform the same type of operation in ten microseconds — ten millionths of a second.[16]

Imagine, a 100,000-fold increase in speed over this short span of time!

If transportation speed kept pace with gains in computer speed, Oliver observed, man today would be able to travel at 500,000 miles per hour. And if transportation costs paralleled computer costs, man would probably not bother about driving through the streets seeking a parking place, but instead would junk his car and purchase a new one when ready to return home.[17] These analogies are staggering. They emphasize the fact that computers have unlimited potential and that they are financially feasible.

How can these information-processing breakthroughs affect education generally and elementary school organization specifically? Agencies such as the United States Office of Education, state departments of education, and local school districts that gather, assemble, and report data can and do use computers to expedite school matters. Local school districts currently use computers to process financial data, to schedule classes, to plan schoolbus routes, and to pinpoint future school sites.

Few elementary school classrooms have felt the influence of computers to date. Several feasibility studies have been initiated, however, that may be harbingers of tomorrow's elementary school organization. One approach amounts to placing in the classroom consoles which are linked to a centrally located computer. Children use the consoles, which look like typewriter keyboards, to interact with the computer when studying specific topics. In these experiments, the computer shares the instructional responsibility with the teacher.

Another approach relegates the computer to the role of an information retriever. A number of classrooms or schools are linked to a computer which has been programmed with selected social science, or mathematical, or literary information. Children use the computer as a data source or a calculation aid during their study of designated topics.

[16]James R. Oliver, "Social Implications of Computers," *Educational Data Processing Newsletter*, 3, No. 9 (October, 1964), 2-3.
[17]*Ibid.*, p. 3.

FIGURE 14

A TEAM TEACHING ORGANIZATION*

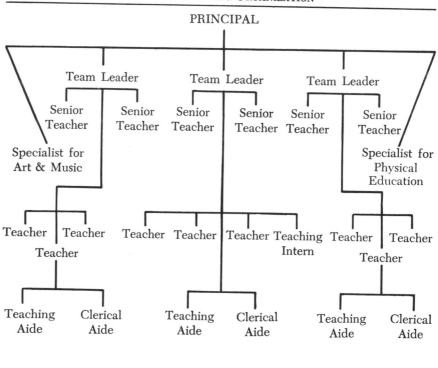

PRINCIPAL

Team Leader Team Leader Team Leader

Senior Teacher Senior Teacher Senior Teacher Senior Teacher Senior Teacher Senior Teacher

Specialist for Art & Music Specialist for Physical Education

Teacher Teacher Teacher Teacher Teacher Teaching Intern Teacher Teacher
Teacher Teacher

Teaching Aide Clerical Aide Teaching Aide Clerical Aide Teaching Aide Clerical Aide

ALPHA BETA OMEGA

*Ellis A. Hagstrom and Beverly S. Stone, "A Brief Description of the Teaching Teams Project, Franklin School," unpublished document (November, 1960), p. 12. Reprinted with permission.

Each of these pilot probes is pregnant with possibilities. Can the reader envision a computer-based elementary school which eliminates the need for classroom groupings, grade levels, scheduled lessons, and testing as we know it? What specific changes might occur within such a school? What will become of Miss Ritter in this kind of school?

TEAM TEACHING

Team-teaching experimentation is usually undertaken by school leaders who are seeking means of improving instruction and attracting and holding professional personnel of superior quality. Salient aspects of these experiments include joint teacher responsibility for the educational program and some teacher specialization within the instructional program (see the instructional team description on page 120). More team-teaching innovations have been conducted by secondary than elementary school leaders to date, as the secondary school organizational plan seems to lend itself more readily to a team-teaching pattern.

One of the pioneering projects in team teaching at the elementary level was initiated in the Franklin School in Lexington, Massachusetts, during the 1957 school year. Franklin was selected by a Harvard University study group as the experimental site because it contained two large multipurpose rooms and a new ten-room building addition. The organizational plan employed in this school for 1960-1961 is illustrated in Figure 14. Alpha, Beta, and Omega are names arbitrarily assigned to the school's three instructional teams. How does this plan differ from Miss Ritter's school pattern?

Even though team teaching is still in its infancy, its structure has materialized sufficiently to enable a perceptive educator to anticipate aspects of the present elementary school organization which are likely to be altered by a team-teaching pattern. Can the reader, on the basis of information presented in this chapter, identify some of these conceivable changes in the elementary school? Several alternatives which seem within the realm of probability are discussed in the following paragraphs.

Team-teaching patterns function most effectively within physical facilities containing a few very large rooms and a number of small rooms. Consequently, before most school systems can undertake an instructional team plan within the elementary school, appropriate building facilities must be provided. A major renovation or building program seems to be essential for most school systems in order to provide adequate facilities for a team-teaching pattern. The Estabrook Elementary School in Lexington, Massachusetts, was designed and built with a team-teaching arrangement in mind. Experimentation which originated in the Franklin School is being extended in this school environment. If team-teaching plans are adopted on a wide scale during the next several decades, tomorrow's school structure will certainly differ from the uniform cell-type structure now in operation.

How can a team-teaching plan, which necessitates specialized building facilities, influence the teacher's role in the school? Most existing instructional teams include teaching specialists. These people assume a responsibility for developing their specialty within the framework of the entire instructional program. Tomorrow's teacher will need specialized training in addition to (or in place of) the usual teacher training requirements, in order to qualify for certain positions in a team type of elementary school. It is not unreasonable to believe that more teaching specialists will function within the framework of a team structure.

The classroom teacher usually assumes a direct responsibility for a particular group of children within a team plan. He has classroom contact with the entire group or certain members of the group during the major part of the school day. When instructional situations involve all pupils within the team, a given teacher may or may not be directly involved in face-to-face contact with the children. Therefore, the team approach may afford tomorrow's classroom teacher more opportunities than present organizational structures for preparing instructional materials in the course of the school day.

One further point deserves comment as a part of this discussion. Teaching teams consist of a hierarchy of levels of responsibility. While no current team-teaching practices seem hampered by power struggles within the team, the arrangement could be hampered by internal conflict.

If team-teaching practices capture the imagination of tomorrow's educational leaders, new building designs, new staff relationships, and an extremely flexible instructional program can be anticipated. Two references, which present opposing viewpoints on the matter, are recommended for additional clarity.

1. Robert H. Anderson, "Team Teaching," *NEA Journal*, 50 (March, 1961), 52-54.

2. Anne Hoppock, "Team Teaching: Form Without Substance?" *NEA Journal,* 50 (April, 1961), 47-48.

NONGRADED CLASSES

The nongraded organizational structure that is evolving takes advantage of current insights into individual differences, curriculum, and theories of personality. Individuals who initiate such a school commit themselves to a comprehensive revision of education. The Goodlad and Anderson book, *The Nongraded Elementary School,* deserves the attention of students who wish to study the ramifications of this organizational pattern more rigorously.

OTHER RESEARCH POSSIBILITIES

Most of the pioneering research currently under way in schools across the United States is designed to investigate the feasibility of an isolated technological or administrative innovation. Preliminary data from these experiments have been most encouraging. More impressive data may result from research probes which incorporate two or more new pedagogical innovations within the framework of a research design. Imagine the opportunities for using teaching machines or television programming as parts of a team-teaching project. Imagine the outcome of an experimental structure to merge desirable aspects of team teaching within a nongraded classroom arrangement. Can the reader visualize himself directing programmed instructional devices as a member of a teaching team in a nongraded classroom situation?

The NEA Center for the Study of Instruction has been established to advance the frontiers of such knowledge. It is dedicated to providing a continuing study of educational issues, to searching for new ideas, to initiating and assisting in educational innovations, and to acting as an information clearing house. Pertinent materials on school organization prepared by the Center staff and consultants include *Planning and Organizing for Teaching* and *Schools for the Sixties.* In the latter publication, 33 specific recommendations respond to 12 crucial issues facing education in the sixties.

It is the writers' hope that novice teachers will cherish the memory of Walter De La Mare's "Jim Jay" throughout their professional experience. Jim's plight is summed up in one sentence:

> Poor Jim Jay
> Got stuck fast
> in yesterday.

QUESTIONS FOR DISCUSSION

1. You are appointed to a committee charged with the responsibility of recommending an elementary school building design and organizational plan that will reflect exciting aspects of contemporary educational experimentation.
a. How would you relate the form of the building to the organizational scheme you prefer?
b. What methods would you employ to justify whatever decisions are made by your committee?
c. How can such a committee plan for the future?

2. James R. Oliver reported the following data in the November, 1964, *Educational Data Processing Newsletter*.[18]

A. The distribution of work in our society:

	Farmers	*Laborers*	*White Collar*	
1880	49%	43%	8%	of labor force
1955	11%	44%	45%	of labor force

B. Power sources used for the production of goods:

	Man	*Horses*	*Machines*	
1880	14%	69%	17%	of power output
1955	2.5%	1.5%	96%	of power output

These data reveal startling and profound changes that have occurred in our social order. How do you think these changes are reflected in the elementary school? Do you think elementary educators anticipate changes like these and plan for them, or do you think such individuals make provisions in the school after the impact of the change has been manifested? Defend your position with concrete examples.

3. Describe the instructional adjustments you think Miss Ritter would have to make if she were transferred to Celia Porter's elementary school (see page 86). What contemporary organizational practices in elementary schools seem to run counter to popular practices like individualizing instruction, providing for children's physical, social, and emotional development, and employing multisensory

[18]*Op. cit.,* p. 4.

aids in the classroom? How would you correct the conditions which are identified?

ADDITIONAL REFERENCES

Darnowski, Vincent, *Computers — Theory and Uses.* Washington, D.C.: National Science Teachers' Association (NEA), 1964. 108 pp.

Edling, Jack V., *et al., Four Case Studies of Programmed Instruction.* New York: The Fund for the Advancement of Education, 1964. 120 pp.

Educational Leadership. The theme of the November, 1960, issue is "Elementary Education: Issues and Prospects"; the theme of the February, 1961, issue is "Teaching Methods and Devices"; the theme of the April, 1963, issue is "New Aids — New Opportunities."

Hillson, Maurie, *Change and Innovation in Elementary School Organization.* New York: Holt, Rinehart, and Winston, Inc., 1965. 416 pp.

NEA Journal. A special feature of the April, 1964, issue is "Education Technology."

Oliver, James R., "Social Implications of Computers," *Educational Data Processing Newsletter,* 3, Nos. 9 and 10 (October and November, 1964), 1-10 and 1 13.

Stolurow, Lawrence M., *Teaching by Machine,* Cooperative Research Monograph No. 6. Washington, D.C.: U.S. Office of Education, 1963. 173 pp.

Chapter Six

CURRICULUM DEVELOPMENT
IN THE ELEMENTARY SCHOOL

Frequent reference is made to Miss Ritter's instructional program in Chapter Three. Her instructional program encompasses the social sciences, the natural and physical sciences, reading, spelling, language skills, arithmetic, art, instrumental and vocal music, physical education and recess, a classroom student council, independent research, and a library period with occasional scheduled times for work in other curricular areas. Many elementary school leaders employ another term—curriculum—to describe all of these school experiences. Curriculum is used throughout this book to describe the total influence of the school upon children.

Today's typical elementary school curriculum attempts to convey content, skills and processes, and attitudes, values, and appreciations to children. Content refers to subject matter derived from the various disciplines (especially the social and general sciences) for instructional purposes. Skills and processes pertain to the "three R's" and other building blocks necessary to our way of life. Attitudes, values, and appreciations are less tangible aspects of the curriculum which are specifically focused upon in art and music, but which also pervade all parts of the school program. This pattern reflects contemporary educational thought on the nature of the elementary school curriculum.

The emphasis placed upon various aspects of the curriculum varies from one grade level to the next. Ordinarily, instruction in the skills sphere consumes the major portion of the day in the lower grades (grades one, two, and three), whereas instruction in the content sphere involves a sizable portion of the day in the upper grades (grades four, five, and six). It is not at all unusual for first-grade children to spend one and one-half hours each day studying reading skills. These same children spend less than half that time studying specific reading skills as sixth graders. Similarly, a social science unit of instruction may receive about 15 minutes daily or every other day in the first grade, and one or two hours daily in the sixth grade. Instruction in the skills areas initially, then instruction in how to apply the skills in study situations, generally sums up what teachers attempt to accomplish during the elementary school years.

Curriculum patterns used in today's elementary schools did not materialize out of the blue. They are a contemporary phase of hundreds of years of evolution. Yesterday's patterns were much narrower in scope. Tomorrow's patterns may take on entirely different proportions. One purpose of this chapter is to trace the development of the elementary school curriculum from colonial America to the present. Prospective teachers possessing this historical perspective derive a threefold benefit. They are in a better position to profit from methods courses that focus upon contemporary curriculum practices. They are in a better position to apply such knowledge when curriculum problems are encountered in the field. And, finally, they are in a better position to assume a leadership role in directing curriculum changes for tomorrow's school. A second purpose of the chapter is to acquaint the reader with contemporary curricular practices. And a third is to introduce the reader to several current innovations that could potentially alter the nature of tomorrow's elementary school curiculum significantly.

THE CURRICULUM IN RETROSPECT

CURRICULUM PRACTICES BEFORE THE INAUGURATION OF OUR FIRST PRESIDENT

Throughout the Colonial period, the curriculum of the common schools reflected the feelings of the various religious and national groups who settled in America. The schools established by the Puritans differed from those established by the Dutch of New Amsterdam and by the English in the southern colonies. Each represented a type of organization that suited a majority of the people within the particular area. Although areas varied in their approach to education, it was apparent that whether a child was tutored, attended a dame school, a reading and writing school, a pauper school, or some other educational institution during this era, his education was influenced by the Protestant emphasis upon moral discipline. Since Bible reading was a vitally important skill in most communities, people who assumed the responsibility for local education placed considerable emphasis upon teaching reading. Hence, the elementary school curriculum prior to the Revolutionary War centered on the rudiments of reading and encompassed spelling, writing, and ciphering. The availability of paper and the development of commerce in a community usually determined the amount of writing and ciphering in the curriculum.

Most Colonial elementary school programs provided instruction for children between the ages of four and eleven. The programs were generally designed for boys who aspired to go on to secondary school and college. It was not at all unusual to find public notices advertising schools, curricula, and tutors during the eighteenth century. The following advertisement appeared in *The South Carolina Gazette* on September 3, 10, and 17, 1744.

White Point

> Reading, Writing in all the Hands us'd in Great Britain, Arithmetic in whole numbers, and Fractions vulgar and decimal, Merchants Accompts, in the true Italian Method of double entry, by Debtor and Creditor, and Dancing are taught at the House of Mrs. Fischer on White Point by
>
> George Brownell and John Pratt.[1]

Messrs. Brownell and Pratt were probably supported by fees obtained from the few children who attended their school.

Many New England communities established and supported a common school during the latter part of the eighteenth century. An example of a school day in Middlesex County, Connecticut, in 1799 is depicted in Figure 15. Since printed materials were limited and writing tools were scarce in common schools throughout the Colonial period, children were forced to spend many idle, unproductive hours at their seats. Young children, inadequate materials, and often an incompetent teacher all contributed to a sterile school atmosphere during this phase of our country's history.

The elementary school curriculum at the time of Washington's

[1]E. W. Knight and C. L. Hall, eds., *Readings in American Educational History*, p. 42. Copyright 1951 by Appleton-Century-Crofts, Inc. Reprinted with permission.

FIGURE 15

AN EXAMPLE OF A DAY IN A COLONIAL SCHOOL*

Morning Session

First half hour: *Bible* study

Second half hour: Older pupils recite morning lessons; younger prepare to spell and read

Third half hour: Writing

Fourth half hour: Hearing under classes (younger children) read and spell

Fifth half hour: Assisting writing and ciphering

Sixth half hour: Hearing under classes read and spell again; receive and deposit pens, writing, and reading books

Afternoon Session

First half hour: Children spend time in review

Second half hour and

Third half hour: Hearing under classes and assisting writers and ciphers

Fourth half hour: Hearing upper classes (older children) read

Fifth half hour: Hearing under classes read and spell

Sixth half hour: Receiving and depositing books, etc.

NOTE: Pupils were dismissed after a psalm or hymn, the Lord's Prayer, and an evening prayer. On Saturday the children reviewed the week's work and focused upon lessons on religion and morality.

*E. W. Knight and C. L. Hall, eds., *Readings in American Educational History*, pp. 476-477. Copyright 1951 by Appleton-Century-Crofts, Inc. Reprinted with permission.

inauguration reflected a spiritual and an increasingly important utilitarian influence: spiritual in the sense that Bible reading was of vital importance in colonial America; utilitarian in the sense that reading, writing, and ciphering were essential aspects of the country's communication.

CURRICULUM PRACTICES BEFORE THE CIVIL WAR

During the nineteenth century, the seeds of the American public school system were sown. The elementary school evolved from a private, one-room, church-controlled entity to a public, nonsectarian, six- or eight-year graded structure by the middle of the century. As the graded school pattern evolved, so did the curriculum of the institution. In fact, an authority on educational history suggested that the development of these two aspects of our public school system is one story. Curriculum development throughout this period slowly began to reflect the needs of a young, expanding nation.

Citizens living in the northeastern area of young America contributed significantly to curriculum development between 1800 and the Civil War. For example, the course of study adopted for the elementary schools of Providence, Rhode Island, after 1800 read:

> The principal part of the instruction will consist in Spelling, Accenting and reading both Prose and Verse with propriety and accuracy, and a General knowledge of English Grammar and Composition: Also, writing a good hand according to the most approved Rules, and Arithmetic through all the previous Rules and Vulgar and Decimal Fractions, including Tare and Tret, Fellowship, Exchange, Interest, etc.[2]

Compare the Providence instructional program with practices noted by Cubberley in 1825 and 1850 (see Figure 16). It is obvious that the three basic skills were refined and extended during the early nine-

FIGURE 16

CURRICULAR PRACTICES IN 1825 AND 1850[*]

The Elementary School Curriculum	
1825	1850
Reading and Declamation	Reading and Declamation
Spelling	Spelling
Writing	Writing
Good Behavior, Manners and Morals	Manners and Conduct
Arithmetic	Mental arithmetic and ciphering
Bookkeeping	Bookkeeping
Grammar	Elementary language
Geography	Grammar
Sewing and Knitting	U.S. History
	Object Lessons

[*]Ellwood P. Cubberley, *Public Education in the United States* (Boston: Houghton Mifflin Company, 1934), p. 473. Reprinted with permission.

[2]Ellwood P. Cubberley, *Public Education in the United States* (Boston: Houghton Mifflin Company, 1934), p. 301. Reprinted with permission.

teenth century. Also bookkeeping, geography, sewing and knitting, United States history, and object lessons became an integral part of the curriculum for the first time.

By the onset of the Civil War, the curriculum had become so diversified that graded structures were employed extensively as a practical means of coping with the range of knowledge surveyed. Clearly, the widespread one-room school pattern of the day was unable to keep pace with the rapidly expanding elementary school instructional program.

CURRICULUM PRACTICES BEFORE THE TWENTIETH CENTURY

The period following the Civil War was characterized by an intensive examination of educational practices in American schools. European pedagogical influences, the increasingly complex social, political, commercial, and industrial life of the American nation, and compulsory attendance enactments forced communities to evaluate critically the existing school's capabilities. These evaluations and examinations contributed to the refinement and organization of the elementary, secondary, and higher educational spheres of American education in the twentieth century.

The expansion of the elementary school curriculum during this era was not without incident. New courses seldom replaced existing courses. Rather, both were provided for within the available time. For example, reading, writing, arithmetic, geography, history, and grammar were initially taught in the graded elementary school at Quincy, Massachusetts, in 1848. Then came music, drawing, and gymnastics. Nature study, domestic science, and manual training were also added. Various attempts were made from time to time to include courses in civics, German, Latin, physiology, hygiene, agriculture, bookkeeping, current events, some geometry and algebra, and aspects of such trades as carpentry and printing.[3] As the curriculum expanded, less time was spent studying the basic aspects of the instructional program.

Countless teachers, innumerable community leaders, and many unsympathetic public presses actively criticized the inclusion of "fads and frills" in the elementary curriculum. The obvious result was an elementary curriculum that burst at the seams.

Ways of solving the problem of an overburdened elementary level

[3]William E. Drake, *The American School in Transition* (Englewood Cliffs, N.J.: Prentice-Hall, Inc., 1955), p. 349.

curriculum were a live issue during the late nineteenth century. Many educators engaged in heated debates on the matter. Unprofitable practices and experiences caused many professional heads to roll. Several practices of this period deserve comment, as they stemmed the tide of expansion to some degree.

Educators influenced by the work of the German Herbart introduced "type studies" into the curriculum as one method of eliminating useless subject matter. These studies organized many isolated facts around a topic or theme such as "the Farm." Herbart's type studies aroused much interest and experimentation on the problem. Some educators extended the Herbartian idea by proposing a plan which concentrated instruction about a few main subjects like history and related the rest of the school work to the main subjects. Others attempted to eliminate the impractical and insignificant from subjects taught and focused upon the parts remaining. Much useless content was purged from arithmetic instruction in this manner. Another noteworthy attempt to solve the problem emanated from John Dewey's experimental school at the University of Chicago. He tried to teach children via projects rather than by means of subject classifications in his school.

Each of the above-mentioned practices sought to restructure the rapidly expanding elementary school curriculum in some manner. These practices served as the basis for many experiments and curricular innovations after the turn of the century. A number of terms (such as "correlate," "integrate," "broad field," "core," and "child-centered") employed in the twentieth-century education literature stem from the Herbartian type study and the Dewey project idea.

CURRICULUM PRACTICES BEFORE THE 1960's

At the turn of the century, the elementary curriculum continued to be a subject of considerable controversy. This was partly due to the fact that curriculum innovations pioneered in the urban school districts often were not easily adapted to one- and two-room elementary schools. A majority of the elementary schools at the turn of the century were of this type. Consequently, curriculum offerings in the graded urban schools were apt to be more attractive than offerings in the multigraded rural schools. Some educators in progressive urban districts were thus inclined to view one- and two-room institutions as archaic. In turn, some rural educators tended to view urban curricula as being overburdened and subject to fads. Criticism and countercriticism were the order of the day.

Cubberley pointed out that a representative curriculum pattern for an urban area in 1900 included approximately 20 subjects.[4]

Since children spent about 25 to 30 hours in school each week, the teacher was confronted with the task of scheduling 20 subjects in this amount of time. To make matters worse, the teacher had no guarantee that the curriculum would be restricted to 20 subjects. Pressures were constantly being exerted to add new courses. Fortunately, capable leaders were on hand to accept the challenge for improving the elementary school curriculum. Frederic Burk, Carleton Washburne, James McDade, William Wirt, Helen Parkhurst, and John Dewey are frequently included on a list of twentieth-century curriculum pioneers. These educators not only experimented with the curriculum, they also devised administrative and methodological innovations to cope with the evolving elementary school institution.

Wirt, Washburne, and Parkhurst each developed a pedagogical plan which treated selected subjects in a historically unique manner. Wirt experimented with a novel administrative pattern, while Washburne and Parkhurst, inspired by the work of Burk, experimented with novel methodological patterns. Wirt grouped selected subjects into what he called the fundamentals and the specialities. Washburne organized his curriculum in terms of common essentials and group and creative activities. Parkhurst structured her curriculum in terms of academic subjects and physical, social, and emotional subjects. In each case, these educators preserved the subject areas of the curriculum.

Since these plans incorporated subjects, they really did not solve the problems of unlimited curriculum expansion. Therefore, other avenues of study were opened. A number of educators employed a variety of "broad-fields" plans in an effort to merge relevant subject areas around a reasonable common core of knowledge. Social studies, general science, and language arts are broad-field areas which emerged in the curriculum. In practice, social studies involved history, geography, civics, economics, sociology, and anthropology. General science surveyed knowledge from physics, chemistry, biology, botany, zoology, and hygiene. Language arts touched upon reading, spelling, writing, grammar, and literature. The state of California, by enacting a law reducing the number of elementary subjects from 27 to 15 (with 12 prescribed and 3 optional) in 1925, provided the impetus for the development of integrated spheres of knowledge in that state. Even though few state legislatures exerted legal pressure,

[4]*Op. cit.*, p. 473.

the broad-fields plan was widely accepted as one means of reducing the number of subject areas in the curriculum.

Another pioneering venture in curriculum construction around 1900 was inspired by a better understanding of the psychology of learning, the recognition that the child's needs and interests are important ingredients of learning. John Dewey's laboratory school at the University of Chicago is an excellent example of an early venture into a child-centered curriculum. A basic aspect of Dewey's and other child-centered schools was that the curriculum emerged from the felt needs and interests of children. Hence, subject boundaries were subordinated to projects or problems undertaken for study. While this curriculum plan eliminated the problem of organizing an indeterminate number of subject areas within a given amount of time, it was not widely adopted in American elementary schools — probably because it created other, equally cumbersome problems.

Even though the child-centered curriculum per se was not extensively practiced, several features of the plan were incorporated within the framework of many traditional curricula. One example of this influence can be noted in the organization of numerous contemporary subject-centered or broad-fields plans. Many subjects or blocks of time are based upon areas, problems, and functions of living instead of upon logically organized subject matter. Another influence is reflected by teachers who strive to provide for children's needs and interests in their instructional program. It seems safe to conclude that some salient features of the child-centered idea have become an integral part of today's curriculum.

Local interest in curriculum construction increased by leaps and bounds after 1930. Since that time, more than 50,000 curriculum guides have been prepared and distributed. The Association for Supervision and Curriculum Development customarily gathers and displays thousands of these at their annual convention. The guides usually list aims of the school system, a curricular framework, and content appropriate for children of various age levels. Occasionally, they describe preferred methods of teaching content. It is not at all unusual for beginning teachers to become actively involved in curriculum developments early in their teaching careers.

THE CONTEMPORARY CURRICULUM

The scope of Miss Ritter's curricular offerings can be ascertained by examining Figure 7 in Chapter Three. It is apparent that several broad fields (social sciences, language skills, etc.) and separate subjects (spelling, arithmetic, etc.) form the basis of her curriculum. She also incorporates opportunities for child-directed activities like recess, independent study, recreational reading, and clubs within the scheme. Each area of the curriculum is allocated a designated amount of time, so that Miss Ritter is able to provide a "balanced" program on a weekly basis. The Long Beach, California, plan, also described in Chapter Three, is quite similar to the one implemented by Miss Ritter.

Three contemporary organizational practices were reported in Chapter Five. Miss Ritter's curriculum and the Long Beach curriculum could function within the framework of Harry Meyers' organizational plan quite readily. Would this be true of Celia Porter's learning ability plan or Eleanor Starling's nongraded, multiaged plan? If not, what adjustments or alternatives would be required?

When curricula for the nation's fourth-grade classes are considered as a whole, how representative is the plan attributed to Miss Ritter? The representativeness of her curriculum can be assessed by contrasting it with other plans discussed in the professional literature. Five recently published textbooks, currently employed in the beginning course of an elementary teacher education sequence, and numerous journal articles describe the contemporary elementary school curriculum in terms of broad fields and subject areas. One of these articles, "Today's Elementary School," by Henry Harap, has been selected and reproduced so that the reader can examine and contrast another educator's view of the curriculum.

TODAY'S ELEMENTARY SCHOOL[5]

Henry Harap

The new elementary classroom bears no resemblance to the gloomy room of yesterday with its dark-hued walls and heavy, fixed desks in straight rows. New buildings have more space, movable furniture, and more equipment for active and creative learning.

As a result, the classrooms are more flexible and informal. Altho many existing classrooms still have a rigid and formal atmosphere, the new room is gradually becoming a center where children live and work together.

Today virtually every American elementary school child has access to free textbooks purchased with state or local funds. The

[5]Henry Harap, "Today's Elementary School," *NEA Journal*, 46 (February, 1957), 78-80. Reprinted with permission.

textbook, more than any other factor, still determines what the elementary-school child learns in school. The textbooks include the whole range of school subjects — reading, spelling, handwriting, English usage, geography, history, science, health, music, and others.

In addition to the basic collection of textbooks, the pupils have access to several sets of supplementary books and a small classroom collection of books and pamphlets.

Twenty years ago it was not uncommon to see a whole primary class begin a reading period with, "Mary, turn to page 30 and read aloud." The children would then take turns reading until they came to the end of the story.

Today, reading is taught to small groups of the same level of ability or need, and reading aloud is the last of several preparatory steps.

Before the child begins to read books, such activities as telling a story from pictures, sharing an easy picture book, and listening to stories that are told or read help him develop readiness to read. The amount of emphasis on phonics varies widely.

The basic texts and directed reading are continued in the upper grades, but the child also reads more independently and more widely. Using the classroom or the library collection, he reads extensively for information and pleasure. The child becomes more familiar with poetry, short stories, plays, biographies, and books of travel.

Written expression often begins with the writing of group stories dictated by the children and written on the chalkboard by the teacher.

Later, pupils write simple letters to invite their mothers to a party or for some other useful purpose. As the pupils move to the upper grades, they have many occasions for original writing with correction of individual errors. Many teachers assign formal writing tasks suggested in language texts and workbooks. Creative writing of poems and stories is encouraged by the imaginative teacher.

Generally speaking, the elementary schools are putting greater emphasis on the development of good speaking and listening habits. The long-neglected art of conversation is engaging the attention of many teachers. As the opportunities to plan, to share and to evaluate become more plentiful, the children are learning to think quickly, talk fluently, and listen attentively.

Grammar is part of the language-arts program. The simpler definitions and rules are incorporated in the language text, which is usually a part of the pupil's collection. This language or English book is one of the important tools used in the child's study of punctuation, sentence structure, word study, and the elements of good usage.

Spelling as a separate subject is generally taught from a text or workbook in which the child encounters the new word in context and in isolation. The words learned in the spelling book are supplemented by new words used in all subjects and by words that have been misspelled in pupils' written work.

In this generation, the teaching of handwriting has undergone a phenomenal change. Today few children learn cursive writing until they reach the end of the second grade or the beginning of the third grade. The mechanical exercises in writing rows of ovals to the rhythmic timing of the teacher have disappeared.

Beginning writing involves learning the letter forms. Soon thereafter, the child writes for a purpose such as telling about a trip to a farm. The child continues to learn to write legibly, not in isolated exercises, but as the need for written communication arises in all subjects throughout the school day. Purposeful writing is supplemented by drill given to groups on their common difficulties.

The whole range of arithmetical processes from simple addition to the division of decimals runs thru all the elementary grades. The skeleton upon which figuring is hung consists of the four fundamental operations — addition, subtraction, multiplication, and division — applied successively to whole numbers, fractions, and decimals, as well as to measures and graphs.

Each grade or group of grades gets its special emphasis from the particular arithmetical steps for which the children are supposedly ready. There is a tendency to introduce topics several years before they are presented for mastery and to extend them beyond the mastery to provide for maintenance of skill. The applications of numbers to real situations in home and community living are being increasingly used in the classroom and in textbooks.

Drill still has a dominant place in the teaching of arithmetic, altho it is more commonly introduced after the child has encountered the number fact in a familiar setting and is more likely to understand it.

The sequence of steps is largely determined by the particular textbook in use. The addition and subtraction of whole numbers are learned in the first and second grades, and the multiplication and division of integers in the third and fourth grades, altho some schools continue them into the fifth and sixth grades.

While fractions and decimals are learned simply and concretely in the earlier grades, their formal learning is confined to the fifth and sixth grades. The children study the simpler uses of money, time, length, and weight in the primary grades and the more difficult applications in the upper grades. The study of graphs is assigned to the three upper grades.

The schools are devoting more time and are giving greater emphasis to the social studies. There is a growing tendency to push the school house walls farther outward into the community. The sequence of social studies in the first six grades parallels the expanding environment, beginning with the home and school and radiating outward to include a view of the world. While the *here* and *now* are studied in all grades, the emphasis on the *far away* and *long ago* is not begun until the fourth grade.

On the basis of curriculum guides that have come to my attention, I can report that seven school systems have fused science with social studies in recent years. The more adventurous teachers are using the lengthened period as a bridge to a larger ongoing unit of work. With this approach, pupils have ample opportunity to do group planning and to have an abundance of active and creative learning.

Science, which originally made its way into the elementary school as nature study, appears to be attaining a broader and more important status. The teaching of science at the elementary level is still in its formative stage. To my observation, the content is largely dominated by the text with very little experimentation and practical work.

Many teachers have been influenced by those courses of study and series of textbooks which are based on a classified list of concepts. For example, the concept, "Plants need air, sunshine, water, and food," is introduced in the first grade and is expanded as the child moves up from grade to grade.

The categories into which study of this concept most commonly fall are: weather and climate, earth, living things, health and nutrition, and energy and machines.

Arts and crafts, stories, music, dance, and dramatics are quietly gaining greater acceptance. The once violent widespread criticism of these so-called fads and frills is now barely audible. In fact, the public is demanding artistic and musical training for its children.

Many schools still devote a separate period to art, altho the theme of the children's work is frequently related to reading, social studies, and other subjects.

Teachers do not follow a sharply defined grade sequence of mediums or skills as they do in arithmetic. The children work with clay, finger paint, crayons, water colors, charcoal, colored paper, cloth, wood, and metals. The particular art mediums used in a school, however, vary from place to place.

On the art frontiers, one finds children weaving, making

puppets, block prints, and cloth design. The appreciation of master-pieces of art is usually limited to the upper grades.

The most common types of musical experience in all the elementary grades are singing, listening, playing instruments, and creative and rhythmic activity. Rhythm bands, folk dancing, and group dances frequently supplement the customary musical activi-ties. Note reading develops from the rote singing of new songs.

The teachers of the upper elementary grades are giving greater emphasis to appreciation of classical music. In the better classrooms, music permeates the total life of the children. For example, one group of third-grade children whom I observed had developed an extensive repertory of songs pertaining to sea life, to which they were giving special study at the time.

Since most of the elementary teachers are women, the pro-gram of physical activities is informal and consists largely of outdoor free play and seasonal games. Where the teaching of physi-cal education is organized, it consists of group games, individual activities, dancing, and singing games as well as other rhythmic activities.

The sequence of activities follows the seasonal pattern of games and sports. (Altho educational leaders disapprove of compet-itive athletics for elementary-school children, the fathers in some schools have succeeded in overpowering their influence and in launching baseball and football tournaments for boys.)

Some teachers are required to follow a rigorous time schedule of subjects and others have considerable freedom to plan the weekly program of studies. A teacher who adheres slavishly to a time schedule tends to allot a fixed period to each of the 10 or more subjects for which he is responsible, unmindful of their relative importance.

Some schools are tardily beginning to give some attention to balance in the total life of the school. In such schools, teachers are helped thru supervision to determine how much emphasis to give to the suggested basic components such as social living, basic skills, expressive arts, individual needs, and routine activities.

It is not unreasonable to believe that Harap has described a number of Miss Ritter's curricular practices in his article. Are there any sections of his paper that obviously conflict with her practice? By relating his description of the elementary school to the historical perspective provided earlier in the chapter, it can be seen that today's curriculum does not deviate very far from the curriculum pattern in vogue fifty years ago. How can this seeming inflexibility be explained?

139

Have the schools offered the kind of program society required during the twentieth century? Or have the alternatives been so undesirable?

There are signs of significant changes being made in today's curriculum. Harap's article provides a point of departure for an examination of some of these signs.

INSTRUCTIONAL MATERIALS

While the textbook still usually determines what children will study in the classroom, it is now subject to rather stringent competition. Curriculum innovators are offering instructional kits, programmed materials, televised lessons, and other multisensory aids as an alternative to the text. Pronounced changes are apparent in mathematics and foreign language programs for children, for example. The new materials not only offer a new form, they frequently provide new content.

READING

Probably because of extensive parental and professional pressure, reading programs are evolving from dependence upon a single basic reading series, which often was characterized by stories of questionable value, uninteresting follow-up study activities, and excessive vocabulary controls, to dependence upon much more stimulating and varied textual and other literary resources. Current basic reading materials usually include respectable literature, reflect the multiethnic background of our nation, and aim at encouraging extensive recreational reading.

Another innovation in reading instruction attracting considerable interest is a new alphabet, known as Pitman's New Initial Teaching Alphabet, consisting of 44 symbols. Children are introduced to Pitman's Alphabet because it makes the English language more consistent in its sound symbol structure, and they later make the transition to the 26-symbol alphabet.

More vigorous efforts are also being made to develop independence in reading. Critical reading, listening, and drama activities are becoming a part of many contemporary reading programs. The extraordinary energies being exerted by educators to build these dimensions into reading programs may reflect their acute awareness of the fact that a healthy democracy demands an enlightened populace.

CREATIVITY

Creativity is a concept that has markedly affected instructional offerings in language and the arts. Children are encouraged to explore on their own—to be unique, rather than imitate the performance of others. Creative writing is encouraged for its message rather than its grammatical accuracy. Varied art forms are utilized in the classroom to orient children to texture, color, form, and so forth. Their creations no longer have to resemble a recognizable entity. These activities focus upon self-concept development—encouraging individuality in a world that has a predilection toward conformity.

ARITHMETIC

Arithmetic is rapidly being replaced by mathematics as the descriptive term for number experiences within the elementary school curriculum. Both the form and content of this instructional area are undergoing drastic changes. Mathematical set concepts are now introduced in the primary grades; algebraic and geometric concepts pervade the entire grade range; the study of computers, probability, and variable number bases is not uncommon in the upper grades of an elementary school; and the nature of mathematical proof receives considerable emphasis. While the development of technical arithmetic skills continues to be an important instructional goal, the development of insight into the warp and woof of mathematics has become equally prominent as an instructional end. Since discussions of the scope and sequence of an ideal elementary school mathematics experience evoke heated controversy, further change can be anticipated in the near future.

SOCIAL SCIENCE

Many individuals, motivated by the belief that elementary school social and general science programs offered too little too late, have explored the application of more complex, demanding, and crucial topics within the curriculum. As a result, children can now be observed (1) studying previously ignored disciplines that deal with man and his social world; (2) treating particular disciplines like economics, anthropology, and chemistry with considerable rigor; (3) utilizing a scientific mode of inquiry that encompasses theorization, experimentation, and interpretation; and (4) reflecting critically upon the outcome of topics studied. The logic of the popular social science expanding-environment sequence and the expository orientation of the general science sequence are now being seriously questioned.

Ground is just being broken in these areas of the elementary school curriculum, so future directions remain rather vague. Further consideration of organizational structure for the social and general sciences is essential to continued progress. That is, how should social studies relate to the social sciences? Which dimensions of the general sciences should be presented to children initially? How can the social and general sciences be interrelated effectively? There are dozens of studies under way at present to find answers to such questions.

This sampling of topics is broad enough to reveal an apparent across-the-board movement under way to alter the form, the content, or both spheres of the curriculum. Some of these alterations may survive the test of time and actually succeed in changing its complexion. Can the reader predict which, if any, will have a significant influence upon the lives of tomorrow's children?

CURRICULUM CHANGE AGENTS

The elementary curriculum is an evolving entity in American society. It is a composite barometer of a multitude of societal factors at a given time. Students of history can easily perceive its changing nature, but identifying reasons for such change is a more complex task. A series of problem situations have been structured to exemplify the nature of curriculum change and to serve as a point of departure for an analysis of curriculum change agents.

The first problem pertains to a frequently stated notion of the elementary school's purpose. A large number of educators adhere to the belief that the elementary school must provide for children's mental, physical, social, and emotional growth in school. The curriculum naturally serves as the vehicle for expediting these four goals. Can the reader determine an approximate point in the evolution of the curriculum when each phase of growth began to receive recognition?

A second problem involves a new course for the elementary curriculum. A large aircraft corporation offers to build and equip science laboratories for all the elementary schools in a district on one condition. Since the corporation directors are vitally concerned by a persistent shortage of aeronautical engineers, physicists, and other scientists, their condition for the financial assistance is that the school district agree to incorporate a series of units of study on basic aeronautics in the fourth-, fifth-, or sixth-grade instructional program. Has a historical precedent been established for school leaders to follow when they are confronted by such an attractive offer?

A third problem arises as a result of a survey of courses offered in the elementary curriculum during the past 250 years. More than 30 different courses have been included in the curriculum at one time or another since the Colonial era. Yet, most of these courses became a part of the curriculum within the past 100 years. Can we safely assume that new course additions in the coming decades are improbable?

Another problem relates to Miss Ritter's curricular plan. A close examination of her instructional program reveals that no provision is made for teaching literature or any foreign language to the fourth-grade children. If the reader were in Miss Ritter's shoes, would he be concerned by these apparent deficiencies? Also, could the reader justify separate time allocations for related areas like reading, spelling, and language skills in the program?

A fifth and final problem pertains to several societal influences upon the curriculum. The nineteenth century was an age of transition for Americans. During this time, commercial and industrial progress changed the economic nature of society, the development of science markedly altered man's view of himself and his environment, and the United States became an important national entity. How did these developments influence the nature of the elementary curriculum in the nineteenth and twentieth centuries?

Each of these problem situations, either directly or indirectly, emphasizes the influence of society upon the school curriculum. Should one conclude, then, that society in general prescribes a curriculum parameter and sets the pace for curriculum change? Or, is it foolhardy to believe that an entity as important as the elementary school curriculum is prescribed by the fortuitous whim of social evolution? An awareness of the agents influencing curriculum change might shed some light on society's actual impact upon the curriculum.

Gordon Mackenzie has categorized modern curriculum change agents according to their potential for instigating action. Students, teachers, principals, supervisors, superintendents, boards of education, local communities, state legislatures, state boards or departments of education, and state and federal courts represent agents whose influence rests upon the authority of position or upon a legal base. Foundations, industrialists (primarily the producers of materials and facilities), national governments (primarily the legislative and judicial branches), other noneducationists (individuals and groups such as Admiral Rickover or the Council for Basic Education), academicians (primarily university professors in the various disciplines), and educationists (individuals and organizations including teacher education institutions, accrediting agencies, and professional educational organizations) are agents that function outside the immediate social or legal system of the schools.[6] There are few, if any, hard and fast rules that apply to the nature of the agents' roles, their interaction, and their relative impact.

Which of these agents might have been responsible for the inclusion of social and emotional goals within the curriculum? Would the aircraft corporation interested in aeronautical study mentioned in problem two qualify as a change agent? What is the probable process of adding a new course to the elementary school curriculum in terms of the potential human presses described above? What really constitutes a "balanced curriculum"? How may the cybernetics revolution affect the scope and sequence of the elementary school? These five questions probe at the heart of curricular change. The literature abounds with educators' answers that vary from a few paragraphs of discourse to pamphlets, booklets, and large sections of books devoted to school curricula. Perspectives on these and other relevant questions can be gleaned from the following resources:

1. William M. Alexander, *Changing Curriculum Content* (Washington, D.C.: Association for Supervision and Curriculum Development [NEA], 1964).
2. Gilbert Burck, "The Boundless Age of the Computer," *Fortune,* 69 (March, 1964), 101-110.
3. Gilbert Burck, "Machines That Man Can Talk With," *fortune,* 69 (May, 1964), 153-156.
4. Gilbert Burck, "Will the Computer Outwit Man?" *Fortune,* 70 (October, 1964), 120-121.
5. *Educational Leadership.* The theme of the May, 1961, issue is "Values: Their Impact on Curriculum"; the theme of the October, 1961, issue is "Who Should Plan the Curriculum?"
6. John I. Goodlad, *School Curriculum Reform* (New York: The Fund for the Advancement of Education, 1964).
7. George Manolakes, *The Elementary School We Need* (Wash-

[6]Gordon M. Mackenzie, "The Social Context of Curricular Changes," *Theory Into Practice,* 1, No. 4 (October, 1962), 186.

ington, D.C.: Association for Supervision and Curriculum Development [NEA], 1965).

8. NEA Project on Instruction Staff, *Education in a Changing Society* (Washington, D.C.: National Education Association, 1963).

9. NEA Project on Instruction Staff, *Deciding What to Teach* (Washington, D.C.: National Education Association, 1963).

10. *Theory Into Practice.* The theme of the October, 1962, issue is "Curriculum Planning and Development."

11. Max Ways, "The Era of Radical Change," *Fortune,* 69 (May, 1964), 113-115.

Let us imagine that the following letter appeared on the editorial page of a newspaper serving Jackson. Points it raised aroused the interest of the paper's editorial staff. Their interest materialized into a series of editorials which amplified specific aspects of Mrs. Fischer's letter. Before you read it, take note of these questions:

1. Is the approach used by Mrs. Fischer apt to have much if any influence upon the Jackson schools?
2. How are school officials likely to react to Mrs. Fischer's message and approach?
3. Are community newspapers a potentially powerful change agent in a community?

Dear Sir:

Today there is a restlessness among many laymen caused by the belief that too many of our children are not learning enough in school — are not being challenged to assimilate enough of the huge bulk of available knowledge. Some of this lay opinion is misguided. Yet it seems neither fair nor wise to discount as unjustified a lay restlessness nationwide in scope. A major portion of this restlessness necessarily centers around the unsettled and unsettling question: *What should we expect our children to learn in twelve years of schooling?* Perhaps the lay community is awakened and thoughtful and ready to accept bold, new ideas in answer to this question. In this search the layman must look to the professional educator for leadership.

The fairly thoughtful layman is worried because he senses around him a certain inertia that he believes could be disastrous. Perhaps all of us, professional educator and laymen alike, have too much the "business as usual" attitude. We seem to think in terms of all out energy expenditure and daring only in time of war. So to use the language of war, the times call for a "crash program." The times demand the national concentration of brains and energy of a Los Alamos project on educational content. We need all of the imagination, vision and courage that we can muster and we need it now!

In the opinion of the layman who is setting down these ideas, many of the problems confronting the schools and worrying the lay public today could be solved by small classroom loads, some kind of ability grouping, and adequate pay for teachers and administrators — together with more flexibility and some revision in offerings of teacher training institutions. Many laymen are trying to help in any way they can be useful in bringing these things about. Yet even if the above were accomplished, the lay restlessness about content and adequate challenge would still remain a basic question worthy of serious consideration.

As the accumulated knowledge increases it seems that we meet the problem of handling this expanding accumulation to the next generation by adding more and more "courses" to our traditional curriculum. We may even "revise" a few courses to take in more information. But what we need to do is to transform, not revise — not add — to transform from grades one through twelve.

A young atomic scientist, the father of three children, said one day: "Our children draw pictures of horses, cows and trees — but the galaxies are very beautiful and none of our children draw pictures of galaxies." Are we really bringing the "galaxies" into the kindergarten? These are now as meaningful a part of our daily world as are the horses, cows and trees — maybe more so than the horses. The world is changing — expanding and contracting at the same time — at such a rapid pace that we can no longer speak of a change in "degree." It is a change in "kind." It is truly a "new" world. We need "new" curriculum content — grades one through twelve.

It has been said that in the time of Columbus so few of the people knew how to read that hardly anyone was aware of the fact that Columbus had discovered a new continent and that the world was round. Are we teaching the next generation to "read" our new world — or are we in our own way failing? To point up the difficulties does not excuse us. We must stop defending and begin creating.

Is Knowing "How to Learn" Enough?

Some of us answer that the vast and increasing quantities of information in all fields present an impossible assignment. Content will be outdated so rapidly that there is no point in trying to absorb it. The best that we can hope to do is to stimulate interest and teach how to learn. When we need any given information, if we know where and how to acquire it, that is sufficient. The experts in a given field will need to know that field, but the great mass of average citizens do not intend to and are not capable of and need not become experts. But is it that easy? Are there not certain things which everyone who is capable of learning (labeled in I.Q. terms or any other such indicator, as being of average intelligence) must know merely in order to be able to function as a citizen in our democratic society of 1960, 70 or 80? Does one not need enough content to understand the society in which one finds oneself and to establish a relationship to it? How does one formulate values on the basis of knowing *how* to acquire information? Pointing to the vast body of knowledge to be assimilated does not excuse us. It rather intensifies the urgency.

If we agree that certain content is required by all who are capable of learning in our society and that this content needs re-examination now, then we should at the same time examine our teaching process to see how it affects content. For example, we speak of a child's being "ready" to learn as if this moment of readiness were a kind of scientific absolute for any given child. This tendency to establish and accept "readiness" limits curriculum content. We acknowledge that a child whose parents have taken him to the library and have encouraged him to take home and read books, is usually "readier" to learn at school than a child who has not had this kind of opportunity. What then is to prevent the possible conclusion that the expectations and attitudes of the total society toward learning—of the parents, the teachers, and the children—as to what *can* be done will surely influence what is finally done? It would follow then that it might be entirely reasonable to expect the average fifth grade child to learn to understand and to use exponents, by way of example. Perhaps much depends upon our attitudes and their effect upon our capacity to motivate. The school can be severely handicapped by an uncooperative community. But perhaps in this field of expectations the lay community needs stimulus—or possibly is ready and waiting for bold professional leadership and vision.

The selection of a *particular* process can limit content. A process that establishes cooperative attitudes and teaches democratic procedures is excellent and indispensable but perhaps not all inclusive. To give an extreme example, one cannot sensibly vote on whether 2 and 2 make 4. Here there is no substitute for drill. One more extreme example—if a cooperative project method of studying the geography of India leads each child into specialized avenues, so that one child becomes an expert on Indian elephants, but cannot answer any questions on mountains and rivers and cities of India, then one might conclude that this process has certain things to recommend it, but also certain limitations if content is of importance to educated citizens.

Let us not allow process to become the giant that swallows up content. It should be our servant, not our master.

The classroom teacher must be of nearly heroic stature to survive the semester under today's conditions in many parts of our country. Teaching is an exacting and exhausting job, physically and emotionally. It requires constant and skilled in-service training just to help the teacher keep abreast with developments in his own discipline. So far we have not devised very effective ways to help him to be well informed in two, three, four or more related disciplines. Yet it is just this kind of knowledge and scope which is vital in the outlining of curriculum content.

In 1893 we had a Committee of Ten who gave leadership the decisions regarding content of high school curriculum. In 1918 another commission distilled the thought on education into Cardinal Principles. Perhaps the time is come again for a new thoughtful committee. It should have on it leaders in thought in the technical sciences, the social sciences, the arts, government, and education — including administrators and classroom teachers. They should sit down together and answer the question: What should be taught in grades one through twelve to help each child answer for himself the question — to quote the ASCD 1956 Yearbook — posed in a novel by Remarque: " 'I would like to know how far I am involved in the crimes of the last ten years.' To this one might add the words of James Farrell, '. . . in a world I never made.' "[1]

The suggestions which the new thoughtful committee would make for curriculum content would be just that — suggestions. These then would be examined and discussed in the [50] states and the thousands of school districts by similar committees. And ultimately they would be interpreted by committees of teachers in each school so as to modify and improve them in any way possible so that they would serve not only the needs of our total society, but on the particular community as well.

So far concern with curriculum content has been centered on the child as a potential *citizen* in our democratic society. But this layman believes that a similar case could be made in relation to the

[1]Association for Supervision and Curriculum Development. *What Shall the High Schools Teach?* Washington, D.C.: the Association, a department of the National Education Association, 1956. p. 133-34.

need for the individual to be a complete, interested, alert, and possibly even creative human being. Learning how to learn and how to acquire knowledge are important but not enough.

All that has been said of content in regard to the average child is certainly applicable even to a greater degree to the gifted. They need a thorough and revolutionized general education if they are to become wise and responsible leaders in our "new" world.

We have had a national advertising campaign of some eight years' duration to arouse interest in schools, primarily in the financing problem. We have had a national White House Conference on Education which aroused still wider lay interest which is broad in scope. Who will now take the initiative on a nationwide scale to coordinate the highest quality and most searching and imaginative consideration possible on: *What* should we expect the teachable child to learn — grades one through twelve? Or to put it another way: What should be the content of general education in a free society? Will it be the government, the laymen or the professional educators? The layman seeks the leadership of the professional educator. He wants to work with him in every way possible.

All of us of average intelligence or above must have some appreciation of the "galaxies" and what they imply for all of the disciplines. It is merely a question of how it can best be accomplished and how soon. Our Congressmen are elected from among us average people. They and we must wrestle with problems involving nuclear energy and budgetary figures that carry nine and ten zeros after the first digit. If we do not have sufficient factual information assimilated to grasp a vision of our universe and our relationship to it — who will do it for us? Will we act in time?

Mrs. Aaron Fischer
St. Louis, Missouri[7]

Editorials that stemmed from this letter might have focused upon the role of content in elementary schools, in-service education practices, learning outcomes of the elementary school, or the breadth of knowledge to be tackled by today's teachers. These are provocative topics that seldom fail to generate verbal exchange. They are also unwieldy topics that continue to challenge the best minds in our society. Individuals who tackle such problems today become tomorrow's change agents.

Norman Douglas observed in his book *South Wind* that it is

---

[7]Mrs. Aaron Fischer, "Random Lay Thoughts on Curriculum," *Educational Leadership*, 15 (October, 1957), 553-557. Reprinted with permission.

possible to tell the ideas of a nation by its advertisements. Little did he realize that the public school curriculum affords a comparable vantage point.

A PREVIEW OF TOMORROW'S CURRICULUM?

The elementary school curriculum is in a stirred-up state at present. The Sputnik influence, a popular notion that many talented children are not challenged by today's school program, and a widespread belief that moral and spiritual values should be a vital aspect of school life are three potent reasons why the curriculum is subject to change. Elementary schools have already felt the impact of each of these influences. Both laymen (a term used to describe individuals who are not professional educators) and educators have been especially vigorous in their efforts to resolve school problems of this nature. Historically speaking, the net result of their activity may be insignificant, as the traditional curriculum pattern has survived many attempts to alter its basic structure. On the other hand, who predicted the stock market crash in 1929, the Philadelphia Phillies' National League Pennant in 1950, or the fantastic German economic recovery after the Second World War?

Since it is unlikely that all or even most of the important variables that influence the curriculum can be pinpointed for analysis, the writers have chosen to focus upon several contemporary ideas and practices that are worthy of attention. Each of the ideas or practices discussed reflects the thought of a prominent figure in education or the influence of a prominent governing body. What specific impact do you believe these ideas or practices will have upon the elementary school curriculum of 1984 or 2000?

A NATIONAL COMMISSION FOR CURRICULUM RESEARCH AND DEVELOPMENT

Professor Paul R. Hanna of Stanford University has proposed a national commission for curriculum research and development. He believes that the United States needs a permanent nationwide commission on curriculum that is nongovernmental, widely representative, and continuously at work on educational goals and balanced curriculum design. He described the function of such a commission in *The Phi Delta Kappan.*

We visualize that a national commission for curriculum research and development would continuously:

> Research, formulate and reformulate the basic purposes of education for our national community in a world setting. Such a set of objectives would help assure the perpetuation and better achievement of the Bill of Rights, the values on which our way of life is built, and the great generalizations in the humanities, social sciences, and sciences drawn from the pages of history.
> Research and formulate alternative curriculum models to provide the teaching-learning experiences through which children would come to understand, appreciate, and have loyalty to our national values, laws, and institutions.
> Research systematically all the expanding horizons of man's mind and spirit and abstract therefrom those values, generalizations, and competencies that are of vital interest to the survival and progress of our national community.
> Interpret these new ideas from all the academic disciplines and make the appropriate ones available to all concerned with curriculum development.
> Emphasize the need to keep in balance the second purpose of education — development of the individual.

There is concern in some quarters that the recommendations of such a national commission could be damaging to discussion in schools of the wide variety of views held by people in a democratic society. There are those who believe schools should discourage any discussion that raises questions concerning historic or popularly accepted positions on controversial issues. But if a closed position were taken by a national commission, the results could be disastrous to a nation that needs to explore every issue and every point of view.

We believe that one of the major contributions of the proposed commission should be the clear identification of the divergent ways of viewing important problems and the encouragement of provisions in the school curriculum for study and discussion of a wide range of views. The job of the national commission would be to encourage and facilitate the creative genius of a democratic society.[8]

Dr. Hanna contends that a nationwide discussion of how best to accomplish desired curriculum improvements is needed because

[8]Paul R. Hanna, "Proposed—A National Commission for Curriculum Research and Development," *The Phi Delta Kappan*, 42 (May, 1961), 331-338. Reprinted with permission.

change can be influenced, because great strides have been made by science and technology that place demands upon school curricula, because local and state systems of education are not usually staffed to accept and to expedite curriculum challenges affecting the national interest, and because a comprehensive body responsible for curricula necessary to our continuing national progress does not exist.

The Curriculum Improvement aspect of the Cooperative Research Program within the United States Office of Education and the Course Content and Improvement Section of the National Science Foundation have assumed some dimensions of Dr. Hanna's proposal. Both administrative units are relatively new, and both are subject to change as reorganizations alter their respective parent agencies. Each has already exerted considerable influence upon the elementary school curriculum.

SCHOOL CAMPING

Dr. L. B. Sharp, known as the father of the "outdoor education" movement, championed school camping as an integral extension of the regular curriculum to the out of doors. He argued that the out of doors offered unlimited opportunities for learning experiences that could not be duplicated vicariously in the classroom.

An example will serve to point to the unique kind of learning experience that camp can offer a child. Five boys plan to go on a camping trip with their counselor. This expedition involves group planning, group execution, and group evaluation. In each of the experiences that take place in the planning, execution, and evaluation of this trip, learning occurs because the act is a direct result of vital necessity. When things go wrong, as they sometimes do, the evaluation becomes as much a necessity as is planning and cooking the meals. Some of the outcomes of the trip experience will be:

1. Gaining an awareness of the importance of health, since first aid and care of one's health are planned for, taught, and experienced on every camping trip
2. Planning, cooking, and eating balanced menus
3. Working co-operatively to achieve an end (making a fire, pitching a tent, cleaning up, leaving the camp grounds clean, preparing the meals, and so on) ·
4. Learning to use, respect, and take care of equipment
5. Making a map and following it
6. Practicing consideration for others (in this close, intimate liv-

ing, the individual begins to appreciate the effect that he has on others in the group)

7. Developing deep and abiding friendships
8. Developing a keen awareness of beauty
9. Making direct observations of animals and other natural surroundings
10. Exercising social tact, a necessity in this close group
11. Enjoying the "simple life"
12. Learning camping skills
13. Experiencing a closeness to God and to nature
14. Talking around the campfire about thoughts, problems, and desires
15. Solving some social difficulty
16. Developing courage when the going is rough
17. Developing loyalty to the group
18. Having fun and adventure
19. Developing a sense of responsibility and sometimes the ability to meet an emergency
20. Developing dependability[9]

This list is by no means exhaustive, but it shows how far-reaching a camping experience can be.

A number of public and private schools have incorporated camping within their pedagogical program, but they represent a small percentage when all schools are considered. Day-camping experiences predominate, as they tend to be administratively feasible. Few school systems have the staff and fiscal support to provide effective resident camp experiences.

If the school year were extended to ten and one-half, eleven, or even twelve months, and if school systems were able to share the facilities provided by more than 12,000 established camps (especially during nonpeak periods), school camping opportunities would become widespread.

LEGISLATION

Virtually every state has enacted laws pertaining to the elementary school curriculum. These statutes may vary from requiring instruction in some specified area of knowledge to spelling out courses which must be taught and how much time must be allocated

[9]Reprinted from Retha Jane Mason, "Camping—An Extension of Elementary School Education," *The Elementary School Journal,* 58 (February, 1958), 275-278, by permission of The University of Chicago Press, publisher. Copyright 1958 by The University of Chicago.

for such instruction. Glen Robinson of the NEA Research Division has divided the enactment of legislation prescribing curriculum into three major periods: First is the period preceding the late 1920's, in which states enacted a large amount of curriculum prescription legislation; the second period, ranging between the late 1920's and the early 1950's, was characterized by the elimination of much curriculum prescription legislation; and the current period reflects a reversion to the pattern preceding the 1920's.[10] The current trend seems to reflect a public concern for tightening the curriculum along more rigorous academic lines.

Interest shown by the American public in its schools can often be gauged by legislative activity directed toward the school curriculum. Legislators often introduce bills and enact statutes pertaining to education as an outgrowth of pressures brought to bear by the voters. Considerable pressure of this sort has become quite apparent in a number of states in the 1960's.

This pressure is being exerted by a populace that, according to public opinion polls, lacks a "balanced" education. For example, about 70 per cent of the American people do not know the length of the term of a United States Senator; 56 per cent cannot name either of the two senators from their own home state; two-thirds have never heard of or have only a vague awareness of important foreign issues. About 50 per cent of college graduates surveyed could not locate the state of Illinois on a map of the United States, few among this group could describe the most direct route between England and India, and most did not have the slightest notion of the population of China.

Heightened interest in more prescriptive curriculum legislation by a populace that lacks a "balanced" education seems to sum up this potent influence upon America's schools.

A New View on Intellectual Development

There is a belief adhered to by scholars that children are subject to a natural ordinal scale of intelligence rather than to a relative intelligence determined by heredity. According to this belief, a child's position on such a scale indicates his stage of intellectual progress, and future progress is contingent upon the nature of experiences planned for him. Implicit in this notion is the possibility of some degree of acceleration in the rate of intellectual development.

[10]Glen Robinson, "Legislation Influences Curriculum Development," *Educational Leadership*, 19 (October, 1961), 26-30.

Dr. J. M. Hunt focused upon some possibilities of this new view in a book entitled *Intelligence and Experience*. He observed,

> ... It might be feasible to discover ways to govern the encounters that children have with their environments ... to achieve a substantially faster rate of intellectual development and a substantially higher intellectual capacity. Moreover, inasmuch as the optimum rate of intellectual development would mean also self-directing interest and curiosity and genuine pleasure in intellectual activity, promoting intellectual development properly need imply nothing like the grim urgency which has been associated with "pushing" children.[11]

Hunt recognized the need for a tremendous amount of research aimed at this belief before educational procedures might be altered.

One current trend in curriculum experimentation, which encompasses fracturing specific disciplines into their component parts and relating the learning of these to the developing intellectual abilities of the children, is a practical manifestation of Hunt's observation. Work conducted by Dienes in England on the mathematics curriculum is an example of this experimentation. He has designed a set of materials — blocks of varying kinds, abacuses, and so on — with which children in the early school years can teach themselves the basic mathematical concepts. Teach themselves, that is, under the aegis of a teacher who understands children. Such a teacher refrains from reinforcing correct or eliminating erroneous responses, but does provide the child with apparatus that enables him to make his own discoveries and to correct his own errors. In such situations, the child moves at his own pace and is rewarded by his increasing mastery.[12]

Experiments similar to Dienes' work are under way in reading, foreign language, science, economics, and linguistics. These probes may yield answers to some of the provocative questions pertaining to the nature of intellectual development. And they may alter significantly the concept of a "course" or a "subject matter area" as we now know them in the elementary school curriculum.

De Tocqueville wrote, in *Democracy in America*, these words:

[11]J. McV. Hunt, *Intelligence and Experience*, p. 363. Copyright © 1961 The Ronald Press Company.

[12]Millie Almy, "New Views on Intellectual Development in Early Childhood Education," *Intellectual Development: Another Look* (Washington, D.C.: Association for Supervision and Curriculum Development [NEA], 1964), p. 23.

America is a land of wonders, in which everything is in constant motion and every change seems an improvement. The idea of novelty is there indissolubly connected with the idea of amelioration. No natural boundary seems to be set to the efforts of man; and in his eyes what is not yet done is only what he has not yet attempted to do.[13]

Ideas offered by Hanna, Sharp and Hunt and the behavior of legislatures characterize the "constant motion" apparent in today's elementary curriculum. Their activities may or may not result in improved education for children. Time will judge their relative merits.

QUESTIONS FOR DISCUSSION

1. Charles Guy is the father of three children of elementary school age. To date, he has always assumed that schools knew what should be included in the curriculum. Recently, he read in a national magazine how valuable a specific method of teaching mathematics would be for his children. This method was not presently used in his community's school program. He discussed the situation with both the principal and teachers at his neighborhood school. How does Mr. Guy interpret the following situations?

a. The principal explained why he wasn't interested in the new mathematics program.

b. The teacher of one of his children indicated a preference to teach the "new" material but was not allowed to.

c. Mr. Guy was informed that, since he was the only one seemingly excited about the material, nothing would be changed at that moment.

2. Paul Hanna proposed a national commission for curriculum research and development, because he believes that such an entity would be strategically situated to bring about curriculum improvement in the schools. He is of the opinion that such centers can help determine basic facts, principles, and processes about curriculum matters.

a. What do you think such a centralized research and development commission might offer that existing facilities cannot duplicate?

b. If this commission is established, would you prefer to see a local,

[13]Alexis Charles de Tocqueville, *Democracy in America* (New York: J. and H. E. Langley Company, 1840), Part I, p. 516.

state, or federal agency serve as its sponsor and guardian? Explain your selection.

c. How might innovations pioneered by the commission be diffused into Miss Ritter's and other teachers' classrooms?

3. Reference was made in the chapter to the fact that virtually every state has enacted statutes pertaining to the elementary school curriculum. A number of these are quite explicit and descriptive in their charge to educators. Suppose a right-wing reactionary faction manages to gain control of the legislature in a midwestern state. This faction immediately passes a series of laws that (1) spell out a state-wide curriculum, (2) prescribe instructional materials, (3) establish a commission to approve books intended for school libraries, (4) require teachers to assert their allegiance to the state and federal governments by affiliating with designated patriotic societies, and (5) require students to attend school-sponsored "Americanization camps" for a period of two weeks every three years.

a. Could a state legislature legitimately enact statutes of this sort?

b. What limits are placed upon legislatures in terms of influencing the elementary school curriculum?

c. What alternatives might Miss Ritter pursue if she taught in this state and was subjected to the laws mentioned above?

ADDITIONAL REFERENCES

American Educational Research Association, "Curriculum Planning and Development," *Review of Educational Research*, 30 (1960), 184-279.

Association for Supervision and Curriculum Development, *Balance in the Curriculum*, Washington, D.C.: the Association, a department of the National Education Association, 1961. 194 pp.

Association for Supervision and Curriculum Development, *Using Current Curriculum Developments*, Washington, D.C.: the Association, a department of the National Education Association, 1963. 118 pp.

Beauchamp, George A., *Planning the Elementary Curriculum*. Boston: Allyn and Bacon, Inc., 1956. 295 pp.

Beck, Robert C., Cook, Walter W., and Kearney, Nolan C., *Curriculum in the Modern Elementary School*. Englewood Cliffs, N.J.: Prentice-Hall, Inc., 1960. 513 pp.

Bruner, Jerome, *The Process of Education*. Cambridge, Mass.: Harvard University Press, 1960. 97 pp.

Conant, James B., "Trial and Error in the Improvement of Education," address given before the 16th Annual Association for Supervision and

Curriculum Development Conference, Washington, D.C.: National Education Association, 1961. 24 pp.

Educational Leadership. The theme of the October, 1961, issue is "Who Should Plan the Curriculum?"; the theme of the March, 1962, issue is "Mathematics in the Schools"; the theme of the February, 1965, issue is "Social Ferment and the Social Sciences"; the theme of the March, 1965, issue is "Reading as a Social Skill."

Fleming, Robert S., ed., *Curriculum for Today's Boys and Girls.* Columbus, Ohio: Charles E. Merrill Books, Inc., 1963. 662 pp.

Fraser, Dorothy M., *Current Curriculum Studies in Academic Subjects,* prepared for the Project on Instruction. Washington, D.C.: National Education Association, 1962. 102 pp.

Lee, J. Murray, and Lee, Doris May, *The Child and His Curriculum.* New York: Appleton-Century-Crofts, Inc., 1960. 596 pp.

"Opinions Differ on the Initial Teaching Alphabet," *NEA Journal,* 53 (September, 1964), 20.

Passow, A. Harry, *Curriculum Crossroads.* New York: Teachers College, Columbia University, 1962. 123 pp.

Ragan, William B., *Modern Elementary Curriculum.* New York: Holt, Rinehart and Winston, 1960. 521 pp.

Smith, B. Othanel, Stanley, William O., and Shores, J. Harlan, *Fundamentals of Curriculum Development.* Yonkers-on-Hudson, N.Y.: World Book Company, 1957. 685 pp.

Taba, Hilda, *Curriculum Development.* New York: Harcourt, Brace & World, Inc., 1962. 525 pp.

Chapter Seven

METHODS OF TEACHING
IN THE ELEMENTARY SCHOOL

Today's elementary school teacher is not only expected to be proficient in the best procedures of modern teaching, but contemporary society expects him to assume occasionally such diverse roles as that of counselor, psychologist, philosopher, social worker, sociologist, physician, administrator, and what have you. His job has become so diverse that few people attempt to proscribe a specific role for him in today's school system. Since a prospective teacher can profit from some insight into the nature of a classroom teacher's responsibilities, this chapter has been structured with this thought in mind. First, three divergent viewpoints on teaching are described. Second, the evolution of methodology from Colonial days to the present is traced. And finally, contemporary problems pertaining to methodology are described. It is hoped that these descriptions will make the reader aware of the evolving character of methodology and of reasons for the considerable diversity in practice in contemporary schools.

CONTEMPORARY METHODOLOGY

Three distinctly different ways of teaching children are described as a point of departure for an examination of methods of teaching in the elementary school. As you study the descriptions, think about the logic, the management, and the possible outcomes of each.

MISS RITTER

Miss Ritter and her teaching associates believe that every child who enters school has a right to two basic considerations: First,

159

nothing fundamental will be omitted from his education, and second, his time will not be wasted on trivial matters. These teachers hold that a program of studies must be carefully planned in order to guarantee each individual's maximum development in school. In order to carry out such ideals, the teachers in Miss Ritter's school spend a great deal of time planning and preparing for each day's instruction.

Previously, it was mentioned that Miss Ritter developed her instructional plans within a prescribed frame of reference. Within this framework, she fitted together her instructional program. The instructional program which she employs is referred to as a modified separate-subjects approach in the professional literature. A modified separate-subjects approach is characterized by (1) instruction in both distinct subject areas (such as spelling, reading, and arithmetic) and areas which transcend subject boundaries (such as unit study), and (2) some integration of the content, skills, and aesthetic spheres of the curriculum during the school day. This is one of several approaches utilized by teachers in Miss Ritter's school district.

She also has complete freedom within the prescribed frame of reference to group her pupils for instructional purposes. Sometimes, she works with the entire group. At other times, she rearranges the children into two, three, or four subgroups. Often, she works with individual pupils. The grouping pattern adopted at a given moment usually reflects her plans to provide for children's individual differences and personal involvement in topics being studied.

A series of observations in Miss Ritter's classroom would reveal these basic features of her daily methodology. Motivation is an important aspect of most of her prepared lessons. Time spent in motivating a lesson may vary from a few moments in a reading group to several days arousing interest in a new unit of study. Getting children to assume a responsibility for learning the important elements of a study is a second aspect. For example, pupil identification of problems to be studied as part of a social science unit reflects this feature. Provision for individual and small-group study is a third aspect. Another basic feature involves analyzing and evaluating individual and group study progress. Deriving and reinforcing appropriate generalizations from material studied is a fifth aspect. Miss Ritter makes a conscious effort to incorporate these five points as part of her teaching methods.

The nature of the curricular area probably influences the extent to which Miss Ritter succeeds in incorporating the above-mentioned features of her methodology. Unit study lends itself quite well to each of the five aspects, whereas spelling does not, due to its unique characteristics. Also, the kind of topic being studied at a given moment probably affects the methodology employed.

Miss Ritter not only strives to develop knowledge, attitudes, and skills systematically, she also gives attention to the child's social and emotional development in school. She puts forth every effort to assist children to overcome troublesome behavioral difficulties. Teacher guidance is aimed at aiding the child to see the need for developing personality traits important to his present and future success. In an atmosphere that is natural and informal, children are helped to achieve freedom through self-discipline and the acceptance of responsibility.

Methods utilized by Miss Ritter are based upon considerable training and classroom experience.

MR. NORTON

Mr. Norton, who teaches sixth graders in another school district, shares Miss Ritter's basic educational considerations. Since he believes that it is important to maintain high standards of excellence throughout his instructional program, and that children must be held responsible for knowledge presented in the classroom, however, he structures classroom activities quite differently from Miss Ritter.

A series of observations in Mr. Norton's classroom would reveal these basic features of his daily methodology. Daily instruction in his classroom is geared to available basic textbook series. Usually, the teacher clarifies the learning task and then assigns work which is carried out by the children. Teacher explanations and questions following the pupil study serve to summarize and supplement the material covered. Next, written assignments and classroom tests are used to reinforce material studied by the children. Occasionally, the pupils undertake follow-up study projects to clarify certain aspects of the instruction. These points typify Mr. Norton's methodology.

The subject-centered curricular structure adopted by Mr. Norton is not geared to topic integration or unit study which transcends subject boundaries. Integrated learning situations develop, but they are the exception rather than the rule. He makes little specific provision for children's social and emotional development in his classroom, because he believes that the school serves society best as an academic institution. Mr. Norton is regarded as a purveyor of basic education by his teaching associates.

Instruction. Note that in the upper photograph all the children are engaged in exactly the same activity, whereas in the lower one the children are performing a variety of activities. Do both pictures illustrate sound educational practice?

Courtesy H. Armstrong Roberts

163

Instruction. Many teachers engage in small-group instruction, especially in teaching reading and developing a "unit" of work. What can children who are not a part of the small group receiving the instruction do during such lessons? What kinds of problems can easily arise in this kind of instructional situation?

Instruction. Foreign language instruction in the elementary school has certainly captured the imagination of educators since World War Two. Today, scenes like the one in this picture are commonplace. Try to develop a short list of probable outcomes of foreign language instruction in the elementary school. Would you be willing to introduce such instruction into an elementary school on the basis of your listed outcomes?

165

Instructional Materials. Many teachers use multisensory materials to enhance their classroom environment. Here are some scenes showing ch.'dren engaged in an arithmetic activity (using Cuisenaire rods), science activities (using laboratory equipment to conduct an experiment), and a social studies activity (making a three-dimensional map). How can materials like these contribute to a learning situation? Do you think these and similar materials can be obtained easily by classroom teachers?

Courtesy Carl Purcell, NEA

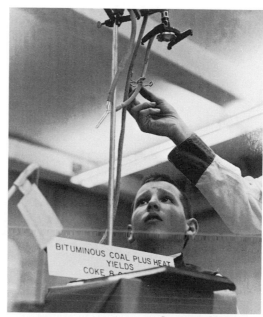

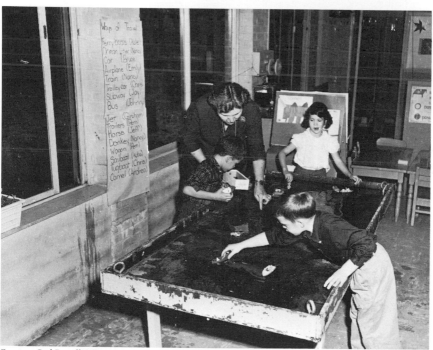

Technological Influences on the School.   The following photographs reveal a potential "pedagogical revolution" in the elementary school. In three of the four situations, specific instructional responsibility is relegated to a mechanical device, rather than to a human being. To what extent can a human being be replaced in the classroom by technological devices? Is it conceivable that a machine can teach children as well or better than a person?

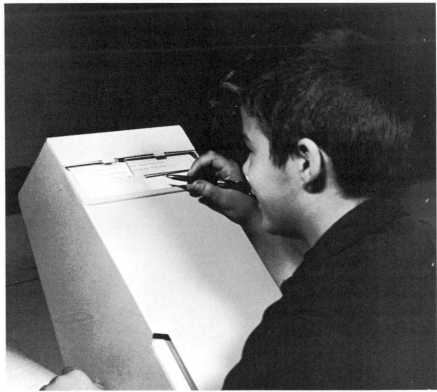

Harper—Courtesy Center for School Experimentation, The Ohio State University

Harper—Courtesy Center for School Experimentation, The Ohio State University

169

Courtesy Carl Purcell, NEA

Courtesy Carl Purcell, NEA

The Elementary School: A Perspective

MRS. SHEETS

Mrs. Sheets, a second-grade teacher in a third school district, also agrees with the two basic educational considerations previously mentioned, but differs from Miss Ritter and Mr. Norton in the way she conducts classroom activities. She believes that areas of study must arise from the felt needs, interests, and experiences of children. Subject areas per se have no place in her program, because they do not depict lifelike situations. Neither does most preplanned instruction, for essentially the same reason. Learning and living are complementary terms in her classroom.

A series of observations in Mrs. Sheets's classroom would reveal these basic features of her daily methodology. The identification of problems or topics to be studied which are real and important to the children is one important aspect. Such problems usually emerge from group planning sessions. Structuring the study and obtaining appropriate materials for study purposes is a second element. Skills and aesthetics are incorporated within the topic as they become relevant. A third aspect relates to summarizing and deriving pertinent conclusions from material studied. Reinforcing conclusions via culminating activities (especially small-group projects which involve making and doing) is a final point. These four features are characteristic of Mrs. Sheets's methodology.

Provisions for children's social and emotional development are also important parts of her methodology. She believes that children are best prepared for the problems of life when they have had an opportunity to experience life by degree in a controlled situation. Mrs. Sheets's approach is referred to as child-centered in the professional literature.

Miss Ritter, Mr. Norton, and Mrs. Sheets all seem to agree that nothing fundamental should be omitted from a child's education and that his time should not be wasted on trivial matters. Yet, considering classroom methodology, these individuals have little in common. It does not seem possible for three elementary school teachers who adhere to three distinctly different methods of teaching to share similar educational objectives. Can one of the teachers possibly be right and the other two wrong in their classroom approach? Can one approach be more fruitful than the other two, even though all three are defended by some educators as appropriate? Or is it within the realm of probability that all three approaches can appropriately be utilized in the classroom? Some answers to these questions may be obtained by studying the historical evolution of methodology in the American elementary school.

METHODOLOGY IN RETROSPECT

METHODOLOGY BEFORE THE INAUGURATION OF OUR FIRST PRESIDENT

Knowledge of effective teaching methods seldom helped an individual to become a teacher in a Colonial elementary school. If he were reasonably literate, a church member in good standing, and if he gave promise of being a firm disciplinarian, he was well qualified for any available teaching position. In all probability, few teachers possessed a knowledge of effective teaching methods, since teacher training facilities were nonexistent throughout the seventeenth and eighteenth centuries.

The Colonial teacher's knowledge of methods can readily be evaluated in the light of his environment and his daily classroom procedure. School was conducted in a living room, kitchen, barn, or in some instances a one room building especially constructed for educational purposes. Since the special building usually was a drafty, rat-infested eyesore, the teacher derived little solace from the fact that he had his own structure. Teaching materials usually consisted of the Bible and a few books published in England, quill pens supplied by homemade ink, and copy books. (Near the end of the eighteenth century, two American texts — Noah Webster's *Blue Backed Speller* and Nicholas Pike's *Arithmetic* — were widely used in the elementary schools.) Throughout the school day, the teacher assigned tasks, heard individual and some group recitations, and kept order. Probably the most widespread practice of this era was to assign work, provide time for the pupil to memorize the material, then hear the pupil recite his lesson.

While present-day elementary school teachers would question their value, Colonial teachers did utilize certain methods of teaching. William Drake described methods used before Washington's inauguration to teach children reading, spelling, and arithmetic.

> In learning to read, the child followed the ABC method, that of first learning the letters of the alphabet, then syllables, then words, and finally, the formation of sentences with words. Often,

weeks and months were consumed by a child in mastering his letters. Such a method was utterly mechanical. In spelling, the emphasis was upon the mere length of the word. The daily method in teaching spelling was to have the master call out a word and then have the whole class bellow it back. The class was detained after school in the event that the master detected an error and if the pupils would not inform him as to who was the guilty party. In learning to read, the child memorized his words in the pattern of the catechism and often in rhyme. Here again, the group method was often used, and the reading was fast and loud. There was a stopping at punctuation points, but without variations in tone. In arithmetic, which was optional, the work was equally monotonous. The student had no book. He was given a problem to work on, for several days if necessary. The whole procedure was catechetical with questions and answers written out. Students expressed no opinions. There was no challenge to think. No problem-consciousness was developed. There were no contributions from members of the class.[1]

These methods were probably handed down from one generation of teachers to the next.

A more descriptive account of how children should be received and treated in school in 1750 is reported in *The Life and Works of Christopher Dock*. Several pages from his book are quoted to depict a day in the life of a hardworking, sincere teacher of young children.

CHRISTOPHER DOCK TELLS HOW CHILDREN SHOULD BE RECEIVED AND TREATED IN SCHOOL, 1750[2]

The children arrive as they do because some have a great distance to school, others a short distance, so that the children cannot assemble as punctually as they can in a city. Therefore, when a few children are present, those who can read their Testament sit together on one bench; but the boys and girls occupy separate benches. They are given a chapter which they read at sight consecutively. Meanwhile I write copies for them. Those who have read their passage of Scripture without error take their places at the table and write. Those who fail have to sit at the end of the bench, and each new arrival the same; as each one is thus released in order

[1]William E. Drake, *The American School in Transition* (Englewood Cliffs, N.J.: Prentice-Hall, Inc., 1955), pp. 78-79. Reprinted with permission. Copyright © 1955 by Prentice-Hall, Inc.

[2]Martin G. Brumbaugh, *The Life and Works of Christopher Dock* (Philadelphia: J. B. Lippincott Company, 1908), pp. 83-86. Reprinted with permission.

174

he takes up his slate. This process continues until they have all assembled. The last one left on the bench is a "lazy pupil."

When all are together, and examined, whether they are washed and combed, they sing a psalm or a morning hymn, and I sing and pray with them. As much as they can understand of the Lord's Prayer and the ten commandments (according to the gift God has given them), I exhort and admonish them accordingly. This much concerning the assembling of pupils. But regarding prayer I will add this additional explanation. Children say the prayers taught them at home half articulately, and too fast, especially the "Our Father" which the Lord Himself taught His disciples and which contains all that we need. I therefore make a practice of saying it for them kneeling, and they kneeling repeat it after me. After these devotional exercises those who can write resume their work. Those who cannot read the Testament have had time during the assemblage to study their lesson. These are heard immediately after prayer. Those who know their lesson receive an O on the hand, traced with crayon. This is a mark of excellence. Those who fail more than three times are sent back to study their lesson again. When all the little ones have recited, these are asked again, and any one having failed in more than three trials a second time, is called "lazy" by the entire class and his name is written down. Whether such a child fear the rod or not, I know from experience that this denunciation of the children hurts more than if I were constantly to wield and flourish the rod. If then such a child has friends in school who are able to instruct him and desire to do so, he will visit more frequently than before. For this reason: If the pupil's name has not been erased before dismissal the pupils are at liberty to write down the names of those who have been lazy, and take them along home. But if the child learns his lesson well in the future, his name is again presented to the other pupils, and they are told that he knew his lesson well and failed in no respect. Then all the pupils call "Diligent" to him. When this has taken place his name is erased from the slate of lazy pupils, and the former transgression is forgiven.

The children who are in the spelling class are daily examined in pronunciation. In spelling, when a word has more than one syllable, they must repeat the whole word, but some, while they can say the letters, cannot pronounce the word, and so cannot be put to reading. For improvement a child must repeat the lesson, and in this way: The child gives me the book, I spell the word and he pronounces it. If he is slow, another pupil pronounces it for him, and in this way he hears how it should be done, and knows that he must follow the letters and not his own fancy.

Concerning A B C pupils, it would be best, having but one child, to let it learn one row of letters at a time, to say forward and backward. But with many, I let them learn the alphabet first, and then ask a child to point out a letter that I name. If a child is backward or ignorant, I ask another, or the whole class, and the first one that points to the right letter, I grasp his finger and hold it until I have put a mark opposite his name. I then ask for another letter, etc. Whichever child has during the day received the greatest number of marks, has pointed out the greatest number of letters. To him I owe something—a flower drawn on paper or a bird. But if several have the same number, we draw lots; this causes less annoyance. In this way not only are the very timid cured of their shyness (which is a great hindrance in learning), but a fondness for school is increased. Thus much in answer to his question, how I take the children into school, how school proceeds before and after prayers, and how the inattentive and careless are made attentive and careful, and how the timid are assisted.

Further I will state that when the little ones have recited for the first time, I give the Testament pupils a verse to learn. Those reading newspapers and letters sit separately, and those doing sums sit separately. But when I find that the little ones are good enough at their reading to be fit to read the Testament, I offer them to good Testament readers for instruction. The willing teacher takes the pupil by the hand and leads him to his seat. I give them two verses to try upon. But if I find that another exercise is necessary after this (such as finding a passage in Scripture, or learning a passage, in which case each reads a verse), I give only one verse, which is not too hard for those trying to read in the Testament. If pupils are diligent and able, they are given a week's trial, in which time they must learn their lesson in the speller with the small pupils and also their lesson in the speller with the Testament pupil. If they stand the test they are advanced the next week from spelling to the Testament class, and they are also allowed to write. But those who fail in the Testament remain a stated time in the A B C class before they are tested again. After the Testament pupils have recited, the little ones are taken again. This done they are reminded of the chapter read them, and asked to consider the teaching therein. As it is the case that this thought is also expressed in other passages of Holy Writ, these are found and read, and then a hymn is given containing the same teaching. If time remains, all are given a short passage of Scripture to learn. This done, they must show their writing exercises. These are examined and numbered, and then the first in turn is given a hard word to spell. If he fails the next must spell it and so on. The one to spell correctly receives his exercise.

Then the first is given another hard word, and so each receives his exercise by spelling a word correctly.

As the children carry their dinner, an hour's liberty is given them after dinner. But as they are usually inclined to misapply their time if one is not constantly with them, one or two of them must read a story of the Old Testament (either from Moses and the Prophets, or from Solomon's or Sirach's Proverbs), while I write copies for them. This exercise continues during the noon hour.

It is also to be noted that children find it necessary to ask to leave the room, and one must permit them to do this, not wishing the uncleanness and odor in the school. But the clamor to go out would continue all day, and sometimes without need, so that occasionally two or three are out at the same time, playing. To prevent this I have driven a nail in the doorpost, on which hangs a wooden tag. Any one needing to leave the room looks for the tag. If it is on the nail, this is his permit to go out without asking. He takes the tag out with him. If another wishes to leave he does not ask either, but stands by the door until the first returns, from whom he takes the tag and goes. If the tag is out too long, the one wishing to go inquires who was out last, and from him it can be ascertained to whom he gave the tag, so that none can remain out too long....

Now regarding his second question: How different children need different treatment, and how according to the greatness of the offense punishment must be increased or lessened.

I should gladly tell my friend all of this truly, but as the subject is such a broad one, I really do not know where to begin or end. This is because the wickedness of youth exhibits itself in so many ways, and the offenses which are taught them by those older than themselves are so various, and as God himself declares ... Corruption is so great, and increases daily in so many ways, that I am convinced that it is impossible to do anything of one's own power. Where the Lord does not help build, all that build work in vain. The slap of the hand, hazel branch and birch rod are means of preventing wicked outburst, but they cannot change the stubborn heart, which hold us all in such sway since the fall, that we are all inclined more to the bad than to the good, so long as the heart is unchanged and not renewed by the spirit of God. But while the seed of wickedness is present, we must strive to remove it, not only from ourselves, but from our fellow man and from our youth. As this old evil and serpent's sting is the same in all, we all are enabled to seek earnestly the same surgeon and apply the means of recovery which He prescribes for such evil, to ourselves and our youth. For without recovery we cannot reach peace, for the worm that forever gnaws our conscience through the serpent's sting leads to eternal damnation. May God mercifully assist us all, that we may not neglect the promise to enter into His rest, and none of us remain behind. Amen.

Because, as has been said, it would take too long to enumerate all cases, I shall give my friend only a few, together with the means that I have sought to apply. But these means cannot cure the damage. The Lord of Lords, who holds all in His hand, and for whose help we need much to pray in such cases, deserves all the praise if we see improvement.

First, among many children swearing or cursing is so common, expressing itself variously in so many wicked words. If this evil is not warded off, such sour "leaven leavens the whole lump," therefore such children are carefully examined, whether they understand what they are saying. As it is frequently very evident that they do not, they are asked whether they have thought of the words themselves or have heard them; they usually reply that they heard them from So and So. If asked why they say it also, the answer is usually again, because So and So said it. Thus often ignorance is shown. They do not know why they are saying it. To such it must be explained that they must guard against such words; that they are against God's will and command. If they hear So and So use them, they shall tell the person that he or she is doubly sinning, for they got into trouble in school by repeating the words. If such children then promise not to use the words again, they go free the first time. But if after being warned they persist in the bad habit, after being certain that the accusation is true, they are put upon the punishment seat, with the yoke on their neck, as a sign of punishment. On promising to be good in the future they escape with a few slaps. If they again offend, the punishment is increased, and they must furnish surety. The oftener the offense, the more bondsmen. These bondsmen's business is to warn and remind the offender and prevent repetition. This is the rein and the bit to be put into their mouths for such offense, but the change of heart must come from a higher hand, and must be sought with diligent prayer. The import of God's word must also be explained to the offender and the other pupils. What great weight is in all this (if one persist and is found guilty to the end) and that man must render an account of himself, on the judgment day, of every idle word spoken. Such passages they must look up and read, and for their further instruction they are given a song or a psalm to learn. . . .

It does not seem unreasonable to conclude that most people were unaware of effective teaching methods before Washington's inauguration. Methods employed in Colonial schools tended to be inefficient, impractical, and usually ineffective. Children taught by an individual capable of using reasonably stimulating methods of conveying knowledge (which were probably developed on a trial and error basis) were indeed fortunate.

METHODOLOGY BEFORE THE CIVIL WAR

During the first half of the nineteenth century, elementary school teachers were made aware of a variety of teaching procedures, were introduced to many different teaching materials, and were given the opportunity to improve their methodology. In effect, people began to examine the societal vehicle for transmitting knowledge much more critically during this century than during any previous period in history. The outcome of such investigation in the United States was the loosening of public purse strings for educational purposes.

A number of Europeans and Americans recognized the great need for better methods of teaching children in school. These individuals objected to the deplorable status of pedagogy in their society. Efforts of some of these individuals to provide better for children in school received widespread attention. Among the most popular European reformers were Johann Pestalozzi, who championed object teaching and oral instruction; Friedrich Froebel, who suggested incorporating manual tasks with various studies to stimulate children's self-activity; and Johann Friedrich Herbart, who (1) correlated history and literature to make instruction more effective, (2) suggested a scientific approach to study, and (3) stressed character formation as the main aim of education. An American, Horace Mann, pioneered the word method in the teaching of reading and sought to enrich the curriculum with music and drawing. These and other perceptive individuals called attention to the fact that some methods of instruction may be more effective than others. They opened the door to the study of methodology.

American textbook publishers became aware of the evolving elementary and secondary schools during the early years of the nineteenth century. Davenport's *History of the United States* and McGuffey's *Eclectic Readers* appeared in 1831 and 1834, respectively. Both were widely accepted in the schools. By 1845, numerous titles were available in arithmetic, reading, spelling, grammar, history, geography, and science. These books served to facilitate teaching and broaden course offerings in the curriculum. While teachers were able to obtain many and varied text materials during the third, fourth, and fifth decades of the nineteenth century, they continued to use them in a manner reminiscent of their mid-eighteenth-century predecessors.

The evolving nineteenth-century elementary school demanded a teacher who possessed skills in addition to being literate. As a result, the state of New York, in 1827, appropriated funds to a private institution for the purpose of training teachers. This venture was supplemented by the establishment of county institutes for in-service teacher training ten years later. In 1839, Massachusetts established the first state normal school. These early efforts paved the way for the development of teacher education programs in numerous colleges and universities later in the century. Teacher education was clearly initiated during this period of history.

What impact did the new teaching procedures, materials, and training have upon the typical American elementary school at the middle of the nineteenth century? Cubberley provides some insight into this question.

> Teaching was conducted on the individual basis, and progress through the schools was on the same basis. The master remained at his desk throughout the day, and called the pupils up one by one to repeat the lesson learned, to examine slates, or to give needed help or explanation. The teaching and questioning was directed to one pupil only, the rest of the pupils not participating in the instruction given....
>
> At the close of the term it was customary to give the pupils merit cards.[3]

If this description is compared with procedures utilized in Colonial schools a hundred years earlier, the only apparent variation in practice appears to be in the adaption of an incentive device, the merit card. While much educational progress was made in some quarters, the typical elementary school was not markedly affected by it before the Civil War.

METHODOLOGY BEFORE THE TWENTIETH CENTURY

The period between the Civil War and the turn of the century was characterized by intensive efforts to transform the nature of the elementary school. Many educational leaders began to view the teacher's role as that of an instructional guide rather than that of an authority figure. Teachers who relied upon the memoriter method of teaching

[3]Ellwood P. Cubberley, *Public Education in the United States* (2nd ed.; Boston: Houghton Mifflin Company, 1947), p. 327. Reprinted with permission.

were frowned upon by progressive educators. Teachers who directed rather than guided instruction also felt the sting of disapproval. Nevertheless, few teachers emerged who were capable of guiding the learning experiences of children effectively, because there were too few perceptive educators available to train such teachers.

Many effective teaching methods which were known before the Civil War found their way into the elementary classroom during the latter part of the nineteenth century. According to Cubberley:

> Oral instruction, the word method in teaching reading, language lessons, instructions about realities, elementary science, geography built on the child's environment instead of the pages of a book, arithmetic by analysis instead of sums by rule, music, drawing, reasoning instead of memorizing, and teaching that comes from the full mind of the teacher rather than from the pages of a book ... appeared after 1860 in the better schools.[4]

Progress of this sort paralleled the rapid development of teacher training programs across the country. By 1870, a number of three-year programs were extended to four years. These teacher training programs focused upon and disseminated proven methods of teaching in a manner unknown earlier. While many people still regarded teaching as an art, there were also many people who now believed that teaching skills could be acquired.

Francis Parker, who represented the latter point of view, took an active part in the improvement of elementary teaching during the latter part of the nineteenth century. He was instrumental in communicating the ideas of Spencer, Pestalozzi, Froebel, and Herbart to educators in America. Children who experienced firsthand and meaningful learning through planned instructional activities and children who studied skills subjects in a functional setting in all probability owed their stimulating school experiences to the work of Parker. Unfortunately, these children were the exception rather than the rule before the turn of the century.

A typical elementary school teacher in 1900 ruled as master in the classroom. He depended upon textbooks to impart information in the various curricular areas; he resorted to both group and individual recitations to assess learning; his instruction was essentially academic with some provision for extracurricular and enrichment activities; and he seldom involved children in concrete activities designed to make

---

[4]*Ibid.*, pp. 327-328. Reprinted with permission.

the instruction meaningful. Nevertheless, he was able to offer children a broad program, varied instructional materials, and more effective teaching methods than his counterpart in 1850 or 1750. Developments in teacher education and certification by 1900 indicated that better days were ahead for children in the elementary schools of the twentieth century.

METHODOLOGY BEFORE THE 1960'S

Knowledge of the fact that children possess different capabilities for learning is nearly as old as the educative process itself. Teachers probably have recognized that some children learn faster than others for thousands of years. Methods of equalizing pupil performance in school have traditionally been punishment and intensive drill. These methods were employed because teachers believed slow learners were not taking their lessons seriously. New insight into the nature of the growth process early in the twentieth century caused teachers to re-examine the implications of children's individual differences. Also, research contributions from education and related fields of knowledge during this time facilitated the development of many other effective classroom procedures.

The application of developments in philosophy, psychology, and sociology after the turn of the century markedly influenced methods of teaching in the elementary school. John Dewey and others championed a pragmatic philosophy of education which manifested itself in the elementary schools in a historically unique way. Dewey advocated an educational program that focused upon the child rather than upon his environment in order to make instruction child-centered rather than content-centered. Dewey's ideas became identified with a "progressive" education movement which enjoyed widespread popularity for several decades.

The contributions of psychology to education have been invaluable. Not only have psychologists provided vehicles for measuring the academic aptitude of children, their achievement in school, and aspects of their personality, they have also provided extensive data on the nature of human behavior itself. Many psychologists have probed the learning process to determine ways in which children acquire knowledge. Their data suggest that learning—contrary to widespread belief—is not a logical affair in the usual sense. Children learn many things in a seemingly unorganized manner, psychologists discovered.

Sociologists pointed out that twentieth-century schools in America are to all intents and purposes middle-class institutions to which children from the upper and lower classes are forced to adjust. These and other contributions from philosophy, psychology, and sociology have affected the teacher's instruction in the classroom.

Research designed to evaluate and improve instruction is another innovation of the twentieth century. Educational research related to methods of teaching in recent years yielded data pertaining to the role of the teacher in the classroom, the relative merits of various patterns of teaching, and specific phases of the instructional process.[5] Methods of teaching reading and arithmetic, for example, have been as extensively investigated as any category of education during this century. Highly refined teaching procedures have been developed in these curricular areas. While research advanced the frontiers of knowledge in methods of teaching, at no time was evidence obtained which suggested that there is any best pattern of instruction for every teacher in every situation.

Recent developments in philosophy, psychology, sociology, and education have increased the need for well-trained elementary school teachers. It is doubtful that the complexity of modern-day metho dology can be grasped by the unskilled or partially skilled individual who chooses to venture into the classroom. Today's effective teacher is expected to be acquainted with many content areas, to make learning meaningful, to provide for children's needs and interests, to involve children in the planning stages of instruction, to provide for children's self-expression and emotional release, and to allow for flexibility in the instructional program. Most of these job responsibilities were not a part of elementary teaching until this century.

A knowledge of proven classroom procedures enables the teacher to expedite these tasks efficiently. If he understands the relationship between the sight and phonetic methods of word analysis, if he recognizes the need for both expository and exploratory elements of arithmetic, if he knows how to carry out units of work in the content areas of the curriculum, and if he can individualize his instructional program, he possesses the kind of knowledge requisite to effective teaching. Societal demands upon the elementary school have increased to the point where few teachers are able to master all the

[5]Walter S. Monroe, ed., *Encyclopedia of Educational Research* (Rev. ed.; New York: The Macmillan Company, 1950), p. 745.

subjects in their instructional program. An effective teacher in today's elementary school is not a master of subject areas, but a master of methodology.

Just as Martin Brumbaugh captured the flavor of eighteenth-century teaching methodology in his portrayal of Christopher Dock, John Bartky has preserved some of the subtleties of twentieth-century methodology in a treatise entitled "The Nature of Teaching Method." While his analysis of contemporary attitudes toward teaching methods is characterized by a folksy, tongue-in-cheek literary style that may offend some individuals, it is a thought-provoking approach that uncovers some methodological skeletons seldom revealed in the professional literature. The article is reproduced for the reader's enlightenment.

THE NATURE OF TEACHING METHOD[6]

All through the history of education, theory and practice have defined varying roles for the teacher in interaction with pupils. Some of these roles suggested that the teacher be directive; others, that he adopt a permissive attitude; and still others that he abandon himself to a laissez faire policy. There almost seems to have been an alternation between the extremes of direction and laissez faire in teaching, as education developed its methodology. For example, the ancient Greek Philosophers were often directive in their teaching, though the Socratic method is permissive. The teaching method advocated in Rousseau's *Emile* is laissez faire.

My generation has seen a complete swing from the authoritarian directive role for the teacher to the laissez faire role, plus a partial swing back to the permissive approach—from the teacher-directed assignment through pupil-teacher planning to the child-centered school and now back to the planned experience. It is my thesis that such alternations are essentially reflections of fashion in philosophy and that the true role of the teacher must be determined by the situation in which he finds himself—that it may be directive, permissive, or laissez faire, depending upon the variables involved in that situation. I contend that failure to recognize this fact results in teacher and pupil frustration and produces ineffective instruction.

Education prior to the thirties concerned itself with a directive method of instruction called the "administration of the assign-

[6]Reprinted from John A. Bartky, "The Nature of Teaching Method," *The Elementary School Journal*, 58 (January, 1958), 199-203, by permission of The University of Chicago Press, publisher. Copyright 1958 by The University of Chicago.

ment." "Assignment" is a comparatively old term that reflects those methods in which the teacher operates as a dominating force. "Assignment," therefore, is hardly a respectable term for use by the child-centered teacher, who looks upon a teacher-dominated method as autocratic and threatening to democratic values.

"Assignment" developed out of the concept that teachers "assigned" learning tasks to children and then heard recitations on that assignment. In a curriculum which accepts teacher direction, the word "assignment" is used to include the process of considering all the variables in a learning experience and communicating the resulting plan for that experience to the children for their action upon it.

Three possible concerns confront the teacher who would administer an assignment properly: (1) Is the assignment properly planned? (2) Is the assignment understood? (3) Is the assignment motivated? The educational theory which centers on the assignment considers these questions.

There are, however, those who feel that the assignment is excessively teacher-directed and that teachers should be more permissive in interacting with pupils. These teachers employ a method in which the child has a strong voice in the determination and planning of his learning experience and in which the child and teacher co-operatively evaluate the success of that learning experience. This method is called "pupil-teacher planning." Pupil-teacher planning, thus, is the co-operative determination of curricular experiences by pupils and teachers alike. It is a permissive approach to teaching.

In the pupil-teacher-planning method the teacher is primarily concerned with the group dynamics of a situation. Like the teacher who uses the assignment method, he is also concerned with planning the learning experience, but he need not attend to such things as communicating the assignment or motivating it. These are assumed to be innate to the planning experience itself.

There are some educational philosophers who would place the teacher in the non-participating role of a catalytic agent that facilitates the learning but does not enter too actively into the learning experience. The teacher is considered nothing more than part of the environment to which the child must adjust, and learning emerges from the experience resulting from environmental adjustment. We call the method of these educators "child-centered," and we speak vaguely of it as being the technique which meets the needs of the children.

"Meet the needs of the children," as a matter of fact, has

become one of the many cliches that provide shelter for the professor in the school of education who must hide behind something when he cannot provide teachers with a more realistic answer. For the child-centered teacher, "meeting the needs of the children" means meeting those needs which emerge as the child is confronted with a challenging environment to which he must respond. The child-centered teacher is concerned neither with planning the learning experience nor with motivating it. These take care of themselves as the child strives to meet his needs. The teacher's worry is with the environment which he recognizes must stimulate needs.

Within my lifetime I have been bombarded by the propaganda of proponents for the assignment, pupil-teacher-planning, and felt-needs methods, and I have fallen victim to all three. If I had it to live over again, when I was faced by a change in educational approach, I would lie down and wait for the pendulum to return to its original position. As it was, I was always a victim of methodological change and a "sucker" for a new method.

As a very young principal, I learned that the proper administration of the assignment was the goal of all educational method. Hence I strove for competency in this area. I arranged with the teachers with whom I worked to take over their rooms every day for a few hours of practice teaching to learn my business. I was too naive to recognize that it would take the poor teacher a week to undo the damage I could cause in an hour.

My first attempt at learning how to administer the assignment was undertaken, innocently enough, in a first grade. The children informed me that they were all birds. "A" class were "bluebirds"; "B" class, "robins"; and I renamed "C" class "crows" because it never ceased to cackle. It took me until almost 9:30 a.m. to get the aviary on its roosts. (Whatever one may think of workbooks, without them I would still be trying to calm down "A" class.) To "B" class I gave clay, upon which some of the members dined. Then I was ready to have the crows come to the reading circle. Not knowing that there is a trick to communicating an assignment, I merely said, "O.K., crows, come up to the little chairs."

This was the cue for a violent game of musical chairs. Three children sat down on the same chair. Two children fought over one chair until they pulled the back off. My assignment degenerated into chaos and violence, which I could not control. I sent for the teacher. She gave me the magic formula. It seemed that you proceed as follows. You say: "Children, we are going to see how orderly and quietly the crows can pass up to the reading circle.

When I say 'move,' each one of us will go in on tiptoe. Let me hear a pin drop. Move."

I never did manage satisfactorily the technique of administering the assignment. So when pupil-teacher planning came into vogue, I grasped at it because it promised that communication of the assignment no longer would be a problem for me. Also, the proponents for pupil-teacher planning waxed so romantic about their method that I could not resist. Here is a typical propaganda account of pupil-teacher planning.

Mrs. Brown's fourth-grade class came to her full of enthusiasm. "Mrs. Brown," said the children, "we have decided to have a picnic. Will you join us in our planning?" Ever alert to the opportunity for using children's emergent needs as a motivating force, and seeing that in the planning experience children would practice and learn real democracy, Mrs. Brown concurred. In her wonderfully permissive way she suggested that the children divide their work among committees. The children were delighted with the idea and created, first, a refreshment committee, then an entertainment committee, and finally a finance committee.

After considerable discussion the refreshment committee decided on having "cokes" and referred the question of cost to the finance committee, in true democratic fashion. The finance committee deliberated over the problem and concluded that the money could be obtained by collecting old newspapers and selling them to the junkman. This meant organizing a canvass of the neighborhood for old papers. The children drew a map of the school district. They divided the district into areas to be canvassed, and they assigned each child a district—a wonderful experience in local geography and map-making. The project netted ten dollars. The refreshment committee divided the ten dollars by the price of a "coke" and found this would provide each child with ten bottles. Even they recognized that this was a little beyond most children's capacity, so they considered the problem of how better to spend the money. This taught them arithmetic and even introduced the subject of health and nutrition. They had their picnic, and everyone (including Mrs. Brown?) had a wonderful time. This despite the fact that the children had learned geography, arithmetic, health, and democratic action in the process of pupil-teacher planning of the picnic. . . .

As an elementary-school principal, I saw the advertising possibilities in the child-centered school. The propaganda for that school just oozed with the sentimentality, love, and respect for the child that makes good copy. All teachers except child-centered teachers were sadists, brutes, and perverts. Also the neighboring university preached child-centered methods, and, needing a Doctor's degree, I ran with the mob.

I completely frustrated my teachers by prating about "felt needs," "whole child," "emergent experiences," and "learning environments" without interpreting these phrases into realities for them. I insisted that the child be allowed to grow. The combination of frustrated children, who "growed" like Topsy and who became uncontrollable "monsters," and frustrated teachers caused my eventual demise as a school administrator but qualified me for the role of college professor.

I would hate to admit that all of my thirty years of experience with method have been unproductive. Therefore I have striven for some functional conclusion about method. Are all methods bad? Is there one best method? Are all methods good?

The administration of the assignment, pupil-teacher planning, and the child-centered school are each an *aspect* of method. (You note I insist that they are *aspects* of method and not methods in themselves!)

If it is essential that a child experience an activity to meet a need which he himself does not feel immediately, the assignment is the course of action for a teacher to follow. The administration of the assignment, however, is an aspect of method that is too remote from a child's emergent and felt needs to be functional. These needs can better be satisfied by a more permissive attack.

Pupil-teacher planning, on the other hand, only partially does what it pretends to do. For example, pupil-teacher planning says (1) that, having been invited to choose and plan an educational activity, the pupil will be better motivated to indulge in it and (2) that pupil-teacher planning is typical of all democratic action and hence that the method teaches the democratic process.

I both agree and disagree with these assumptions. Pupil-teacher planning when a child's educational need is intense and emergent is a very effective motivating force for an educational experience. But, when a need is not apparent and it is necessary to create one, the assignment is more functional. For example, I have tried for years to get my own children involved in the consideration of the problem of cutting the grass at home. Not only have I failed to encourage them to participate with the lawn mower, I have even failed to get them to enjoy the joint planning necessary to determine who shall do the job.

With respect to the contention that pupil-teacher planning teaches the democratic process, I am amazed that its proponents have such a naive and limited concept of democracy. Democracy is not solely a matter of participation; the democratic process calls for a nice balance between participation and forebearance on the part of each individual. Functional instruction in democracy will teach the child both when he should participate and when he should refrain from participation and permit the expert to take over. America became great because of its judicious use of expertness and specialization. The person who insists on the right to participate when he cannot contribute is a meddler, and we have far too many of these without encouraging more. The democratic process involves a paired right and obligation—the right to participate and the obligation to refrain from participation when one is not qualified to make a contribution. Teacher-pupil planning can overemphasize the right while it ignores the obligation.

The child-centered school assumes that the school is a place for child living. It is the situs where the challenge to meet the environment initiates learning experiences. But the school has more responsibility than that of just providing a place for living, where the child eventually learns all he needs to know about life through random experience. The job of the school is to hurry the learning process. I will admit that eventually, through living experiences, the child might accidentally meet all those necessary to make him a well-rounded person. But what assurance have we that this condition will not take longer than a generation to accomplish? The success of the child-centered school seems to be a function of the child's longevity.

The assignment, pupil-teacher planning, and the child-centered school came into being as fashions in education. At one time it was chic to use the assignment; at other times, la mode called for pupil-teacher planning; and at still another time, a teacher could not be seen in the classroom except in child-centered garb. But these fashions are like the fashions in ladies' dresses. They do not alter the basic garment; they are merely the new neckline, the new sleeves, and the new hemline. Any teacher who takes the fashion so seriously that she wears only a neckline, a sleeve, or a hemline is pedagogically naked. The task of teaching calls for all natures of approach. As aspects of a complete method, the approaches described are parts of a whole, not separate wholes, as some educators would have them.

Direction, permissiveness, and laissez faire—all are portions of the same continuum. One helps to define the other, and hence one cannot stand alone and have meaning. The degree of direction is measured in terms of permissiveness, and permissiveness is bounded on two sides by direction and laissez faire. There are as many possible educational approaches as there are points on the continuum between direction and laissez faire. Each of these has its own unique use. The adequate teacher employs all.

TOMORROW'S TEACHING METHODS TODAY

Every teacher of elementary school-aged children must decide upon operational answers to a series of problems he encounters when entering the classroom. Since educational authorities seldom are in complete agreement on these matters, his decisions must be based upon the relative merits of the apparent alternatives. Variations in teaching procedures employed in contemporary elementary schools may be attributed in part to individual interpretations of the "best" solution for each of these problems.

Related problems include the following:

1. How do children learn? That is, under what conditions does learning occur?
2. Since children's measured intelligence varies more than 50 I.Q. points in a typical classroom, what provisions must be made for their individual differences in the instructional program?
3. If the children vary considerably in intellectual capacity, how can the teacher effectively evaluate pupil progress in school? Also, how can the teacher effectively report pupil progress to parents?
4. Again, if individual differences are real, what instructional materials must the teacher possess to challenge children at all levels of ability?

A teacher might logically approach these problems by becoming acquainted with the children to be taught. Unfortunately, this is not where most teaching begins. According to John Goodlad, most teaching begins with a determination of what is to be brought to the learner instead of looking for clues to children's drives. Wasted lessons, boredom, or frustration typify instruction that is not in tune with the learners' level. He believes that teachers ought to find out what is in a person, and then provide a setting in which children's goals and what stands in the way of movement toward those goals may be perceived, examined, and perhaps articulated.[7]

A number of pilot projects and experiments now in progress

[7]John I. Goodlad, *Some Propositions in Search of Schools* (Washington, D.C.: National Education Association, 1962).

stemmed from efforts to evolve more effective methods of teaching children along the lines Goodlad prescribed. Not all recent innovations, however, have pursued this course of action. Several have been selected and described below. Which of the following schemes seem to meet Goodlad's criterion? In your opinion, which will have a significant long-range impact upon classroom instruction?

METHODOLOGY IN THE AMIDON SCHOOL

The Amidon School was conceived and put into operation by Carl F. Hansen, Superintendent of Schools in the District of Columbia, as a demonstration of so-called basic education. The Amidon plan has been described by critics as "a sop to all the reactionary forces afloat" and as a "new frontier in education." Rather than engage in an analysis of the relative merits of Hansen's scheme, the writers prefer to focus upon methods employed in the school itself.

Teachers in the Amidon School, like Miss Ritter, adhere to a daily schedule for implementing the school program. Orderly management of all classroom functions from the most routine chores to the planning and presentation of assignments is emphasized by the staff. One of the unique elements of the Amidon concept is that for a major portion of the day the teachers should instruct the whole class at the same time. This is in lieu of subgrouping within the class, which is widely practiced in elementary schools. Ability grouping between classes is employed to facilitate whole-class instruction. Small-group and individualized instruction are used as needed — usually for special purposes.

The whole-class instruction practice is supported by a belief that the teacher is responsible for teaching what she knows to pupils and that she can impart information and stimulate learning most efficiently by direct instruction. "Under the Amidon concept she returns to the front of the room with chalk in hand to explain, discuss, reinforce learning by immediate checks on class responses, to teach what needs teaching, check learning, teach again, and test again."[8] The lecture method of instruction is not to be implied by this method, as the lecture does not provide for interaction with the learner.

Textbooks are considered a central and fundamental necessity in the school, because they select out of the vast range of knowledge

[8]Carl F. Hansen, *The Amidon Elementary School* (Englewood Cliffs, N.J.: Prentice-Hall, Inc., 1962), p. 151. Ideas presented pertaining to the Amidon concept were gleaned from this source.

essential elements that must be transmitted to each generation, they logically organize these elements, and they offer the information in usable form. Textbooks serve as a foundation for the development of the teacher's lesson plan. Hansen feels that judicious use of textbooks provides a basis for control of the teaching time.

PRESENTING ARITHMETIC CONCEPTS BY A DEVELOPMENTAL METHOD

Miss Ritter adheres to a "Developmental Method" of teaching mathematics which was pioneered by Professor Herbert F. Spitzer of the State University of Iowa. The following distinctive features of this method are practiced in her classroom:

(1) A "figure it out" or "problem solving" type of approach to learning is used;

(2) Each area of arithmetic content is introduced through word problems in which a need for, or a use of, the new principle is exhibited;

(3) New facts, terms, and arithmetic procedures are developed from pupil experiences originating from and related to these introductory word problems;

(4) Pupil activity is emphasized through frequent use of directions such as "find the answer by any method" and "show that the answer is correct";

(5) These instructions elicit solutions of varying quality as well as different rates of progress;

(6) The differentiation of instruction achieved in this way makes formal separation of the class into groups unnecessary;

(7) Pupil experience is used as the basis for mastery study and a variety of specific study procedures are supplied;

(8) Understanding is fostered by requesting that the answer be found by more than one way and through use of drawings, number line, evaluations, and reviews.[9]

Spitzer's Developmental Method stresses an inductive approach to mathematical study. He recommends proceeding from immature and often cumbersome means of dealing with quantitative material to more mature and efficient ways. Miss Ritter probably spends more time preparing her lessons and assembling materials to expedite this approach than teachers using other methods, but she believes the extra effort is profitably spent.

[9]Herbert F. Spitzer, *The Teaching of Arithmetic* (Boston: Houghton Mifflin Company, 1961), p. 328.

INQUIRY TRAINING

Inquiry training is a term used by Dr. Richard Suchman and his associates to describe a method of teaching the skills and strategies of scientific inquiry. According to Dr. Suchman, its purpose is to help young students develop the procedures of investigation that are necessary for the autonomous quest for understanding. Children, working as a group, are exposed to concrete problems in physics, economics, and biology by means of motion picture films. They are then asked why the events in the filmed episode occurred. The problem posed to them is one of constructing an explanatory system.

In order to gather needed information, the children ask questions which can be answered by "yes" or "no." This tactic is employed to prevent children from reverting into the open-ended type of inquiry in which the responsibility for structuring is in the teacher's hands. The yes-or-no question forces the children to think through and structure their own questions.[10] The children may not depend on the teacher to provide explanations, interpretations, or principles; they must generate these on their own. Periodic procedural reviews and critiques serve to make the children more aware of the process of inquiry and to help them form productive search models to guide their investigation.

When the mode of learning is inquiry, says Dr. Suchman, the process of data-gathering, analysis, and experimentation is under the control of the learner himself. Through inquiry, he influences and actually programs his own learning in terms of his own cognitive needs, as dictated by his style of learning and his informational needs of the moment.[11] He is given an element of choice in the learning process.

Suchman believes that inquiry training should not be divorced from the regular subjects of the curriculum. He envisions an inquiry-centered curriculum that uses the inquiry approach to launch children into specific areas of study.

Today's studies of responsive teaching methods suggest that teaching in the schools of the future will be less directive and more responsive to children. This means that teachers will pay careful

[10]J. Richard Suchman, "The Child and the Inquiry Process," *Intellectual Development: Another Look* (Washington, D.C.: Association for Supervision and Curriculum Development [NEA], 1964), p. 71.

[11]*Ibid.*, p. 61.

attention to verbal and nonverbal data emitted by children, in order to provide for their learning more effectively. Feedback data will be subjected to rigorous analysis so that optimum classroom conditions may be established.

QUESTIONS FOR DISCUSSION

1. Have teaching methods changed significantly during the past two hundred years? Re-examine the Brumbaugh and Bartky quotations for clues to specific changes that have taken place.

2. Reference was made in the text of this chapter to several problems every teacher of elementary school-aged children must face. How would you answer each of the questions raised?

3. Frequent reference is made in the professional literature to instructional aids like the Stern Blocks and Cuisenaire Rods, educational television, and programmed instruction. Describe ways in which these aids can affect methods used in the classroom. Is it conceivable that any one of these aids might become the principal method of conveying content to children?

ADDITIONAL REFERENCES

Educational Leadership. The theme of the October, 1963, issue is "Focus on Instruction."

Frazier, Alexander, "Improving the Learning Situation," *NEA Journal,* 50 (September, 1961), 40-43.

Hilgard, Ernest R., *Theories of Learning and Instruction.* The Sixty-Third Yearbook of the National Society for the Study of Education, Part I. Chicago: The University of Chicago Press, 1964. 430 pp.

Hock, Louise E., "Classroom Grouping for Effective Learning," *Educational Leadership,* 18 (April, 1961), 420-424.

Joyce, Bruce R., *Strategies for Elementary Social Science Education.* Chicago: Science Research Associates, Inc., 1965. 302 pp.

Morgan, H. G., "How to Facilitate Learning," *NEA Journal,* 49 (October, 1960), 54-55.

NEA Journal. The theme of the December, 1959, issue is "Reporting."

Staff of the Bank Street College of Education, New York City, "Building a Classroom Climate for Learning," *NEA Journal,* 50 (December, 1961), 34-38.

Wahle, Roy P., "Methods of Individualization in Elementary School," *Educational Leadership,* 17 (November, 1959), 74-79.

SUMMARY: PART TWO

An account of Miss Ritter's fourth-grade situation served as the point of departure for a study of purposes, organization, curriculum, and methodology pertaining to elementary education. The reader was acquainted with her classroom facilities, her data-gathering and record-keeping activities, and her instructional program in Chapter Three so that he might obtain a representative perspective of contemporary pedagogy. Problems stemming from her instructional style were introduced to involve the reader in the issues suggested.

Chapter Four focused upon purposes of education in the elementary school. After a model depicting the evolution of a social institution was introduced, presses influencing the evolution of the common school in Western culture were described. R. L. Sharpe captured the essence of this evolution in a memorable poem:

> Each is given a bag of tools,
> A shapeless mass,
> A book of rules;
> And each must make,
> Ere life is flown,
> A stumbling-block
> Or a stepping-stone.

These words tend to summarize the existence of a school which was created to meet the needs of the common people. As the needs of the people changed, the school's function changed. At times, the school functioned as a stepping-stone, at other times as a stumbling-block to the development of Western culture.

In recent years, much stress has been placed upon defining the role of the elementary school in our society. Contemporary educators have attempted to formulate purposes of education in the elementary school that are compatible with American democracy. To date, their undertakings would hardly be described as a smashing success. This is attributed to the fact that a number of conflicting philosophies have

195

been championed by prominent educators. Until educators find a *modus operandi* for resolving these differences, the American elementary school will continue to function as a seemingly rudderless social institution.

The expression "Conform and be dull" certainly would not apply to elementary school organizational practices in the United States since the days of our first president. Quite the contrary, the history of organizing children for instructional purposes in the elementary school is characterized by diversity, diversity, and more diversity. Within the past hundred years alone, a multitude of organization and classification plans have been employed to discover the optimum grouping arrangement for children in classroom groups. These and earlier patterns were reported in Chapter Five. Intensified experimentation of this kind in recent years is mute testimony to the fact that educators are still searching for noteworthy organizational breakthroughs.

In Chapter Six the evolution of the elementary school curriculum was traced from Colonial America to the present, contemporary curricular practices were examined, and innovations that could potentially alter the nature of future curricula were reported.

Societal needs have influenced the elementary school curriculum since Colonial days in our country. In recent years, children's needs have also been taken into account by curriculum planners. Hence, today's curriculum reflects individual and societal needs. These are not stabilized by any means. While a broad core of courses has been a part of the curriculum for many years, many courses appear and disappear with each passing decade.

This history of curriculum development in the United States can be described as a series of chance occurrences rather than as a carefully planned sequence. Sufficient public or professional pressure represents itself as an important criterion for adding new courses to the curriculum. Courses often are deleted when they lack social utility, or when individuals trained to teach them are unavailable. Consequently, today's educators have no precise objective measures for plotting the course for tomorrow's elementary school curriculum.

Many educators believe that teaching methods come and go in a manner reminiscent of the swinging of a pendulum. It is their belief that certain methods are fashionable at some times and not at others. According to this attitude, an individual may be criticized at different times for employing the same methods. Data presented in Chapter Seven do not lend support to such a point of view.

The evolution of methodology in the United States is not represented by the swinging of a pendulum. Rather, this evolution is analogous to a coil spring which has small spirals at its base and large spirals at its apex. Teaching methods have become increasingly complex over a period of several hundred years. Some educators regard methodology as a distinct sphere of knowledge to be mastered as one of the requirements of modern teaching.

Teachers can anticipate a bountiful harvest of new ways to teach children in the years ahead. Research relating to improved methods of teaching is currently as intensive and extensive as mankind has ever known. Even Madison Avenue's motivational research — geared to selling products to the public — has applications in the elementary school classroom. Much exploratory research is under way to determine the role, if any, of devices like television, teaching machines, and programmed materials in the classroom. It seems reasonable to conclude that tomorrow's child will be taught more effectively than today's child, and today's child is experiencing better instruction than his counterpart of yesterday.

Even though purposes, organization, curricula, and methodology were treated separately in Part Two, they are inextricably interrelated in fact. They have been isolated solely for the purpose of analysis. Research into any one of the four must be cognizant of its relationship to the other three.

Part Three

CHILDREN IN SCHOOL:
THE VITAL INGREDIENT

Chapter Eight

UPON ENTERING
THE ELEMENTARY SCHOOL[1]

Miss Caroline began the day by reading us a story about cats. The cats had long conversations with one another, they wore cunning little clothes and lived in a warm house beneath a kitchen stove. By the time Mrs. Cat called the drugstore for an order of chocolate malted mice the class was wriggling like a bucketful of Catawba worms. Miss Caroline seemed unaware that the ragged, denim-shirted and floursack-skirted first grade, most of whom had chopped cotton and fed hogs from the time they were able to walk, were immune to imaginative literature. Miss Caroline came to the end of the story and said, "Oh, my, wasn't that nice?"

Then she went to the blackboard and printed the alphabet in enormous square capitals, turned to the class and asked, "Does anybody know what these are?"

Everybody did; most of the first grade had failed it last year.

I suppose she chose me because she knew my name; as I read the alphabet a faint line appeared between her eyebrows, and after making me read most of *My First Reader* and the stock-market quotations from *The Mobile Register* aloud, she discovered that I was literate and looked at me with more than faint distaste. Miss

[1]Three perspectives of child behavior are included in Part Three. The first perspective is aimed at the child beginning his "formal" education. First grade has been selected rather than kindergarten, because the latter is often not included in school systems, and its program often differs considerably from other levels of the primary school. The middle years of the elementary school—that is, the third or fourth year—provide the second perspective. And the sixth grade, which is usually the culminating experience of the elementary school, contributes the final perspective.

> Caroline told me to tell my father not to teach me any more, it would interfere with my reading.[2]

The casual reader can readily recognize that Miss Caroline is not only insensitive to the needs of her pupils, she functions as if she owns a copyright on all teaching. In business circles, her activities would be viewed as monopolistic. Both educators and noneducators probably wonder why she selected a story about cats for her unique group of children on the first day of school, why a large number of children were repeating the first grade, and why a child's reading capabilities disturbed her. In addition to these questions, many readers are probably wondering how representative Miss Caroline is of all first-grade teachers in America. It is the purpose of this chapter to present data that afford the student of elementary education an opportunity to obtain some insight into questions of this nature.

Historical records indicate that individuals have performed valuable teaching services in various cultures for thousands of years. Yet, intensive scientific study of the child and the educative process was not undertaken until late in the nineteenth century. Since that time, a vast amount of information pertaining to child development and the educative process has been made available to classroom teachers. This new dimension of data has markedly altered the elementary school in the twentieth century.

Contributions to our knowledge of child development and the educative process have become so voluminous in recent years that it is practically impossible for today's classroom teacher to keep abreast of all the data. As might be expected under these circumstances, there is a perceivable lag between the publication of a major research breakthrough and its application in the elementary classroom. Nevertheless, this new knowledge is rapidly changing the character of the school. Teachers who fail to keep pace with current developments become as conspicuous as the American hotel owner who refuses to install plumbing and electricity in his building, or the medical doctor who rejects all wonder drugs because he believes they are fads. Miss Caroline is a perfect example.

Even though the elementary school teacher is confronted with an overwhelming amount of data pertaining to child development and the educative process, it is not unreasonable to believe that he can be

[2]Harper Lee, *To Kill A Mockingbird* (Philadelphia: J. B. Lippincott Company, 1960), p. 134. Copyright © 1960 by Harper Lee. Reprinted with permission.

selective in extracting and utilizing many significant aspects. For example, much is known about children's mental, physical, social, and emotional development today. While it is doubtful that the typical first-grade teacher will master all of these dimensions of child development, it is recognized that certain aspects of the knowledge can appreciably facilitate a successful pupil-teacher relationship. Thus, one task of the modern first-grade teacher is becoming familiar with pertinent knowledge and implementing it in the instructional program.

Some knowledge of child behavior is needed in order to comprehend the implications of the questions raised above. Therefore, behavior patterns characteristic of preschool children and pupils in their first year of school are reported in this chapter. Information of this sort affords the reader an opportunity to assess critically the feasibility of Miss Caroline's pedagogical practices.

THE PRESCHOOL CHILD

It seems logical that teachers who are aware of characteristic behavior patterns of preschool children can implement such knowledge by structuring a stimulating learning situation for first-grade pupils. Knowledge of the needs, interests, capabilities, and development of five-year-old children, for example, should certainly enhance the quality of an instructional program that is geared to six-year-olds. Prospective teachers can obtain such knowledge through careful study supplemented by direct observation of child behavior. Since direct observation of child behavior is not possible in many teacher training programs, this section incorporates several representative descriptions of five-year-old behavior as one means of providing for the latter pedagogical dimension.

A typical late summer day in the life of three preschool children is reported in the following paragraphs. Let us assume for analytical purposes that these and similar records are available to first-grade teachers. The reader is invited to study each description and then identify ways in which this knowledge can influence the first-grade instructional program.

JENNIFER

Since breakfast in the Jones household is an elaborate affair, all the members of the family usually are in their places around the table long before the food is served. The breakfast hour is one of the few times during the day when all the members of the family gather together. Six-year-old Jennifer has become accustomed to seeing her father depart for work and her older brother depart for his summer job each day. She knows that they will return home when the shadows begin to lengthen later in the day.

After breakfast, Jennifer usually turns on the television set in order to view "Captain Kangaroo." The Captain invariably succeeds in captivating her attention for the entire 60-minute show. Not only does he command her attention during the show, his influence frequently carries over into her daily play activity and her spoken vocabulary. "Captain Kangaroo" is one of the few television programs that actually appeal to Jennifer.

Following "Captain Kangaroo," Jennifer often plays with her doll house, her doll with real hair, or her toy piano. Occasionally, she helps her mother with the household chores at this time. She especially enjoys sharing two of the "chores." One is the biweekly trip to a nearby supermarket. At the supermarket, she is permitted to push the food cart, select some food items, and "pay" the check-out clerk for the items purchased. The other chore which she enjoys is operating the vacuum cleaner. The suction action of the cleaner absolutely fascinates Jennifer.

Frequently, Jennifer and Mrs. Jones devote part of the morning to a variety of number and word games. Even though Jennifer is unable to read, she can distinguish her name, a number of proper nouns, and many letters of the alphabet. Also, she knows her age, home address, telephone number, and a few other number facts, even though she has not been formally introduced to the study of arithmetic. Mrs. Jones introduced Jennifer to these games and activities because she felt her daughter might be handicapped in the first grade without a formal kindergarten experience.

Jennifer spends many of her summer afternoons with several neighborhood playmates. These children engage in a variety of activities. They can frequently be observed using their toys or games or engaging in role-playing. Often, one of their parents escorts them to a nearby swimming pool. Generally speaking, the children are able to get along with each other quite well.

After the evening meal, Jennifer and her father usually share a bit of lighthearted fun. He seldom fails to introduce Jennifer to a challenging puzzle or problem situation in the course of the merriment.

She invariably accepts the challenge, and the fun begins. These "sessions" seldom last longer than an hour. Then, Jennifer goes outdoors to play with her friends until her bedtime hour approaches.

Jennifer is accustomed to hearing her mother read a short story before she goes to sleep. She has become so interested in the story sessions that she seldom balks at going to bed. Her day ends around 8:30 or 9:00 P.M.

ERIC

Eric is accustomed to rising with his mother each morning. After breakfast, he gathers a few favored playthings and accompanies her to his grandparents' home. Eric stays with his grandparents until his mother returns from work late in the day. His mother has been employed since the death of his father.

Eric's grandparents live in retirement on a small farm a few miles from his home. The farm serves as a pastime rather than a source of income for his grandparents. Nevertheless, there is enough work to occupy Eric from the time he arrives each morning until his mother picks him up late in the afternoon. Most of the chores fascinate the boy, so he usually is quite enthusiastic about the responsibilities he receives.

When Eric is not performing one of his chores, he usually can be found playing cowboys and Indians with the family's pet German shepherd. A flock of chickens function beautifully as Indians on the warpath. Eric and the dog attempt to capture or wipe out the attacking Indians. This type of imaginative play engages him for many hours each week.

Eric usually eats his evening meal at the grandparents' home, because his mother seldom returns from work to pick him up before 6:00 P.M. He and his mother exchange the news of the day as they return home. Then, she frequently works on office correspondence that must be completed in time for the morning mail. Eric either views television or listens to his record player while his mother works. Often, they step out to enjoy an ice cream concoction at a nearby soda fountain late in the evening.

After the late snack, Eric prepares for bed. His mother seldom has to force the boy to retire, as the activity of the day invariably overtakes him between 9:30 and 10:30 P.M. Eric performs a series of evening rituals with his favorite stuffed teddybear and his mother before he slips off to sleep.

HARVEY

Mr. and Mrs. Holloway usually depart for their respective jobs before Harvey and his younger brother and sister arise. A hired baby-sitter provides breakfast for the children. This baby-sitter chaperones the children until their parents return from work later in the day.

Harvey's first responsibility following breakfast is to feed his pet rabbit and turtles. He has accepted these responsibilities enthusiastically. After feeding the pets, he enjoys playing with his tame rabbit in the yard. Several neighborhood children and his younger brother frequently congregate in the yard at this time. After the children lose interest in the rabbit, they engage in a variety of games, which occupy the children until lunchtime.

Each day after lunch, Mrs. Edwards, the baby-sitter, helps Harvey tackle a series of reading, writing, and number readiness activities that his parents obtained at his kindergarten teacher's suggestion. Harvey's parents felt these readiness experiences combined with his recent kindergarten experiences would enable Harvey to get a good start in the first grade. Since Mrs. Edwards does not employ effective motivational techniques when introducing Harvey to the readiness activities, his interest invariably wanes after 20 to 30 minutes of effort. And, since Harvey's six-month-old sister requires much close attention, Mrs. Edwards is happy to conclude the daily lesson at that time.

During the remainder of the afternoon, Harvey plays with his peers in the neighborhood. The boys enjoy varied running and hiding games when the day is not too hot. On the particularly hot August days, they prefer to assemble in front of the neighborhood grocery store and idle away the afternoon, or spend their time talking to a retired fireman in his workshop.

Soon after Mr. and Mrs. Holloway return from their jobs, dinner is served. Dinner is usually plain, reasonably nutritious, and filling. After dinner, Mr. Holloway catches forty winks while the boys help their mother in the kitchen.

Later in the evening, Harvey, his brother, and his parents gather around the television set and enjoy the evening's programs. The Holloway family spends the major portion of their evening hours viewing television. Harvey's brother often retires around 9:00 P.M. Harvey usually slips off to sleep during the late news and is carried to bed by his father.

Jennifer, Eric, and Harvey were among the 25 children to enroll in Miss Mark's first grade. Before the first day of school, the teacher received permanent record cards describing each child's family background and preschool experience. Illustrations of the kinds of data summarized on these cards are as follows: (1) the number of children who attended kindergarten; (2) the current status of the child's family unit (i.e., deaths, divorce, siblings); (3) the extent of parental education; and (4) the children's travel experiences. Obviously, information of this sort enables the teacher to prepare better for the new group of children. Can the reader cite several specific instances in which such knowledge can help the classroom teacher to establish good rapport with the new group of children?

Many first-grade teachers not only have access to the kinds of data described above, they often possess a wealth of information on developmental characteristics of five- and six-year-old children. This knowledge of children is categorized and detailed in the following section.

DEVELOPMENTAL CHARACTERISTICS OF FIRST-GRADE CHILDREN

Recently, one of the writers overheard several graduating seniors discussing their prospective teaching assignments for the coming school year. One student expressed concern over the possibility that she might be assigned to teach first-grade children. She did not feel that she could "get down to their level." As the writer listened, he wondered whether the student's apprehension about teaching first graders was based upon past experiences with children at this level or upon hearsay and old wives' tales. In all probability, the student possessed only a vague notion of the capabilities of six-year-old children.

Conversations among prospective teachers and teachers in the field frequently reveal varying concepts of the actual capabilities of six-year-olds. These variations can be attributed to each individual's past experiences with the vast amount of knowledge that has been accumulated about first graders. One method of bringing teachers up to date on this matter would be to report the significant contributions to our knowledge of six-year-old children. This is impractical. However, a sampling of what is known about children's mental, physical, social, and emotional development better reflects the purposes of this book.

If the reader imagines that he has been assigned to teach six-year-old children during the next school year, the following data will be more meaningful. It is suggested that the reader survey the sampling of data in order to identify aspects which would probably facilitate appreciably a successful pupil-teacher relationship.

MENTAL

Much knowledge has been accumulated about the mental development of six-year-old children. Three dimensions of this knowledge — mental capabilities, skills, and interests characteristic of this maturational level — can easily be distinguished. Each of these dimensions are developed as follows.

Mental Capabilities. If there is one mental characteristic of six-year-old children that teachers need to recognize, it certainly must be variability. Just because children are about the same age is no guarantee that they will perform in a similar manner. A typical group of first graders will vary considerably in their ability to solve problems, their concept development, their skills, and their interests. Teachers who overlook this variability and attempt to treat all children as if they were cast from the same mold lack insight into the pedagogical process.

By the time many children enter the first grade, they have developed extensive problem-solving abilities. They can perceive relationships, grasp patterns of ideas, generalize from their experiences, analyze logical fallacies, and differentiate between fantasy and reality. Since few children possess well-developed verbal skills at this level, most resort to manipulating concrete objects in their environment as their principal problem-solving vehicle. David Russell pointed out that verbalism aids but is not essential to problem-solving at this point in school.[3] He also observed that children's ability to solve problems increases in both speed and accuracy with advancing maturity.

Just as children vary in their ability to solve problems, they vary tremendously in their understandings of different kinds of concepts. Ernest Horn noted that the success with which a student structures a meaningful and valid mental concept is dependent upon three factors: first, the difficulty and the complexity of the concept to be learned (imagine first graders struggling with the Darwinian theory of evolution); second, the adequacy of the language in which the concept is

[3]David Russell, *Children's Thinking* (Boston: Ginn and Company, 1956), p. 278.

208

experienced; and third, the student's funds (i.e., his knowledge and experience, his interest and motivation, his command of the language, and so forth).[4] The interaction of these three factors may result in a child's knowing a concept thoroughly, partially, not at all, or erroneously. Perceptive teachers have known for some time that children need extensive experience with a concept before it is learned. Hence, these teachers provide numerous concrete learning experiences to facilitate better concept development.

Classroom teachers quickly discover that children's progress in school is not predictable solely on the basis of their maturation and intelligence. Some mature and able children invariably are classified as reading problems, whereas some less able and immature children easily keep pace with reading instruction. In some cases, the explanation for peculiar developmental patterns may be traced to the limitations of a teacher or a teaching method. A better explanation for these patterns, according to William Martin and Celia Stendler, can be uncovered if educators pay more attention to children's personality development.

> In the process of socialization, the child builds up certain concepts about himself which affect the way in which he learns. The child who feels good about himself, who has built up a strong ego, who looks upon himself as a worthwhile person is more likely to utilize his intelligence effectively than the child who lacks self-confidence.[5]

In effect, what children want for themselves affects the way in which they accomplish the tasks required by the school.

Skills. At the age of six, many children become preoccupied with things in their immediate environment. Their school experiences undoubtedly contribute to this preoccupation. In school, most children are exposed for the first time to systematic instruction in skills needed in our culture. The development of reading, writing, speaking, and computational skills is heavily emphasized in the first grade.

Six-year-olds who have spent several months in the first grade can be expected to exhibit many skills. For example, these children are

[4]Ernest Horn, "Language and Meaning," *The Psychology of Learning*, The Forty-First Yearbook of the National Society for the Study of Education, Part II (Bloomington, Ill.: Public School Publishing Company, 1942), pp. 377-413.

[5]William E. Martin and Celia B. Stendler, *Child Behavior and Development* (New York: Harcourt, Brace & Company, 1959), p. 370. Reprinted with permission.

able to understand thousands of words. One study, based upon an abridged dictionary, estimated the six-year-old's level of understanding at better than 2,500 words.[6] Another study, based upon an unabridged dictionary, concluded that the six-year-old's level of understanding varied between 5,000 and 32,000+ words.[7] No matter which estimate best reflects reality, the fact remains that first-year pupils are able to comprehend thousands of words.

Many first graders are exposed to intensive reading readiness experiences early in the school year. These children often are able to recognize printed words, letters of the alphabet, phrases, and, in some instances, simple sentences. Much time and effort is spent in learning the alphabet, words, and sentences at this time. A successful first-grade reading program not only conveys the necessary basic reading skills to children but also instills in them a desire to read books at their level.

After several months of schooling, six-year-olds usually have had an opportunity to experiment with wax and pencil crayons and lead pencils. The product of their efforts varies fantastically. Often, the child's ability to coordinate and control the fine muscles of his body determines his written progress. By this time, the teacher has been able to convey to most children that writing is merely recorded talk.

First-grade children vary considerably in their ability to speak, read, and write. This often is not the case with arithmetic skills. While children vary in their ability to utilize computational skills, the variation is not nearly as extensive as it is for the three skills mentioned previously. After seven or eight months of school, most children have learned the basic symbols of the number system, many have learned to count and add, and some have learned to perform subtraction operations. Few children receive instruction beyond these aspects of arithmetic in the first grade.

Most preschool children view life in terms of the present. Their comprehension of the past and the future is often vague and muddled. Six-year-olds do not vary markedly from this behavioral pattern. However, they do learn a great deal about time early in their first school year. Louise Ames reported that 50 per cent of the six-year-old

[6]Madorah Smith, "An Investigation of the Development of the Sentence and the Extent of Vocabulary in Young Children," *Iowa Studies in Child Welfare*, No. 3 (Iowa City: State University of Iowa, 1962).

[7]Mary K. Smith, "Measurement of the Size of General English Vocabulary Through the Elementary Grades and High School," *Genetic Psychology Monographs*, 24 (1941), 311-345.

children who comprised her study sample correctly answered the following questions about time:

1. What time do you go to school?
2. What do you do in Spring?
3. What do you do in Fall?
4. How long do you stay in school?
5. What grade are you in?[8]

Since most school programs are time-oriented, first graders are exposed to many school experiences that are designed to develop a time consciousness.

Interests. Interests of six-year-olds, according to Jersild, Mackey, and Jersild, are primarily selfish and egocentric.[9] Their activities in the first grade often center on ego gratification. This can best be observed during play periods in the first grade when the children are asked to share certain games and toys. Conflict, usually of short duration, can be expected.

These children enjoy imaginative play, informal role-playing and dramatization, listening to phonograph records, and viewing television. A child can engage in each of these activities without the assistance of playmates. Such behavior further reinforces the statement that children of this age level tend to be egocentric.

PHYSICAL

Extensive data have also been accumulated on children's physical development during the past sixty to eighty years. As a matter of fact, the twentieth century will probably be remembered as a era of intensive child study. Since it is impractical to attempt to report all the significant contributions that have been made to our knowledge in this area, the writers have sampled data pertaining to the physical structure, behavior, and special needs of the six-year-old. It is hoped that such a survey will shed a beam of light on this dimension of child development.

The Physical Structure of the Six-Year-Old. Most six-year-olds range between approximately 44 to 49 inches in height and approxi-

[8]Louise B. Ames, "The Development of the Sense of Time in the Young Child," *Journal of Genetic Psychology,* 68 (March, 1946), 97-125.

[9]Arthur Jersild, F. V. Mackey, and C. L. Jersild, *Children's Fears, Dreams, Wishes, Daydreams, Likes, Dislikes, Pleasant and Unpleasant Memories,* Child Development Monograph No. 12 (New York: Teachers College, Columbia University, 1933).

211

mately 40 to 56 pounds in weight. Skeletally, their growth is not as rapid as previously. The knock knees and protruding abdomens that characterize younger children are beginning to disappear. So are the temporary teeth and the large foreheads. Generally speaking, girls tend to be more mature than boys in their skeletal development.

Physical Behavior.   Six-year-old children probably come as close to the definition of perpetual motion as any age level. They have acquired most of the basic motor skills and actively practice them throughout the day. Both sexes can be observed crawling, tumbling, running, wrestling, manipulating large blocks and furniture, and in some instances tossing a ball. Girls tend to be more graceful than boys when they participate in these activities. Since children work and play vigorously, it is only natural that they tire easily and need frequent rest periods.

Special Needs of the Six-Year-Old.   About 10 per cent of American school children deviate from normal development enough to require special educational services. This figure includes extremely gifted and mentally and physically handicapped children. Unfortunately, many school districts are unable to provide special facilities to meet the needs of these children. Under such conditions, the classroom teacher is called upon to provide educational experiences for them in a regular group.

The greatest challenge to teachers who work with either mentally gifted or mentally handicapped groups lies in exposing these children to suitable learning experiences. Mentally gifted children need to be motivated, then freed; mentally retarded children need to be motivated, then taken by the hand. The greatest challenge to teachers who work with physically handicapped children lies in helping them to develop a positive attitude toward their affliction.

SOCIAL

American educators have been severely abused in recent decades because of their professed interest in the social development of children at the expense of intellectual development (see Chapter One). Critics argue that time spent by teachers on social development curtails the child's intellectual development. Teachers counter with the argument that children's mental development is markedly affected by their social behavior in the classroom. In order to uncover some truth in this controversy, it appears sensible to examine known data pertaining to the social development of six-year-olds. This dimension of knowledge is sampled below.

Social Characteristics of Six-Year-Olds. Karl Garrison, a specialist in child growth and development, sums up the social behavior of the first-grader in the following manner:

> The first-grader has a difficult time at home, in school, and with his friends. He seems either to love or to hate intensively. Often he is domineering and cruel to younger siblings and playmates. It is not beyond him to take delight in telling of the misdeeds of other children and of his own accomplishments.[10]

Garrison's views receive considerable support in the professional literature. Imagine a group of 25, 30, 35, or 40 six-year-old children, who exemplify the above description, living together in the same room for five or six hours, five days each week, for approximately 180 school days. Rather frightening, isn't it?

Actually, there are several good reasons why most first-grade teachers do not fear groups of six-year-olds. They know, for example, that children of this age tend to be quite insecure in new situations. Because of this insecurity, six-year-olds are constantly alert to clues in the classroom environment that might guide their behavior. One of the writers witnessed a beautiful manifestation of this phenomenon during his first teaching experience.

A preschool orientation meeting for five- and six-year-old children was one of the pedagogical duties of the writer late in the school term. The meeting, which functioned as a kind of "shotgun" kindergarten, was conducted for about an hour immediately after the regular school day. Since the preschool registrants were accompanied by their parents, a certain amount of socialization was in order. When the first child arrived with his parents, he was asked to take a seat on a long wooden bench placed beneath a chalkboard in the front of the room while the adults conversed for a moment. He promptly obliged by sitting down on the bench, facing the chalkboard. His position was rather awkward, as his nose was barely four inches from the board itself. Nevertheless, he sat in that position with his hands folded and

---

[10]Karl Garrison, *Growth and Development* (New York: Longmans, Green & Company, 1959), p. 309. Permission to reprint granted by David Mackay Company, Inc.

appeared to study the chalkboard before him. It never occurred to him to turn around and survey the rest of the room while we conversed.

Within a period of five minutes, six children entered the room and proceeded to take a seat beside the first child on the bench in exactly the same manner. As the writer viewed the backs of seven children sitting on a long wooden bench with their noses barely four inches from the chalkboard, he could hardly contain himself. Up until the time the teacher requested that the children turn around in their places and take a look at the rest of the classroom, he controlled his amusement admirably.

Each child entered the classroom and attempted to size up the environment. After the first child was seated, the other children used his position as a behavioral clue. The net effect of their efforts was quite delightful. This illustration focuses upon a characteristic of the six-year-old that can be exploited advantageously by a sensitive first-grade teacher.

Another characteristic of children at this age level — their ability to acquire varied social skills easily — is frequently capitalized upon by first-grade teachers. These teachers know that children will quickly adapt to a set of prescribed rules and procedures if they are sensibly derived, if they take into account the developmental characteristics of children, and, most important, if they are taught positively. It is not accidental that some groups of children quickly respond to the demands and experiences of their teacher throughout the school day, whereas other groups seem to wallow in chaos.

It is improbable that the six-year-old has developed the ability to concentrate upon an assignment for an extended time interval. It is also improbable that he can work effectively on an assignment or play successfully with a group of children. These are important skills that must be acquired by children as they adapt to their school environment.

Group Interaction.   If the reader were able to observe a group of six-year-olds, he would frequently find the members fluidly shifting from one set of activities into another, and he would find that the grouping of the participants was in an almost constant state of flux.[11] A closer analysis of the group would reveal a few mutual friendships, some children who were well liked by most members of the group,

[11]Max Hutt and Robert Gibby, *The Child: Development and Adjustment* (Boston: Allyn and Bacon, Inc., 1959), p. 250.

and some children who were practically outsiders. The criteria for acceptance by the group are ill-defined, but they seem to take into account age and size.

The way in which a child interacts with his peers and his teacher markedly influences his self-concept. His self-concept, in turn, influences his attitude toward school in general. As a result, it is not unreasonable to believe that a child's adjustment in the classroom influences his scholastic achievement.

First-grade teachers can anticipate frequent flare-ups among six-year-olds. These arouse emotions which trigger name-calling, fighting, and other unpleasantries. Fortunately, the emotional state is short-lived and quickly forgotten. Sensitive teachers accept such behavior as characteristic of the age level, but at the same time they strive to teach children more socially acceptable ways of resolving their problems.

EMOTIONAL

This dimension of knowledge is a contribution of the twentieth century. Since the bulk of the available data on children's emotional behavior tends to be descriptive rather than explanatory, man's insight into the operative realm of the emotions is quite limited. Researchers have studied emotional behavior intensively, but as yet, they lack a clear-cut understanding of its why and how. Teachers are learning that children's emotions function like a double-edged sword in the classroom. Aroused emotions can both facilitate and severely impede progress in school. Both sides of the sword are explored in the following paragraphs.

Manifestations of Emotions in School. A six-year-old child is capable of displaying most, if not all, of the emotions known to mankind. Unfortunately, children of this age frequently display extreme emotions in both work and play. Such behavior indicates that few children of this age are capable of emotional self-control. Since uncontrolled emotional behavior can seriously disrupt a school program, modern teachers attempt to teach children more socially acceptable ways of expressing their emotions.

David Russell observed that it is the teacher's responsibility to utilize children's emotional behavior to enhance the purposefulness and efficiency of thought. If a child feels no emotional drive toward learning the basic features of the Hindu-Arabic number system, his chances of improving thinking in such areas are greatly reduced.[12] Effective teachers have learned to use a variety of motivational techniques and devices as one means of involving children positively in a learning experience.

No matter how conscientious a first-grade teacher may be in preparing for each school day, it is improbable that all of the pupils' reactions to the prepared lessons can be anticipated. A child who feels rejected, for example, may fear a new learning situation and resist any changes that are required by it. Or, if he is criticized for failing to measure up to the demands of the new situation, he is apt to react quite negatively. A child who seldom experiences success either at home or in school may withdraw completely from a new classroom activity, or the activity may strike a responsive chord and generate considerable enthusiasm. While classroom teachers cannot anticipate all of these pupil responses, they can take them into account as normal reactions to conflict or frustration.

Fears of Six-Year-Olds. Fears are a normal part of the process of growing up. Teachers know that it is rare for a child to be free from fears, so they focus upon helping children encounter and overcome their fears. This is no easy undertaking, as Willard Olson pointed out, because children's fears often appear irrational, rather remote from the actual hazards that threaten them, and of little value in warding off real dangers. Behind most fears, he wrote, is some threat to security — either the child's individual security or his relationships with other members of the family.[13] Positive, accepting first-grade teachers can take great strides to alleviate children's fears.

A sampling of mental, physical, social, and emotional characteristics of six-year-olds has been reported. These data represent one phase in the human growth process. They attempt to portray children in the initial phase of their school experience.

THE FIRST-GRADE PROGRAM

A knowledge of some developmental characteristics of five- and six-year-olds is invaluable to a first-grade teacher when he structures his instructional program. He needs to take into account the limited

[12]*Op. cit.*, p. 199.

[13]Willard Olson, *Child Development* (Boston: D. C. Heath and Company, 1959), pp. 311-312.

skill capabilities of these children, their short attention span, their asocial behavioral tendencies, their strong emotions, their mental and physical variability, and so forth, in his planning. He must clearly perceive the capabilities and limitations of first graders so that his program is challenging but not stifling.

Two typical first-grade schedules are briefly described below. Each schedule represents the best thinking of an experienced first-grade teacher. Examine each of these programs, compare them, and evaluate them in terms of the data reported in the preceding section of this chapter. Then decide whether one, both, or neither of the programs exemplifies desirable pedagogical thought.

Teacher A: Monday's Schedule

 8:30— 8:45: Opening exercises
 8:45— 9:00: Planning the day's work
 9:00— 9:50: Reading groups and seatwork
 9:50—10:10: Recess
10:10—10:30: Reading groups and seatwork
10:30—10:55: Arithmetic
10:55—11:00: Preparation for lunch
11:00—12:00: Lunch
12:00—12:30: Telling and talking time
12:30— 1:15: Physical education
 1:15— 1:30: Preparation for radio story time
 1:30— 1:45: Radio story time
 1:45— 2:05: Reading groups and seatwork
 2:05— 2:20: Recess
 2:20— 2:55: Reading groups and seatwork
 2:55— 3:00: Preparation for dismissal
 3:00—   : Dismissal

Teacher B: Monday's Schedule

 9:00— 9:15: Opening exercises
 9:15— 9:30: Planning the day's work
 9:30—10:30: Reading groups and seatwork
10:30—11:00: Planned recess
11:00—11:20: Music
11:20—11:45: Arithmetic
11:45—12:00: Review of morning's work and lunch preparation
12:00— 1:15: Lunch

Children. Can you describe vividly a second-grade child? a fifth-grade child? Many experienced classroom teachers might respond affirmatively to these questions, because they have fallen prey to "pigeonholeitis." These teachers become so accustomed to working with second graders or fifth graders that they attach an identity to the group itself. The writers have frequently listened to teachers ascribe classroom problems to the unique characteristics of second graders, fifth graders, or children of whatever grade level they happen to be teaching. While there is some truth in such a statement, the truth can become hopelessly distorted. To illustrate "pigeonholeitis" better, imagine that you are a second-grade teacher. Try to pick a group of second graders from the photographs. How does the group you have selected differ from the groups you did not select? Are there any similarities between your group and the unselected ones?

Courtesy Carl Purcell, NEA

1:15— 1:45: Unit study (stressing either the social, natural or physical sciences)
1:45— 2:15: Reading groups, seatwork, and library period
2:15— 2:30: Free recess
2:30— 3:00: Independent study
3:00— 3:15: Review afternoon's work and prepare for dismissal
3:15— : Dismissal

If neither of the above schedules is satisfactory to the reader, he is invited to structure one that represents his best pedagogical thought. His ideas can then be analyzed critically by fellow classmates, or in some cases by experienced teachers.

OUTCOMES OF A FIRST-GRADE EXPERIENCE

A well-planned program of instruction certainly ought to have some impact upon a group of six-year-olds after approximately 180 school days. The fact that children's behavior is modified can be demonstrated in several ways. Some aspects can be measured (by achievement tests, indices of social development, and so forth), some can be observed (personal tidiness, emotional control, etc.), while some may be perceived only in certain instances (critical thinking skills, group loyalty, etc.). It is a rare child indeed who is able to remain completely oblivious to a school program.

Which aspects of the six-year-olds' modified behavior may be sensibly attributed to the efforts of the teacher and the school program? Obviously, the teacher is not able to influence children's physical maturation a great deal. He can teach effective health practices and be alert to deviations in children's developmental patterns, but beyond these contributions he is merely a bystander. This is not the case insofar as the academic, social, and emotional dimensions of children's behavior are concerned. The teacher can be and often is an important factor in the development of these behavioral dimensions.

An effective first-grade teacher probably accomplishes the following. A teacher who provides for children's individual differences in the classroom will significantly increase the range of achievement (especially in the skills areas) among these children by the end of the first grade. A teacher who implements the belief that first graders need to be taught how to act as group members will develop many socially sensitive children. A teacher who recognizes the extreme nature of children's emotions and who concentrates upon teaching children socially acceptable outlets for them will teach many children how to cope with heightened emotions. Generally speaking, these outcomes are realistic and within reach of the typical practitioner.

QUESTIONS FOR DISCUSSION

1. A first-grade teacher was invited to address her school's Parent Teacher Association about education in early elementary grades. She decided to focus upon variability among children's performance in the classroom, how the parents can help their child adjust to school, and new instructional materials utilized in her classroom when she spoke to the group.

a. What would you have included within each of these topics if you were delivering the address?

b. Do you think the topics selected are particularly appropriate? If not, what topics would you substitute or add?

c. Would you favor distributing to the parents a brochure stressing ways of helping children adjust to school?

2. Obviously, a person can invest a great deal of time in studying about human growth and development. Most undergraduate elementary education majors are exposed to one or two courses pertaining to this topic, and they frequently work with children in school settings. Do you think one or two courses plus interaction with children is sufficient to grasp salient dimensions of human growth and development? Or do you believe that our knowledge of human growth and development is so limited that more than one or two courses of this sort would be superfluous?

3. First-grade teachers usually bend over backwards to provide for children's individual differences. They individualize their instruction, they are cognizant of children's social and emotional behavior, and they usually are warm, positively oriented, and patient.

a. What aspects of their teacher preparation contribute to the development of these sensitivities?

b. Why is it that, as a child moves through the grades established by a school system, he encounters fewer and fewer teachers who evidence the above-mentioned sensitivities?

ADDITIONAL REFERENCES

See the list at the end of Chapter Ten, pages 253-255.

Chapter Nine

THROUGH THE MIDDLE YEARS
OF THE ELEMENTARY SCHOOL

The elementary school program can be described as a series of tasks and experiences that enable children to become an integral part of their culture. Robert Havighurst views this process of assimilation as a series of developmental tasks that are determined by children's maturational changes and the expectancies of society.

> The tasks which the individual must learn – the *developmental tasks* of life – are those things which constitute healthy and satisfactory growth in our society. They are the things a person must learn if he is to be judged and to judge himself to be a reasonably happy and successful person. *A developmental task is a task which arises at about a certain period in the life of the individual, successful achievement of which leads to his happiness and to success with later tasks, while failure leads to unhappiness in the individual, disapproval by the society, and difficulty with later tasks.*[1]

Each child progresses from one developmental task to the next at his own rate. Teachers who treat a classroom group of similarly aged children as if they were all at the same point in their development have lost sight of this behavioral characteristic. Unfortunately, such groups are a reality only in the dreams of a teacher.

A child can be compared with a snowflake, because each is a unique entity. Just because a child happens to be in a room with children of a comparable age or just because a snowflake happens to

[1]Robert J. Havighurst, *Developmental Tasks and Education* (Chicago: The University of Chicago Press, 1948), p. 6. Reprinted with permission.

222

be descending to earth along with thousands of snowflakes is no guarantee that there will be any other resemblance between the child and his peers or a snowflake and other snowflakes. Close scrutiny almost always reveals significant variability among children and snowflakes. Most teachers know that no two snowflakes are structurally alike. It is indeed unfortunate that some are unable to perceive and provide for similar differences among children.

What kinds of tasks and experiences enable children to become an integral part of their culture? According to Havighurst, six- to twelve-year-old children should develop the following:

1. Physical skill needed for ordinary games
2. Wholesome attitudes toward self
3. The ability to get along with age mates
4. Appropriate masculine or feminine social roles
5. Fundamental skills in reading, writing, and computing
6. A scale of values, conscience, and morality
7. An attitude toward social groups and institutions
8. Personal independence[2]

He believes that children who successfully achieve these developmental tasks are putting their best foot forward on the path leading to adulthood.

Carolyn Tryon and Jesse Lilienthal have prepared a similar list of developmental tasks which are expected of all children growing up in American society. In their opinion, each child must:

1. Achieve an appropriate dependence-interdependence pattern
2. Achieve an appropriate giving-receiving pattern of affection
3. Adjust to changing social groups
4. Develop a conscience
5. Learn a psycho-socio-biological sex role
6. Accept and adjust to a changing body
7. Manage a changing body and learn new motor patterns
8. Learn to understand and control the physical world
9. Develop an appropriate symbol system and conceptual abilities
10. Relate to the cosmos[3]

[2]*Ibid.*, pp. 33-62. Reprinted with permission.
[3]Carolyn Tryon and Jesse W. Lilienthal, III, "Developmental Tasks: 1. The Concept and Its Importance," *Fostering Mental Health in the Schools*, 1950 Yearbook of The Association for Supervision and Curriculum Development (Washington, D.C.: National Education Association, 1950), pp. 84-87. Reprinted with permission. Each of these developmental tasks is discussed in detail in the book.

The authors emphasize that these tasks or phases of them can be accomplished most successfully when the child is physically and emotionally ready for them. Even though Havighurst's and Tryon and Lilienthal's lists overlap a great deal, together they provide a composite picture of the major developmental tasks of children in the elementary school.

In this chapter, an attempt has been made to trace some of the behavioral modifications that result from children's exposure to the developmental tasks of the middle years of the elementary school. More specifically, two points are stressed: First, what happens to children during this phase of their elementary school experience; and second, how does the teacher actually influence these happenings? The lists of developmental tasks serve as a loose frame of reference for the illustrations that are used.

CHILDREN'S EXPERIENCES IN SCHOOL

It is difficult to make generalizations about children's experiences in the elementary school, because elementary school programs differ. For example, the way an educator views children affects his school program. Some educators structure a program that enables children to progress from one developmental task to another at their own rate. In such a program, children's individual differences are taken into account at each grade level. Other educators structure a program in which children are expected to master prescribed developmental tasks. In such a program, children's achievements are viewed in terms of established grade-level standards and expectations. This illustration emphasizes one way in which a school program can influence children's behavior. The reader needs to keep this point in mind when he examines descriptions of children's school experiences.

Developmental tasks that children encounter during the middle years of an elementary school experience and ways in which children react to them are reported in a series of selected anecdotes in the following papagraphs. An attempt has been made to encompass mental, physical, social, and emotional dimensions of children's behavior in these anecdotes. This attempt has not been at the expense of realism, as each anecdote has been derived from actual elementary school experience.

FRANKLIN AND JOHN

Franklin and John progressed at a normal rate in school until the latter part of the third grade. At that time, an obstacle (or obstacles) was encountered, because both boys began to experience problems. In the following year, both boys had difficulty in concentrating on their schoolwork and in relating to other children. During free recess periods, John usually volunteered but seldom was invited to participate in boys' games, whereas Franklin studiously avoided all group activities. What factor or factors might account for these behavioral changes?

Havighurst's first developmental task — physical skill needed for ordinary games — provides a clue to the boys' behavior. These boys have reached a point in their life when group games, especially touch football and baseball, become vitally important. A combination of interest in adult versions of football and baseball[4] and physical maturation, which enables many nine- and ten-year-olds to acquire the basic skills of these games easily, probably accounts for their importance. Franklin and John were unable to master this developmental task as readily as most of their classmates because of certain physical characteristics.

Franklin, aged nine, was 46¾ inches tall and weighed 51½ pounds. He was easily the smallest boy in his fourth-grade class. His diminutive size had not been very conspicuous during the first and second grades. However, in the third and fourth grades his size seemed to remain constant, while his classmates grew taller and heavier. Not only was Franklin small in stature, but he was poorly coordinated. He could not toss a ball accurately or catch it consistently. Nor could he run very fast or climb readily. Thus, it was not surprising that Franklin's initial touch football and baseball experiences were quite traumatic. He could be counted upon to make several embarrassing mistakes or to be injured in the course of a game. After a number of experiences of this nature, Franklin decided he had had enough. Even though he withdrew from the organized games, he still evidenced a strong desire to be a good athlete.

Like Franklin, John's problems were related to his size. On his ninth birthday he was 61 inches tall and weighed 112 pounds. Not

[4]Many boys of this age become bubble-gum addicts in order to accumulate baseball and football cards which are wrapped with the gum. Each card includes a picture and brief biography of nationally famous athletes.

only was he a very large, muscular fourth grader, but he was also extremely awkward. His classmates occasionally referred to him as the "Elephant." Because of his size and strength, he frequently — though inadvertently — injured other children in the course of a game. Other children had good reason not to participate in games with John, so he tended to remain apart from their activities. Since John wanted to participate in the football and baseball games, he was sorely disturbed by the group's cold-shoulder treatment.

Not only did the boys' limited physical skill curtail their participation in popular group activities, but this limitation also affected other facets of their school and personal life. Earlier in this account, mention was made of academic and social problems which probably could be related to the boys' inability to acquire needed physical skills. It is improbable, considering these problems, that Franklin and John were developing wholesome attitudes toward themselves during the middle years of the elementary school.

SUSAN

Susan's school progress was quite normal until the fourth grade. At that time, rapid development of secondary sex characteristics created a constellation of personal problems for her. Her problems began when a group of female classmates became aware of her early physical maturation. These girls, through teasing and sarcasm, succeeded in making Susan acutely aware of her uniqueness in the class.

The net effect of the girls' efforts was quite unfortunate. Susan withdrew from their company and from classroom activities that she ordinarily enjoyed. Also, she began to develop extremely poor posture, which probably reflected a sensitivity to her developing anatomy. Not only were Susan's schoolwork and social relationships affected by the maturational change, but her self-concept undoubtedly suffered as well.

HENRY

To Henry, the elementary school was an undesirable place that became less desirable with each passing year. A serious speech handicap and partially crippled hands and legs undoubtedly influenced his attitude toward school. His physical limitations hampered the development of reading, writing, and computational skills, physical skills needed for ordinary games, and social skills. And being a fifteen-year-old fifth grader did not contribute to the development of a wholesome self-concept. These problems contributed to a general insecurity and dependence on his part. Because of his inability to master these and other developmental tasks successfully, Henry literally "gave up" in school. He seemed to be biding his time until he reached the legal age to drop out.

IRENE

High parental expectations and below-average mental capabilities combined to make the academic dimensions of the elementary school exceedingly frustrating for Irene. She had the misfortune of having a series of teachers who adhered to rigid grade-level standards of achievement. Consequently, Irene's work in school usually was judged inferior by her teachers. Irene's well-educated and capable parents refused to accept the possibility that she was mentally retarded as an explanation for her poor performance in school, preferring to believe it was due to laziness and apathy.

Irene, faced with the possible loss of her parents' love and admiration, discovered by accident one day that cheating during a test enabled her to get a good grade. Since her parents praised good schoolwork, she quickly learned that cheating, lying, and in some instances stealing, enabled her to improve her grades in school. While this action tended to pacify her parents, it did not contribute to the internalization of a scale of values, conscience, and morality. Nor did her behavior contribute to the development of a wholesome self-concept. Irene became involved in a serious "frying-pan-versus-fire" dilemma early in her life.

DON

Don, an alert but outspoken and pugnacious third grader, apparently antagonized his teacher too many times, because she failed him at the end of the year. Her justification for this action was based upon his social immaturity. Grade failure in Don's case was extremely painful, since he attended a one-room school. In a one-room school, promotion usually means that children occupy seats in a different part of the room each year. If a child repeats a grade, he remains in the same part of the room, where he is joined by a younger group of children. Hence, a "flunky" is as conspicuous as an American flag in the classroom.

Most "flunkys" are subjected to a great deal of ridicule in school, and Don was no exception. His former classmates and the older boys made his school day unbearable. Consequently, he frequently engaged in fisticuffs, began to have temper tantrums, and periodically cried in an uncontrollable manner. His grade retention did not result in more mature social behavior. Rather, it contributed to a deterioration not only in the boy's social behavior, but his school progress as well. It produced a frustrated, negative ten-year-old boy.

Jo

A distant onlooker who observed Jo battling and tossing a baseball and running would assume that "Jo" was a nickname for Joseph rather than for Joanne. Ten-year-old Joanne not only played like a boy, she even looked like one with her short haircut and dungarees. Few classmates could recall the last time she came to school wearing a dress.

Her interest in boys' things was not confined to the playground. Jo's closest friends were boys, her fondest hobbies were building model boats and collecting baseball cards, and her dearest possession was a boxer puppy. Like many boys, Jo disliked school because she "had to sit still too long doing silly things."

Jo's behavior indicated that she had not learned much about her appropriate sex role during the first ten years of life. Since ten-year-old tomboys are often considered "cute" or are often the apple of their father's eye, their behavior is usually tolerated both at home and in school. This is unfortunate, because the onset of puberty and the development of secondary sex characteristics in the not too distant future could result in serious emotional conflict for the child.

Throughout the middle years of the elementary school, children encounter important developmental tasks. Some children are able to cope with these tasks without much difficulty. Some, like the seven cases cited, encounter a problem that often results in unhappiness, disapproval, and more problems. Adjustment difficulties seem to feed upon themselves—that is, one problem serves as a stimulus for others. A simple difficulty can quickly mushroom into a complexity of woes. Children who reach such a state of mind are not apt to profit from a school's instructional program. Elementary school teachers who are acquainted with the developmental tasks of the middle school years are in an excellent position to lend assistance to children who fail to master successfully the tasks which they encounter.

228

THE TEACHER AS AN INFLUENTIAL FACTOR

Before the twentieth century, most elementary school teachers functioned primarily as disseminators of information, that is, they presented a lesson and expected children — all children — to master its important features. When children did not measure up to their expectations, teachers often employed punitive measures or additional repetition of the lesson. These means were supposed to motivate laggards and loafers to attain greater heights of achievement in the classroom. Teachers of this era had practically no research data to guide their classroom conduct, so they depended upon trial and error methods of instruction.

Today's teacher has at his fingertips a wealth of data that pertain to the pedagogical process. However, availability does not insure implementation. Accumulated research has cast a shadow upon the validity of many nineteenth-century classroom practices. For instance, (1) while "telling" can be an effective teaching technique, it is only one of a number of effective techniques that can be employed; (2) expecting comparable academic performances from a group of children is as ridiculous as expecting all golfers to score in the low seventies or all bowlers to average 200 or better; (3) employing punitive measures as a means of stimulating scholastic achievement is often more detrimental than helpful; and (4) employing additional repetition of a lesson as a means of stimulating scholastic achievement will be as successful as the repetition is meaningful to the child. Now, if research contributions of the twentieth century have influenced the elementary school at all, the impact certainly ought to be reflected by the modern teacher's functions. The best way to determine this impact is to become acquainted with some research breakthroughs, and then spend time observing elementary teachers function in the classroom to see if they take advantage of the breakthroughs. While the advantages of such an approach are obvious, its implementation is dependent upon and limited by available observational facilities.

It is not unreasonable to believe that elementary school teachers try to do their utmost to teach children effectively — be it yesterday, today, or tomorrow. Yet, in spite of these intentions, some teachers are demonstrably more effective in the classroom than others. Operational variables besides teachers' desires probably account for these variations. Few people will dispute the statement that the typical elementary teacher of the 1960's is a better teacher than his nineteenth-century counterpart. Why? Because educators have learned a great deal about children and the pedagogical process in the twentieth century.[5]

If today's teachers are more effective in the classroom, what are they doing that probably differs from the practices of their nineteenth-century counterparts? Since a sampling of children's experiences in school was reported above, these illustrations will serve as a frame of reference for a response to the question. The response is structured to focus upon ways in which modern teachers can be expected to cope with prescribed problems of children.

Children like Franklin, John, Susan, Henry, Irene, Don, and Jo represent the age group Miss Ritter instructs. It is not unreasonable to believe that she would encounter problems similar to the seven described in this chapter—probably not all at once, but over a relatively short period of instructional activity. And it is likely that she would treat each of the children in a manner similar to the responses described in the following paragraphs, even though she is designated as the teacher of only two of the seven children.

FRANKLIN AND JOHN

Teachers can quickly identify children who fail to develop physical skills needed for ordinary games. This is especially true in Franklin's and John's cases because of their respective size and lack of coordination. Once a teacher becomes aware of a child who fails to master an important developmental task, it is his responsibility to determine the degree to which the failure affects other aspects of the child's behavior. Since the over-all behavior of both Franklin and John was markedly affected by their difficulty, it was up to their teacher to initiate positive action.

Even though the teacher cannot alter a child's maturational pattern, several courses of action could be pursued to help the boys resolve their difficulty. Two aspects of the instructional program afforded the boys' teacher an opportunity to launch an offensive designed to resolve their difficulties. A dramatization proved to be an entering wedge into Franklin's problem, while an independent study effort accomplished the same result for John.

Franklin's teacher occasionally used plays as a part of the reading

[5]Refer back to the account of Christopher Dock's teaching for an informative perspective (pp. 174-178).

230

program. He would select a play, cast the needed parts, provide time enough for the children to grasp the flavor of the play (and in a few instances to memorize their parts), and then present the play informally in the classroom, usually without an audience (once in a while another grade would be invited, or a few parents would visit the classroom to observe the end result). During a casting session for *The Pied Piper of Hamelin,* Franklin's teacher encouraged the boy to try out for the Mayor of Hamelin's part. The part called for a blustery, bombastic portrayal, which was quite contrary to Franklin's usual classroom behavior. Not only did he accept, but he undoubtedly would have pleased the playwright with his stirring portrayal of the Mayor's role. The part enabled him to blow off considerable steam and at the same time gain recognition among his peers. The class reacted to him just as a person might react when he discovers a huge pearl in an oyster on his dinner plate. While the play did not resolve Franklin's athletic difficulties, it did open a new dimension of interest for the boy, and it enabled him to relate better to his classmates. Franklin's teacher helped him to accept previous failure and experience new success.

John experienced a similar outlet during an independent study activity that was incorporated into his teacher's school program. Each child was encouraged to become involved during independent study time in a study of an area of knowledge that reflected his own interests. At times, children presented the results of an intensive study to the entire group, but this was the exception rather than the rule. By chance, John's teacher learned that the boy had an unusually strong interest in submarines. It was natural for the teacher to encourage John to pursue the topic as an independent study project.

As John generated enthusiasm for the project, the teacher was able to steer some of his energy into other phases of the school program as well. His efforts were culminated by one of the best-organized and delivered classroom reports his teacher had ever heard. The report had an electrifying effect upon John's peers, because they did not believe that he was capable of such productivity. When John agreed to show several boys how to build a model submarine, he won a major psychological victory. Again, as in Franklin's case, the teacher succeeded in steering John away from past failures toward some rewarding experiences. The teacher also suspected that, in John's case, his size would become a tremendous asset for playground games as soon as he developed better coordination.

231

SUSAN

Time is an important factor in resolving Susan's problem. Once her female peers attained a comparable maturational stage, their teasing and sarcasm would be pointless. Unfortunately for Susan, her problems were immediate, and she was not fully aware of nature's plans for her friends. Therefore, it was up to the teacher to help Susan get back into the swing of things in the classroom.

The teacher first contacted Susan's parents to sensitize them to their daughter's problem and to suggest that the girl wear very loose-fitting blouses or sweaters in school. Next, the teacher structured several situations which required Susan and some of her female classmates to associate with several well-developed older girls for a short period of time. And third, since the teacher recognized Susan's embarrassment whenever she was called upon in the classroom, he minimized these incidents for a while. While these efforts did not eliminate the problem, they seemed to take some of the pressure off Susan in school.

HENRY

The years of frustration and failure that Henry experienced in the elementary school could not easily be corrected by even the most enterprising teacher. This does not mean, however, that all teachers were powerless to act on the boy's behalf. One resourceful teacher who cultivated Henry's capabilities succeeded in bringing about a significant change in his school behavior.

Which capabilities did the teacher cultivate? The teacher recognized, as had Henry's previous teachers, that the boy had a great deal of difficulty in grasping a pencil. Rather than accept his physical limitations as an impossible barrier to written communication, the teacher explored a previously untapped resource—a typewriter. "Hunting and pecking" on the typewriter proved to be well within Henry's physical capabilities; hence, a new dimension of communication was opened to him. As he developed typing proficiency, he also evidenced more confidence in school activities. After all, he was acquiring a skill that no other child in the school could duplicate!

The teacher also capitalized upon Henry's interest in television to help him overcome his fear of speaking in a group setting. Once the boy's interest became apparent to the teacher, it was used to initiate many conversations about television. It was obvious that the boy was an authority of sorts on television programming. This perception was reinforced by another discovery made during a class discussion that Henry's stuttering did not prevent him from entering into the exchange of ideas pertaining to a television program. As a matter of fact, his stuttering practically disappeared when he addressed this topic. Therefore, the teacher used this clue in a variety of ways to involve Henry in classroom activities.

Henry's honesty and responsibility represented other capabilities that the teacher cultivated in school. The teacher placed him in charge of the school's milk fund. In this capacity, the boy collected the children's milk money, ordered the needed milk, and maintained a set of books that indicated the daily status of the fund. He functioned so effectively in this role that his classmates learned to respect Henry's administrative talents. Class confidence in his capabilities reached a pinnacle when they voted to place Henry in charge of all financial matters relating to the end-of-the-year school trip (the teacher functioned as a financial consultant to Henry in this instance).

The four accounts of Franklin, John, Susan, and Henry illustrate ways in which a teacher successfully involved troubled children in the ongoing activities of the school. While these experiences affected their self-concepts, their attitudes toward other children, and their attitudes toward school in general, they certainly did not resolve all of the difficulties. However, these experiences introduced the children to a dimension of school life that proved to be satisfying, enjoyable, and constructive. The teacher was able to establish a firm beachhead in the struggle to resolve their problems. Other teachers must sustain an offensive before the problems can be effectively and completely resolved.

IRENE AND DON

Both children's problems stemmed from their teachers' beliefs in evaluating pupil progress in school. Since Irene's teacher adhered to rigid grade-level standards of achievement, the girl, being mentally retarded, was at a disadvantage the first day she entered the classroom. Don's teacher overlooked the fact that eight-year-old boys will be boys when she established her criteria for promotion and retention. Her failure to recognize children's behavior patterns in school resulted in a policy that severely discriminated against boys. These school policies did not contribute to Irene's or Don's adjustment in school. Instead, the policies actually hampered each child's efforts to master several essential developmental tasks. Neither of these teachers differed significantly from their nineteenth-century counterparts as pedagogical practitioners.

The initiation of several new school policies, a school reorganization, and the addition to the staff of several well-trained teachers proved to be the best therapy Irene and Don could obtain. Both children were assigned to the classroom of one of the new, well-trained teachers. In this classroom, the children were exposed to a teacher with a refreshing concept of progress and behavior in school. The ideas of Miss Ritter — their new teacher — when put into practice in the classroom, penetrated the core of each child's school difficulties.

Miss Ritter's pupil evaluation program reflected known research about child growth and development. It was based upon the maintenance of active files for each child in attendance. In each file, she accumulated samples of a child's work, anecdotal records,[6] personal reactions to the child's progress in school, and intelligence, achievement, and sociometric test data. Data gathered in this manner served as the basis for (1) a report letter sent home to each child's parents several times each year, (2) a parent-teacher conference at least once during the year, and (3) at least two pupil-teacher conferences in the course of the year. In each of these situations, the teacher stressed the child's past and present performance in school and what could reasonably be expected from him in the future. During the parent conference, the teacher also described the child's school progress in relation to a large number of similarly aged children. Hence, the system stressed individual progress rather than group progress. Even though this program required much time and effort, the teacher accepted the burden without question. She felt that the program represented a truly professional method of evaluating pupil progress in school and reporting this progress to parents.

Since Irene's school performance was evaluated in terms of her own potential rather than in comparison with her classmates' potential, nothing could be gained by persistent cheating and lying. Even so, many months passed before she reconciled herself to this fact. This realization, combined with a new sense of dignity (which came about as a result of the teacher's constant efforts to praise her work in school), was reflected by a changed attitude toward school and by

[6]Brief, objective statements of a child's specific behavior in a particular situation. These statements, when accumulated over a period of time, tend to reveal interesting behavioral patterns.

more overt efforts to interact with classmates. The procedures used by Miss Ritter to inform the child's parents of her progress in school did not succeed in changing their attitude toward Irene's school performance. However, the noncompetitive nature of the procedures served to minimize the anxiety of the parents about their daughter.

Don also received a new lease on life with Miss Ritter. Upon learning the facts of the boy's retention, she planned a course of action that was based upon "being a little nearsighted and partially deaf." This teacher knew that many boys were at a serious disadvantage in school, possibly because (1) they had a higher metabolic rate than girls, and (2) they tended to be self-centered rather than sensitive to their school setting. Consequently, Don and others like him were not apt to respond to a teacher's instructional efforts as readily as girls in the middle grades of the elementary school. This statement becomes almost axiomatic when one recognizes that (1) boys predominate in the lowest reading groups in a classroom, (2) many more boys than girls evince speech disorders, (3) many more boys than girls repeat a grade because of academic failure, (4) boys constitute the vast majority of discipline cases in an elementary school, and (5) nearly eight out of ten children of this age range who are called to the attention of juvenile authorities are boys! With this knowledge in mind, Miss Ritter launched an offensive designed to restore Don's self-confidence and self-respect.

The teacher initiated her offensive by guiding Don's energies toward a series of carefully designed classroom activities and responsibilities. As the boy successfully completed each venture, the teacher showered him with praise and recognition. Whenever possible, the teacher subtly informed other children of Don's accomplishments. Through sociometric tests, the teacher discovered a few children in the group who enjoyed Don's company. She worked these children into her plans for Don, so that the boy could reap the benefits of constructive group interaction. Miss Ritter's positive, accepting, understanding attitude toward Don slowly penetrated the boy's exterior shell. As the boy positively identified with his teacher, he began to accept the teacher's values, requests, and perspectives. Once this occurred, the teacher was in an excellent position to influence Don's self-confidence and self-respect.

An altered school program and a compassionate teacher proved to be the pound of cure both Irene and Don needed to resolve their respective problems. Fortunately for these children, their problems were treated before they became so complex that an expert's assistance was required. Treatment of this sort is not at all unusual in today's schools. Many Irenes and Dons have been helped by sensitive teachers in America.

JO

If Jo is fortunate, the development of her secondary sex characteristics will bring about a closer mother-daughter relationship. Once this occurs, she will probably display many feminine characteristics both at home and in school. Her tomboy tendencies will not disappear, but they will not be as apparent as in the past. If Jo is unfortunate, she will react negatively to the development of her secondary sex characteristics and overtly or covertly reject her physical sex. This occurrence may have serious behavioral overtones.

An alert teacher will recognize that he is playing with fire when he attempts to cope with problems as intricate as Jo's. Often, the best move a teacher can make in a case like Jo's is to bring the child's problem to the attention of a specialist. If the child is a latent homosexual, or if the child has a character disorder, the teacher's efforts to help may waste valuable time. An early referral to a specialist in many cases of this nature could bear significantly upon the success of the therapeutic treatment.

The writers of this text each spent one year teaching children in a hospital school setting. Some of their students were children who were being treated in a hospital for the mentally disturbed. One pupil who attended the school—a thirteen-year-old girl—was committed to the hospital because of her failure to accept her appropriate sex role. Her case illustrated the potential severity of this problem. When the girl became aware of the development of certain feminine organs, she began to starve herself. This unconscious reaction thwarted further maturation, but threatened the girl's existence. At the hospital, she was fed intravenously to maintain her health. Hospital officials prognosticated lengthy treatment before the girl's problems would be resolved. Fortunately, few cases reach this proportion.

The cases cited above illustrate ways in which today's well-trained teacher might respond to a variety of children's problems. The teacher's actions in these cases are by no means atypical, nor are they characteristic of all contemporary practitioners. Each situation affords the reader an opportunity to become aware of teaching practices that are taken for granted in many twentieth-century classrooms—functions that were beyond the comprehension of most nineteenth-century teachers. It seems safe to conclude that children who progress through the middle years of the contemporary elementary school are exposed to more effective pedagogical treatment today than at any previous time in the history of the common school.

AN OPPORTUNITY FOR APPRAISAL

Thus far in the chapter, two topics have been developed: first, children's experiences in school; and second, ways in which teachers influence these experiences. These topics were structured to be informative. In the following paragraphs, several problem situations are described that relate to the two topics. These problems have been added to the chapter so that the reader will have an opportunity to evaluate his perceptions of the information presented. A recommended study procedure would entail (1) studying each situation, (2) reacting to it, and (3) comparing personal reactions to data presented in the chapter.

SITUATION ONE: REPORTING PUPIL PROGRESS, A DILEMMA

The teachers at the Wimbly Elementary School were in a quandary. A letter written by Mrs. Cruikshank (a parent who is quite actively involved in motherhood—eight children) to the school principal on the matter of the school's reporting practices instigated the situation. She raised a series of rather embarrassing questions about the A-B-C-D-E reporting system, which is used by the school staff to report pupil progress to parents.

Among the questions raised in her letter were the following:

1. Why does Freddie, her nine-year-old fourth-grade boy, get mostly "C" on his report card, when Charlie, her ten-year-old fifth-grade boy, gets mostly "B" on his report card? It is rather confusing, since Freddie learns more rapidly and retains much more effectively than Charlie.
2. Why did none of her children ever receive any "A" grades as first graders with Miss Burns, whereas all of them received many "A" grades as second graders with Mrs. Peta?
3. How does Mr. Zink arrive at his grades? Since he seldom tests his sixth-grade children in social studies, science, health, music, and art, the basis for his evaluation is rather confusing.
4. How can Miss Burns justify giving six-year-old Myron, the ablest

child in the family, "C" grades in reading because "he is not putting forth much effort in his schoolwork"? Myron recently finished reading *Tom Sawyer* on his own at home (he started reading at three years of age).

5. How can Betsy receive below-average grades in fourth grade, outstanding grades in fifth grade, and average grades in sixth grade?

6. How can teachers trained in child growth and development continually frustrate and thwart low-achieving first- and second-grade children with "D" and "E" letter grades?

Mrs. Cruikshank was of the opinion that grades do not communicate pupil progress to parents very effectively. She believed teachers are so shackled by evaluation peculiarities and and biases that letter grades become practically meaningless in this light.

She suggested that an effective pupil progress reporting system was needed in the school. If teachers focused upon where the child happened to be in his development at the beginning of the school year, where the teacher was guiding him during the school year, and what could be expected from the child in school, then, she felt, the teachers fulfilled their obligation to the parent. Should Mrs. Cruikshank be viewed as a constructive critic of the school's reporting policy, or should the educators write her off as another crank?

SITUATION TWO: TONDALEYA

Tondaleya, while exceptionally able as a student, never raised her voice above a whisper in the classroom during three years of school. Her contributions were essentially inaudible as far as the group was concerned. On the playground and in her home environment, she behaved in a normal manner. What could be done to help Tondy overcome her classroom-associated problem?

SITUATION THREE: THE ANIMAL SCHOOL

Once upon a time the animals decided they must do something to meet the problems of the "New World," so they organized a school. They adopted an activity curriculum consisting of running, climbing, swimming, and flying, and to make it easier to administer, all animals took all subjects.

The duck was excellent in swimming, better in fact, than his instructor, and made passing grades in flying, but he was poor in running. He had to stay after school and also drop swimming to practice running. This was kept up until his web feet were badly worn and he was only average in swimming.

The squirrel was excellent in climbing, until he developed frustration in the flying class, where his teacher made him start from the ground up instead of from tree-top down. He also developed charlie-horse from over-exertion and then got a "C" in climbing and a "D" in running.

At the end of the year, an abnormal eel, who could swim exceedingly well, and also run, climb, and fly a little, had the highest average and was valedictorian.[7]

Is it conceivable that some of these "students" failed to achieve some important developmental tasks? Did the school program lend itself to the needs of the animals as youths and later as adults?

QUESTIONS FOR DISCUSSION

1. Most elementary schools are described in terms of the primary grades and the intermediate grades. If one factor could be identified that might characterize each of these units, it probably would pertain to the child's ability to direct his own study activities.

a. Would it make sense to reorganize the elementary school so that a primary school would be created and the intermediate unit would be merged with the junior high school? Wouldn't such a pattern provide more homogeneous — in terms of growth and development — administrative arrangements?

b. Why do some elementary schools institute departmentalized classroom experiences in the fourth grade? Why is fourth grade selected rather than second grade or sixth grade? How might this action be defended?

2. If facilities were available, would you favor a full-time, school-sponsored camping experience for fourth graders that extended over a five- or ten-day period? Considering their stage of growth and development, what special provisions would you make for the experience?

ADDITIONAL REFERENCES

See the list at the end of Chapter Ten, pages 253-255.

[7]Author unknown.

THE PRODUCT OF AN ELEMENTARY SCHOOL EXPERIENCE

Children's behavior in the first grade and through the middle years of the elementary school has been the focal point of Chapter Eight and Chapter Nine, respectively. In this chapter, the product of an elementary school experience is the main concern. More specifically, behavior characteristic of sixth-grade children is reported. Again, the data are organized into mental, physical, social, and emotional dimensions. Data presented in this chapter serve to complete an overview of children's behavior in the elementary school.

Before an analysis of the behavior of sixth-grade children is undertaken, several points need to be qualified. First, sixth grade is not always the terminal grade of an elementary school. A number of contemporary elementary schools include a seventh and an eighth grade as well. Since eight-grade elementary schools are being replaced by a six-grade-elementary-school — three-year-junior-high-school plan, the latter organizational structure has been emphasized in this chapter. Second, the chronological age of sixth graders is apt to vary considerably. The writers have worked with and have observed ten-, eleven-, twelve-, and thirteen-year-old children enrolled in a sixth-grade class. Therefore, this possible age range must be kept in mind whenever the writers generalize about the sixth-grade population.

BEHAVIOR CHARACTERISTIC OF SIXTH GRADERS

An unknown writer is credited with the following statement on children:

I must not interfere with any child, I have been told; to bend his will to mine, or try to shape him through some mold of thought. Naturally, as a flower, he must unfold. Yet flowers have the discipline of wind and rain, and though I know it gives the gardener much pain, I've seen him use his pruning shears to gain more strength and beauty for some blossoms bright. And he would do whatever he thought right. I do not know — yet it seems right to me that only weeds unfold naturally.

He is of the opinion that intelligent, sensitive adults — like beautiful flowers — are the outcome of careful cultivation. This view is often expounded by school critics. According to the critics, contemporary teachers fail to cultivate children's intellect because they refuse to interfere with the children's "natural" development, and they waste time pursuing too many nonintellectual activities. Most teachers reject this kind of criticism of their classroom function. They point out that the task of inculcating children with the American way of life requires extensive cultivation and guidance, and this function seems to be performed quite well.

One way to assess the positions taken by the critic and the teacher is to subject their viewpoints to a reality test. That is, by examining each viewpoint in conjunction with a description of behavior characteristic of sixth graders, their relative merits ought to become apparent. Familiarity with the data reported below should enable the reader to determine whether teachers contribute significantly to or are incidental to the developmental process during the elementary school years. The data are presented according to mental, physical, social, and emotional categories.

MENTAL

In Chapter Eight, it was pointed out that much knowledge has been accumulated about the mental development of six-year-old children. This statement also applies to sixth graders. Since the data are so extensive, an attempt has been made to present an orderly sampling from them. Three dimensions of the data — mental capabilities, skills, and interests characteristic of this maturational level — are emphasized.

Mental Capabilities. Previously, the mental capabilities of six-year-olds were described. These descriptions revealed that while children of this age level were capable of extraordinary mental feats, certain factors—notably limited skills, a limited conceptual frame-work, and a limited capacity to evaluate mental activity—restricted the scope of their intellectual explorations. Such limitations are usu-ally overcome in varying degrees by the time a child reaches the sixth grade. For example, many sixth graders possess highly refined study skills, evidence extensive conceptual development, and are able to evaluate problem situations critically. Since the reader may question the validity of this statement, further clarification seems appropriate.

Well-developed study skills and access to a wide range of infor-mation open the door to highly refined mental capabilities. In contrast to the first grader's limitations, the sixth grader derives concepts and percepts from a variety of concrete and vicarious learning situations. Children of this age are able to utilize books, pictures, films, and television extensively as they attempt to unravel the world in which they live. Also, they are able to analyze these first-hand and vicarious experiences critically in order to derive appropriate generalizations about a topic being studied. Even though sixth graders are just beginning to grasp the significance of all there is to know, they have already been exposed to mountains of data. Consequently, the ability to simplify and order information becomes an important part of the mental process. All of these mental activities contribute to the struc-turing of the thought process.

Other characteristics of sixth graders' thought processes that set them apart from first graders is their ability to recognize and solve problems and their ability to work with other children in solving problems. Often in the course of a social studies unit, a group of children get together to attack a series of common problems. The problems are usually identified, then divided among the committee members. After the children have surveyed available materials that yield data relevant to the questions at hand, they pool their informa-tion and attempt to solve the original problems. Generalizations that emerge from the group interaction are often recorded and reported to other children in the class. This activity can be observed in numerous sixth-grade classes.

The refined character of sixth graders' mental capabilities is probably best reflected by the concepts they possess. It is not at all unusual for sixth graders to possess well-developed concepts of space, time, life and death, beauty, and humor. Not only do they possess such concepts, but many can verbalize at length about each. Obviously, abstract concepts like these are based upon well-developed skills and a wide range of information.

Skills. Well-developed skills are mentioned several times in the above paragraphs as one basis of sixth graders' mental capabilities. These skills range from familiarity with to mastery of the prime elements of the "three R's," and from familiarity with to mastery of a variety of study skills. For example, many children of this age level possess sufficient skill to read *The Reader's Digest, Life, Look, The National Geographic,* and innumerable full-length books. Many can comfortably utilize the four fundamental arithmetic operations with both whole and fractional numbers. And many can write as legibly as (or more legibly than) most adults; their spoken vocabulary encompasses more than 7,000 words;[1] they comprehend approximately 50,000 words;[2] and they are able to write detailed paragraphs using complex and compound sentence structure.

Numerous well-planned elementary school programs focus upon the development of study skills. Children who are exposed to these programs can be expected to utilize such skills as map reading; outlining; summarizing read material; skimming; selecting appropriate resource materials; use of the dictionary, encyclopedias, and other reference materials; and so forth. Mastery of these skills enables children to solve problems, to obtain information, and to enjoy plenty of leisurely moments both in and out of school.

It is important not to lose sight of the fact that the range of individual differences among sixth graders in the various skills areas is fantastic. Spreads of five, six, and seven or more years are apparent in reading, arithmetic, and study skills sections of standardized achievement tests. How should an elementary school be evaluated when it is apparent that its program causes the range of individual differences among children to increase each year? Is this a desirable outcome of a program, or has this program failed to bring many pupils up to expected standards? What do you think?

Interests. What, how, and why questions of sixth graders are as comprehensive as the universe itself. Their questions may range from a science area, to religion, to the world in general. Unlike six-year-olds, sixth graders seldom are satisfied by simple answers. Interest in a question often leads to an intensive survey of available resources

[1]Cecil V. Millard, *Child Growth and Development* (Boston: D. C. Heath and Company, 1958), p. 155.

[2]Mary K. Smith, "Measurement of the Size of General English Vocabulary Through the Elementary Grades and High School," *Genetic Psychology Monographs,* 24 (1941), 311-345.

that might apply to the problem at hand. When children of this age level are not actively engaged in a research probe, they often pass the time of day by reading books, magazines, and comic books, or by viewing television. These children also spend many hours playing checkers, chess, Monopoly, Parchesi, cards, and other games that involve a group of children. Their interests are often based upon specific skills acquired in school.

PHYSICAL

This growth stage is really a period of transition for children. It is a time when girls mature at a more accelerated pace than boys. While few eleven-year-old boys have entered the pubescent growth spurt, more than one-fourth of the girls have attained this developmental level. What impact does the onset of puberty have upon children? How are the different sexes affected by puberty? And can the onset of puberty affect a child's progress in school? In order to address these and similar questions, data pertaining to the physical structure and physical behavior of sixth graders are reported.

The Physical Structure of the Sixth Grader.   Marked differences in physical development are characteristic of children in the sixth grade. It is not at all unusual to note wide variations in height and weight among them. Probably the safest way to describe eleven-year-olds is to point out that many of these children measure 56 to 59 inches and weigh 80 to 100 pounds. In general, girls are slightly taller and heavier than boys. This differential can be attributed to differences between the sexes with regard to the onset of puberty. When these figures are contrasted with typical adult dimensions, it becomes apparent that boys still have a long way to go physically, whereas girls are approaching their maximum physical development.

Sixth graders not only make rapid strides in height and weight, but they also experience other internal and external changes. Internally, changes in the size and position of vital organs and changes in glandular secretions take place at puberty.[3] Externally, children begin to show adult posture characteristics, the abdomen is drawn in, and the back line straightens appreciably.[4] An unfortunate side-effect of periods of rapid growth that becomes rather obvious at this develop-

[3]Elizabeth B. Hurlock, *Developmental Psychology* (New York: McGraw-Hill Book Company, Inc., 1959), p. 242.
[4]Millard, *op. cit.*, p. 89.

mental stage is instability and poor coordination. Children of this age are apt to evidence more awkward behavior than graceful behavior. Some experts are not convinced that the awkwardness is due entirely to physical growth, believing that children of this age are awkward because of social immaturity. They strive so hard to do the right thing that they appear to fumble in the process.

According to Hurlock, this is a homely age. There are a number of reasons for the unattractiveness of some preadolescents and adolescents, she wrote, most important of which are the following: (1) the transition from baby teeth to permanent teeth; (2) the transition from the fine-textured hair of the young child to the coarser-textured hair of the adolescent (note the stringy, unmanageable hair which characterizes many sixth graders the next time you visit an elementary school); (3) spindly arms and legs which give the child a young-colt appearance; and (4) poor grooming which comes from the child's lack of interest in his appearance.[5] Fortunately, this stage is only a temporary phase in the growth process.

Physical Behavior. The onset of puberty serves as a departure point for boys and girls insofar as their physical activities are concerned. Girls as a rule tend to focus upon physical activities that involve the finer muscles activities like sewing, painting, and knitting. Boys, on the other hand, tend to pursue activities involving the grosser muscles—activities like football, baseball, basketball, and other roughhouse games. Boys appear to be attracted to strenuous group games, whereas girls appear to be attracted to games that demand a minimal amount of physical exertion. This statement should not be interpreted to mean that girls are not capable of more rigorous activity. Nothing could be farther from the truth. Rather, the children's choice of activities vividly reflects the degree to which they are learning their respective sex roles.

Since girls concentrate upon finer muscle activities at this age level, and since sixth graders are confronted with innumerable situations which require finer muscle activity, it is not accidental that sixth-grade girls' school achievements are usually more impressive than sixth-grade boys'. As girls learn their appropriate sex role in our society, they also learn how to succeed in school, because the demands of the elementary school program are more akin to female than

[5]*Op. cit.*, p. 170.

to male activities. This phenomenon, combined with earlier female maturation, serves to set boys and girls apart quite precisely at the sixth-grade level.

SOCIAL

Cecil V. Millard, a specialist on child development, observed that maximum personal-social development is dependent upon the cultivation of three kinds of social skills. The first skill is the ability to utilize social "niceties"; the second pertains to getting along with children and adults in peripheral groups; and the third is the ability to adjust to the demands of intimacy—in personal, family, or group contacts. Most sixth graders have acquired all of these social skills in varying degrees. But, awareness of such skills is no guarantee that children will use them at the appropriate time.[6] Just what can be expected of sixth graders as they interact with each other, their families, and other individuals and groups? It is the purpose of this section to report representative social characteristics of sixth graders.

The following passage, which has been quoted from Elizabeth Hurlock, another specialist on child development, provides an excellent point of departure:

> No longer is the child satisfied to play at home alone or to do things with members of his family. Even one or two friends are not enough for him. He wants to be with the "gang," because only then will there be a sufficient number of individuals to play the games he now enjoys and to give the excitement to his play which solitary play or play with another child lacks. From the time the child enters school until the physical changes at puberty begin to develop, the desire to be with and to be accepted by the gang becomes increasingly strong. This is just as true of girls as of boys.
>
> At this time, social development is taking place rapidly and the child quickly passes from the self-contained, selfish individual, whose social contacts are characterized by constant disagreements and fights, to the point where he is a cooperative, well-adjusted member of a social group composed of his peers.[7]

In the process of expanding social contacts during the elementary school years, children tend to be selective in their choice of friends. They seem to prefer playmates of their own sex more often than of the

[6]*Op. cit.*, p. 234. Reprinted with permission.
[7]*Op. cit.*, p. 183. Reprinted with permission.

opposite sex at this age level. Girls can be expected to exhibit much more interest in boys as "social objects of increasing excitement" than boys in girls.[8]

A desire to be independent is the basis for much of the sixth grader's difficulty with adults. His perceptions of personal capabilities often clash with adult perceptions of his capabilities. Hence, children of this age level turn to each other for consolation and ego gratification. It is interesting to note that these children may continually bicker and argue with their parents, but at the same time refer to them with a great deal of pride when they are absent.

By the time a child reaches the sixth grade, he has usually stereotyped himself in the group. If he smiles often, plays fairly, volunteers for varied group activities, conforms to group mores and values, and presents a pleasant appearance, he probably is a popular pupil. If, on the other hand, he is quiet and withdrawn, aggressive and troublesome, and unattractive, he probably is an unpopular pupil. Social status, race, and family background are variables that also influence the child's degree of acceptance or rejection in school. Most sixth graders have a pretty precise notion of their own status in the group.

Generally speaking, sixth graders are very sensitive to their interactions with peers and adults. They have a pretty vivid conception of the adult world, and they want to become actively involved in it. Unfortunately, adults still view them as children, so conflict is bound to occur. Children, in turn, learn to share their problems with members of the peer group. Thus, peer acceptance becomes an important developmental task of this age group.

EMOTIONAL

Sixth graders are either on the threshold of or they have actually entered another important developmental cycle, puberty. Previously, it was pointed out that major physiological and psychological changes are characteristic of this developmental stage. Children who experience these changes are often bewildered by their altered anatomy, by strange drives and feelings which become a part of their psychical apparatus, and by altered social relationships. If rapid bodily change and growth confusion characterize sixth graders, it seems likely that these children will display considerable emotional instability. One

[8]Virgil E. Herrick, J. I. Goodlad, F. J. Estvan, and P. W. Eberman, *The Elementary School* (Englewood Cliffs, N.J.: Prentice-Hall, Inc., 1956), p. 101.

way to address this assumption is to study manifestations of emotional behavior at the sixth-grade level. Are sixth graders likely to be emotionally stable or unstable?

Manifestations of the Emotions at the Sixth-Grade Level. Previously, it was noted that six-year-olds are capable of displaying most of the emotions known to mankind. It follows, then, that the range of emotions exhibited by first graders and sixth graders is quite similar. While these two age groups may have the range of emotions in common, there is little resemblance between the manner in which each group expresses the emotions.

Few first graders are capable of emotional self-control, whereas many sixth graders are able to present at least a veneer of it. This veneer represents the impact of society upon the child. Beneath the surface lies a seething cauldron of all the extreme emotions known to mankind. Fortunately, these reach the overt behavior level only infrequently. As Hurlock put it:

> The older child soon discovers that violent expressions of emotions, especially of the unpleasant emotions, are socially unacceptable to his contemporaries. They regard temper outbursts as "babyish"; withdrawal reactions in fear as indicative of a "fraid cat;" and hurting another in jealousy as poor sportsmanship. Hence a child acquires a strong motivation to learn to control the outward expressions of his emotions.[9]

Considering all the changes that are taking place at this age level, one might expect these children to display extreme emotions rather frequently. This is not the case for most children. One explanation for this inconsistency is that the socialization process enables sixth graders to control their emotions more effectively than first graders.

Sixth graders seldom succeed in suppressing their emotions. Rather, they have learned how to keep them under control. To illustrate, when a recess privilege is taken away from a sixth-grade boy as a punishment for misbehavior, he is not apt to have a temper tantrum, to throw things, or to talk back to the teacher. He expresses his displeasure by being sulky and sullen. Or, when he has a difference of opinion with a large, muscular playmate, rather than express his anger by attacking the stronger child physically, he makes his point with verbal barbs and sarcasm. Another instance of self-control can be observed

[9]*Op. cit.*, p. 177. Reprinted with permission.

when a boy's mother visits his classroom while school is in session. The boy is more likely to recognize her presence by waving, smiling, or blushing than by rushing over to her and showering her with hugs and kisses. In each instance, the boy expresses his feelings, but not in a conspicuous manner.

Similar changes can be observed among girls. They usually resort to verbal subtleties instead of physical actions to communicate their anger or displeasure. Individuals who subject girls to conflict can expect to be the focal point of sarcastic or disparaging comment. Girls' emotional behavior seems to differ slightly from boys' behavior at the sixth-grade level. First, girls exhibit much more over affection than boys, This affection may be directed toward a peer, an adult in the child's environment, or an idol like a movie star. Second, many girls have learned to use tears as an effective means of accomplishing their desires.

An unusual manifestation of the emotions of eleven-year-olds has been described by Lester and Alice Crow. They pointed out how typical school experiences may become fear-inducing stimuli.

> Children's school experiences often become fear-inducing stimuli. It is quite common for a child who is achieving success in school work to be afraid of failing a test, of being demoted, of earning the disapproval of his teacher, or of failing to gain the friendship of his school mates. Sometimes the less probable it is that any such catastrophe will occur, the greater does the fear seem to become. It sometimes appears to serve as a self-protective covering against loss of prestige in the school community.[10]

This fear can also be observed at both the high school and college level, especially among conscientous students, so the sixth grader is in good company.

Can the reader determine, on the basis of data presented above, whether sixth graders are likely to be emotionally stable or unstable?

A sampling of mental, physical, social, and emotional characteristics of sixth graders has been reported. These data represent another phase in the human growth process. An attempt has been made to portray children at the conclusion of their elementary school experience.

Earlier in this chapter, several conflicting views of the teacher's

[10]Lester D. Crow and Alice Crow, *Child Development and Adjustment* (New York: The Macmillan Company, 1962), p. 243. Reprinted with permission.

role in the educational process were reported. It was suggested that one way to assess the positions taken was to subject them to a criterion measure. In this case, the criterion happened to be the sixth grader, the product of an elementary school. Now that the sixth grader's mental, physical, social, and emotional status has been surveyed, the reader ought to be in an excellent position to determine which position is more tenable.

A LOOK AHEAD

What can the typical sixth grader expect when he enters the junior high school? Originally, the junior high school was intended as a transition between the elementary school and the high school. There was reason to believe that a special school arrangement of this sort offered specific advantages to the student. Educators attempted to combine certain assets of the elementary school with specialized course offerings (such as vocational education, fine arts, and scientific laboratory facilities), teachers who evidenced a command of a given area of knowledge, and increased student responsibility for tasks to be learned in the junior high school.

Operationally, the typical child who entered this institution at the "seventh-grade" level could expect to be placed in a homeroom group. In the course of a school day, he could plan on rather frequent moves from one room to another at designated time intervals. Different teachers provided instruction in different curricular areas in the various rooms. And, all too often, this instruction was rigorous, subject-oriented, and somewhat impersonal.

This operational pattern was supported by a number of widely accepted assumptions that seemed to contradict the original *raison d'être* of the junior high school. Included among these were the following: First, children who enter the seventh grade possess study skills needed at this grade level (this assumption could easily be verified by noting the kinds of texts and other printed materials that were made available in seventh-grade classrooms); second, these children were able to profit from extensive whole-class instruction (this assumption is based upon extensive reports of seventh-grade teachers' classroom behavior); third, all children need to be exposed to the same school program (this assumption is also based upon past teacher performance); fourth, since all children have had the same instructional opportunities, their achievement is evaluated in terms of grade-level expectations (school policy on this point was quite stringent); and fifth, seventh graders are sufficiently mature to be held responsible for numerous homework assignments. Unfortunately, a number of these assumptions continue to serve as a basis for many present-day junior high school programs.

While such pedagogical practices continue to pervade today's school programs, there is another vibrant, exciting movement apparent in the junior high school of the sixties. This movement is rooted in a desire for academic excellence, in a desire to provide for the culturally disadvantaged members of our society, and in an instructional material and methodological "revolution" which is under way. The net effect of this movement upon the junior high school has already been significant. Some of these operational changes are summarized as follows:

1. Increased emphasis has been placed upon sorting students on the basis of intellect, and then providing appropriate academic experiences for the various levels of ability. Improved instructional materials and teaching methods have enhanced these undertakings considerably.
2. Science, mathematics, and foreign language sequences have been extensively revised and expanded within the curriculum. This expansion has been at the expense of the fine arts and vocational offerings. Hence, the student who is interested in music, art, homemaking, industrial arts, drama, and so forth, may be somewhat thwarted.
3. Educators are increasingly taking into account social and economic factors and human development realities when they plan instructional experiences. Hence, school programs are becoming more responsive to individual and community needs.
4. A sense of national urgency in education has resulted in an intensification of study assignments and in a tendency to make certain phases of the junior high school program extremely rigorous. Fortunately, many educators take into account the fact that many students are not able to cope with these expectations.
5. The social and athletic atmosphere of the senior high school has been superimposed upon many junior high schools in America. Consequently, students date earlier, and they become vigorously involved in competitive interscholastic sports.

Hence, the student who enters today's junior high school can expect to find a variety of organizational arrangements. He may enter a school which is organized along the lines of the elementary school he recently moved beyond, or he may enter a school that represents a decided organizational departure. He may enter a so-called traditional school, a so-called ultra-progressive school, or a compromise middle-of-the-road institution. In any event, he will be subjected to a pre-scribed set of expectations, value patterns, and scholastic opportuni-ties. His ability to profit from the new school setting may be predicated upon previous experiences he has had in the elementary school.

Variables which undoubtedly affect children's progress through-out the seventh grade are intelligence, emotional stability, and study skills development. It is not unreasonable to believe that well-ad-justed, able children who command a variety of study skills will fit into a seventh-grade program, whereas slow learners, whose com-mand of study skills is limited, and emotionally disturbed children will encounter many difficulties. The degree to which children will satisfactorily adjust to the typical seventh-grade situation can be predicted on the basis of factual statements like the following:

1. About half of the seventh-grade population is known to have an intelligence quotient of 100 or less.[11]
2. Achievement test results reveal that seventh graders vary six to eight years in reading capabilities. More than two-fifths of these children are unable to utilize profitably materials written at the seventh-grade level.
3. Recent figures indicate that for every two marriage-license appli-cations, one divorce is granted in a large midwestern community. In this community, thousands of children have become the victims of broken homes. Many large urban centers share this problem.
4. Delinquency among young adolescents continues to increase at a fantastic rate in America.
5. Relatively few secondary school teachers are required to take course work in the area of child growth and development.

How would you interpret these statements?

QUESTIONS FOR DISCUSSION

1. The Mental Health Association has invited you to participate in a community program aimed at developing healthful living. They want you to provide perspectives on the school's role in this process. How would you describe:

[11]100 is a theoretical figure that may actually be too low. The median I.Q. of elementary school children surveyed in Iowa recently was 108, for example.

a. The school's impact upon mental and physical health?
b. Traits that characterize teachers who work effectively with emotionally disturbed children?
c. Ways in which the school operates with other community agencies on matters pertaining to children?

2. There is a school in England known as Summerhill that functions in a unique manner. Freedom and permissiveness are paramount features of the school. Children in attendance command their study endeavors to the degree that they can decide not to study or even attend school.

a. Do you think that children are mature enough to assume a responsibility for the direction and extent of their education?
b. What impact might such a philosophy have upon the teaching staff?
c. Could such a school scheme be justified in terms of growth and development data?

3. Most children in South America, Africa, and Asia are not likely to acquire much more formal education than that attained by a typical sixth grader, even if they are fortunate enough to progress to that point. On the basis of what you know about the product of an American elementary school, how would you assess the readiness of children from the above-mentioned continents for citizenship, business and commerce, and self-improvement? What impact is such a level of education apt to have upon the culture, the gross national product, and the receptivity to change of a country?

ADDITIONAL REFERENCES

Almy, Millie, *Ways of Studying Children.* New York: Bureau of Publications, Teachers College, Columbia University, 1959. 226 pp.

American Eucational Research Association, "Growth, Development and Learning," *Review of Educational Research,* 84 (December, 1964), 495-618.

Bonney, M. E., *Popular and Unpopular Children: A Sociometric Study.* New York: Beacon House, 1947. 81 pp.

Burr, James B., Harding, L. W., and Jacobs, L. B., *Student Teaching in the Elementary School.* New York: Appleton-Century-Crofts, Inc., 1958. 459 pp.

Crow, Lester D., and Crow, Alice, *Child Development and Adjustment.* New York: The Macmillan Company, 1962. 514 pp.

Cunningham, Ruth, *et al.*, *Understanding Group Behavior of Boys and Girls.* New York: Teachers College, Columbia University, 1951. 446 pp.

Durkheim, Emile, *Moral Education.* New York: The Free Press of Glencoe, 1961. 288 pp.

Dutton, Wilbur H., and Hockett, John A., *The Modern Elementary School.* New York: Rinehart and Company, Inc., 1959. 530 pp.

Forest, Isle, *Child Development.* New York: McGraw-Hill Book Company, Inc., 1954. 291 pp.

Frazier, Alexander, ed., *Learning More About Learning.* Washington, D. C.: Association for Supervision and Curriculum Development (NEA), 1959. 88 pp.

Garrison, Karl C., *Growth and Development.* New York: Longmans, Green & Company, 1959. 559 pp.

Gesell, Arnold, Ilg, Frances L., and Ames, Louise Bates, *Youth: The Years from Ten to Sixteen.* New York: Harper and Brothers, 1956. 542 pp.

Hanna, Lavone A., Potter, G. L., and Hagaman, Neva, *Unit Teaching in the Elementary School.* New York: Rinehart and Company, Inc., 1956. 592 pp.

Harris, Irving R., *Emotional Blocks to Learning.* New York: The Free Press of Glencoe, 1961. 210 pp.

Hawkes, Glenn R., and Pease, Damaris, *Behavior and Development From 5 to 12.* New York: Harper and Brothers, 1962. 375 pp.

Herrick, Virgil E., Goodlad, J. I., Estvan, F. J., and Eberman, P. W., *The Elementary School.* Englewood Cliffs, N. J.: Prentice-Hall, Inc., 1956. 474 pp.

Hurlock, Elizabeth B., *Developmental Psychology.* New York: McGraw-Hill Book Company, Inc., 1959. 645 pp.

Hutt, Max L., and Gibby, R. G., *The Child.* Boston: Allyn and Bacon, Inc., 1959. 401 pp.

Jersild, Arthur T., *In Search of Self.* New York: Bureau of Publications, Teachers College, Columbia University, 1952. 141 pp.

Jersild, Arthur T., *Child Psychology.* Englewood Cliffs, N. J.: Prentice-Hall, Inc., 1960. 506 pp.

Klausmeier, Herbert J., and Dresden, Katharine, *Teaching in the Elementary School.* New York: Harper and Brothers, 1962. 622 pp.

Logan, Lillian M., and Logan, V. G., *Teaching the Elementary School Child.* Boston: Houghton Mifflin Company, 1961. 900 pp.

Loomis, Mary Jane, *How Children Develop.* Columbus: The Ohio State University, 1964. 68 pp.

Lowenfeld, Victor, *Creative and Mental Growth.* New York: The Macmillan Company, 1957. 541 pp.

McCandless, Boyd R., *Children and Adolescents.* New York: Holt, Rinehart and Winston, Inc., 1961. 521 pp.

Martin, William E., and Stendler, Celia B., *Child Behavior and Development.* New York: Harcourt, Brace & Company, 1959. 618 pp.

Millard, Cecil V., *Child Growth and Development*. Boston: D. C. Heath and Company, 1958. 512 pp.

Moustakas, Clark E., *The Teacher and the Child*. New York: McGraw-Hill Book Company, Inc., 1956. 265 pp.

Ojemann, Ralph H., *Personality Adjustment of Individual Children*. Washington, D. C.: Department of Classroom Teachers, American Educational Research Association (NEA), 1962. 32 pp.

Olson, Willard C., *Child Development*. Boston: D. C. Heath and Company, 1959. 497 pp.

Passow, A. Harry, ed., *Intellectual Development: Another Look*. Washington, D. C.: Association for Supervision and Curriculum Development (NEA), 1964. 119 pp.

Passow, A. Harry, ed., *Nurturing Individual Potential*. Washington, D. C.: Association for Supervision and Curriculum Development (NEA), 1964 91 pp.

Piaget, Jean, *The Construction of Reality in the Child*. New York: Basic Books, Inc., 1954. 386 pp.

Prescott, Daniel A., *The Child in the Educative Process*. New York: McGraw-Hill Book Company, Inc., 1957. 502 pp.

Ragan, William B., *Teaching America's Children*. New York: Holt, Rinehart and Winston, Inc., 1961. 344 pp.

Redl, Fritz, and Wattenberg, William W., *Mental Hygiene in Teaching* New York: Harcourt, Brace & Company, 1959. 562 pp.

Strang, Ruth, *An Introduction to Child Study*. New York: The Macmillan Company, 1959. 543 pp.

Waetjen, Walter B., ed., *Human Variability and Learning*. Washington, D.C.: Association for Supervision and Curriculum Development (NEA), 1961. 88 pp.

Waetjen, Walter B. ed., *New Dimensions in Learning*. Washington, D. C.: Association for Supervision and Curriculum Development (NEA), 1962. 96 pp.

SUMMARY: PART THREE

An *attempt* was made in Chapter Eight to depict children at the initial phase of their school experience. The word "attempt" is emphasized because of the overwhelming amount of data that have been accumulated to describe and account for the developmental process. Because of the extensive available data, the writers were forced to sample carefully aspects of the data that in their opinion best portrayed behavioral characteristics of children at this point in their development. It must be kept in mind that this chapter was designed to survey rather than to analyze methodically children's behavior.

An overview of a typical day in the lives of several preschool children and a survey of four dimensions—mental, physical, social, and emotional—of first-grade children's behavior were included in the chapter. Also, several representative school programs were described to illustrate how classroom teachers take into account what is known about first-grade children. A brief description of some reasonable outcomes of a first-grade experience served to culminate the chapter.

Descriptions of children's experiences during the middle years of the elementary school and ways in which the classroom teacher is able to influence these experiences were incorporated into Chapter Nine. Such an approach sheds light upon the over-all pattern of children's behavior and also focuses upon a sampling of children's specific adjustment problems at this time.

To summarize a chapter that deals with the product of an elementary school experience is indeed an imposing task, because there is so much ground to cover. In Chapter Ten, the sixth-grade child was viewed in terms of his mental, physical, social, and emotional development. Data sampling each of these developmental categories were reported as one means of portraying the child who is about to conclude his elementary school experience. According to the data, sixth graders evidence a great deal of variability in their developmental status. Even so, it seems safe to conclude that many children of this age possess an intricate thought mechanism and elaborate study skills; they are in a developmental stage known as preadolescence or adolescence; they are in command of extensive social skills; and they seem to be able to control their emotions more often than not. This account suggests that the sixth-grade child is approaching the threshold of adulthood.

More than 2,500 years ago, Solon wrote, "I grow old learning something new every day." His statement catches the flavor of the child's elementary school experience. It is a most unusual day when a child spends five or six hours in school and fails to encounter a single new facet of knowledge. The impact that this accumulation of knowledge has upon children is dramatically revealed when behavior characteristics of first and sixth graders are compared.

Part Four

THE ELEMENTARY
SCHOOL TEAM

Chapter Eleven

THE NATURE OF
AN ELEMENTARY SCHOOL TEAM

Who comprises the elementary school team? This is a difficult question to answer, because the team differs from one school district to another. One of the writers served as the administrative officer, teacher, clerk, custodian, school psychologist, and health official during his first teaching experience. He was located in a one-room rural school. In contrast, twelve full- and part-time individuals combined forces with the same writer to provide for a group of fourth-grade children in another teaching situation. The elementary school team appears to vary in proportion to a school district's needs and ability to pay for specialization and related services. It is the purpose of this chapter to analyze the team held responsible for providing children with the best possible education.

Homeroom and special-area teachers and a building principal were mentioned in conjunction with Miss Ritter's school. In all probability, there are other individuals who assume some responsibility within Jackson's elementary school operation. Try to identify from among the following list of positions other possible members of the elementary school team in Jackson:

Secretarial staff
Custodian
Dietician and staff
Speech and hearing therapist
School psychologist
Guidance counselor
Assistant principal

Supervisors
School doctor
School dentist
School nurse
Noncertified teaching assistants

Can the reader add any positions to this list? Try to restrict the frame of reference to individuals who spend a considerable portion of their time in the elementary school building itself.

THE INGREDIENTS

The above-mentioned positions can be categorized into three spheres: (1) positions primarily concerned with instruction, (2) positions primarily concerned with the administrative process, and (3) positions primarily concerned with specific services other than teaching or administration. Descriptive data relating to each of these spheres are presented in the following paragraphs for further clarity.

THE INSTRUCTIONAL SPHERE

Homeroom and special-area teachers, some building principals, and some supervisors assume a responsibility for the instructional sphere of the school team. Full-time teachers may deal with a large number of children as a team, they may specialize in teaching one or two disciplines to different groups of children, or they may assume the major responsibility for teaching a single group of children (see Chapter Five). The building principals may have formally assigned teaching responsibilities in addition to their administrative duties, or they may function as instructional leaders in the school without a teaching assignment.

The supervisors' instructional responsibilities are quite varied. In some instances, supervisors focus upon improving instruction in one area of the curriculum—such as art—for a specified number of elementary schools in the district. These supervisors are frequently employed by large school districts. Often, supervisors are identified as instructional leaders specializing in elementary education. Whether supervisors are identified with a particular discipline or the entire elementary school program, they serve as consultants to teachers, as demonstration teachers, as disseminators of instructional materials, and as initiators of program change. Each supervisory situation embodies a few unique characteristics.

These individuals assume the major responsibility for planning, implementing, and revising the instructional program in the elementary school.

THE ADMINISTRATIVE SPHERE

Pupil enrollment probably determines the extent of the school's administrative sphere more than any other factor. A teacher assumes the administrative duties in a one-room rural school. When enough children are enrolled in a school to provide for a number of grade-level groups, one teacher may be designated as the head teacher. His teaching load may or may not be reduced, and his salary may or may not be increased. Or an individual may be hired as the building principal. He may serve as principal of one building or of several buildings in the district. When an elementary school unit houses close to 1,000 children, it is not at all unusual to find an assistant principal serving in a part- or full-time capacity.

Building principals soon discover that as their administrative unit increases in size, administrative problems demand more and more of the time which they previously devoted to instructional leadership in the school.

THE SERVICE SPHERE

Many school districts have become accustomed to providing a number of professional and nonprofessional services in the elementary school. For example, it is not at all unusual to discover a full- or part-time nurse housed in an elementary school. Dentists and doctors are also employed periodically by school districts to examine children in attendance. Guidance counselors, psychologists, and speech and hearing therapists spend increasing amounts of their time working with children in the elementary school. Since these professional services are rather costly, only well-endowed school districts can afford them.

Nonprofessional services are equally vital to the operation of the elementary school. The custodian and the principal's secretary are well-established institutions in the school. In recent years, nonprofessional teaching aides have been used to assist classroom teachers, and food handlers have been employed to provide hot lunches for children in attendance. These are examples of nonprofessional services rendered in many of today's elementary schools.

Instruction, administration, and service are three important dimensions of the elementary school team. The complexity of each of these dimensions in a school district depends upon pupil enrollment, income from taxation, and professional initiative. School districts vary markedly in this respect.

EVOLUTION OF THE TEAM

Today's elementary school team can vary markedly in its size and complexity. This variation is an innovation of the late nineteenth and the twentieth centuries. Before the nineteenth century, team variation was practically nonexistent. What occurred between the time of Washington's presidential inauguration and the present century that changed the status of the elementary school team so drastically? The following paragraphs are directed toward this question. Can the reader recollect some of the developments mentioned in Chapter Six which would bear upon it?

Throughout the seventeenth and eighteenth centuries, the elementary school team usually consisted of a single individual. This individual assumed all the responsibilities that were necessary to provide for the children in school. Such a pattern persisted until a multiroom structure began to appear. Multiroom schools encouraged teachers to divide school responsibilities systematically for the first time in America. (Does the reader remember the reference to the reading and writing schools and the Lancastrian schools?) Multiroom schools proved to be a stepping-stone toward the multigraded elementary school that flourished after the Civil War.

Grouping children in a multigraded school, providing teachers for each of these grades, and keeping records of the children in attendance are very time-consuming tasks. People in authority recognized the necessity of designating an individual to take care of these administrative duties. The building principal evolved out of this need. The individual who served without specified teaching responsibilities as a full-time administrator in the elementary school was quite an exception to the pattern of the late nineteenth century and the early decades of the twentieth century.

After the principal's position was established, a need arose for an individual to operate and maintain the physical plant and an individual to relieve the principal of his clerical obligations and routine tasks. Taxpayers in many communities were quick to recognize that tax dollars were wasted when a high-salaried principal was required to function as a clerk and a custodian. Thus, the custodian and the secretary eventually became a part of many school teams.

The rapid development of teacher training programs in institutions of higher learning during the latter part of the nineteenth century and the twentieth century tremendously affected the nature of the elementary team. These training programs produced teaching specialists. Graduates from these programs tended to specialize in specific areas of education such as science, English, industrial arts, or elementary education. Even the sphere known as elementary education was eventually subdivided into specialties like teaching at the preschool, primary, or intermediate level and teaching children art, music, manual training, or some other curricular area. If the reader surveyed his fellow elementary education majors to determine their teaching plans following graduation, he would very likely discover that the majority intend to specialize at a particular level or within a particular area of elementary education.

Graduate training in education, which has flourished in the present century, has also altered the composition of the elementary team. Many elementary school teachers return to institutions of higher education to pursue advanced degrees. A large percentage of these individuals specialize in administrative and supervisory programs. However, increasing numbers are attracted to programs in school psychology, guidance and counseling, special education and remedial teaching, and speech and hearing therapy. Graduate programs provide numerous specialty people for the elementary team.

The pattern of the elementary team is well defined. As our social order assumes more complex and intricate dimensions, the elementary team expands accordingly. What lies ahead for the elementary team in the light of this pattern? Several Danish schools currently provide fully equipped and staffed dental clinics. In West Germany, many mothers obtained employment to help alleviate a serious labor shortage following the Second World War. A number of West German schools have established elaborate nursery facilities since that time to care for employed parents' children during the working day. In America, some individuals predict that television and programmed instructional materials will significantly alter the role of the classroom teacher. Is it unreasonable to believe that medical services, child care facilities, technological innovations, and other similar developments may influence tomorrow's elementary school team considerably?

AN ANALYSIS OF SEVERAL TEAM POSITIONS

Early in this chapter, a list was made of positions that might be included as a part of an elementary school team. These positions were categorized into instructional, administrative, and service spheres. Two of these positions—the classroom teacher and the elementary principal—have been selected from this list for further analysis at this time. It is the purpose of this section to present data relevant to such questions as:

1. What preparation is necessary to obtain a teaching position or a principalship in the elementary school?
2. How are candidates selected for these positions?
3. What is known about in-service teachers and administrators? Do these individuals represent the best minds in our society? Are they satisfied with their choice of professions?
4. What is meant by certification of teachers?
5. What is the principal's role in the elementary school?

The teacher's position is viewed initially; an analysis of the elementary school principal's position follows.

THE TEACHER

The reader was briefly introduced to his future professional associates, typical classroom assignments, financial returns of teaching, and job prestige in the first chapter of this book. Then an actual classroom situation was detailed to illuminate the functions of the classroom teacher. At this time, additional data are presented to help clarify the concept elementary school teacher in our society.

What Is Required of A Person Who Wishes to Teach? All an individual has to do in the United States to obtain an elementary school teaching position is to convince a local board of education that he is able to handle the job! His qualifications may vary from little if any college training to extensive undergraduate and graduate work in elementary education. His employment or rejection will depend upon the number of applicants a district has on hand, its financial status, location, physical facilities, and community attractions. For example, compare Winnetka, Illinois (a well-endowed suburb of Chicago which is nationally recognized for its outstanding educational program), with West Blueberry Falls (an impoverished school district located in a depleted mining area in a Rocky Mountain state). In which of these communities is an unqualified teacher apt to be located?

The contention that practically anyone can teach in today's elementary schools may be disputed on the grounds that many states establish requirements for teaching. In 1955, these requirements ranged from a college degree in 31 states to less than a year's collegiate preparation in one state. By 1960, the requirement of a bachelor's degree was enforced in 42 states and territories. If the various states did not provide innumerable loopholes for prospective teachers, these requirements would be extremely impressive, but exceptions are made because of teacher shortages and increasing numbers of students enrolled in elementary schools.

Most states provide two types of teaching certificates, standard and substandard. In order to obtain a standard elementary teaching certificate, an individual must meet the specified academic and professional requirements for the state. Academic requirements may vary from about a dozen to more than six dozen semester hours. Professional requirements may range to more than three dozen semester hours. Substandard certificates are issued to unqualified individuals who are the best applicants available for an unstaffed position. These certificates are commonly limited to a single year. Many states permit an individual to renew the certificate yearly. The substandard certificate serves as the major loophole in a state's certification scheme. It not only licenses unqualified persons to teach, but it also perpetuates the existence of inefficient school districts.

Prospective elementary school teachers who qualify for a standard teaching certificate in the state of their choice are in an excellent employment position.

What Factors Influence Teacher Selection? Officials held responsible for hiring new classroom teachers in a district face an imposing task. The complexity of their task stems from the fact that adequate measures for predicting teaching success are nonexistent. Researchers have (1) studied college and practice teaching grades, (2) devised comprehensive written examinations, (3) conducted interviews, and (4) analyzed human behavior in order to derive a predictive vehicle for a hiring official. Their efforts have not been particularly fruitful. Consequently, hiring officials are likely to be influenced by such tangible factors as certification status, previous successful teaching experience, age, personal recommendation, and appearance when they seek individuals for employment.

One of the prime difficulties involved in predicting teaching success relates to a definition of teaching success. How can a successful teacher be identified? Fred Tyler is of the opinion that successful teachers are little less than paragons, if one is to judge from recent discussions and from reports of empirical observations and experimental research dealing with teachers' personalities. He has supported his position as follows:

> One writer lists nineteen desirable qualities, including integrity, maturity, dominance, and diligence. Another investigator catalogues twenty-nine attributes, such as introversion, vitality, punctuality, and persistence. A third researcher tabulates only six traits, but among them is competence in computing with two-digit numbers. A fourth author reports that "speed of tapping" and "right and left hand coordination" (supposedly measures of temperament) distinguish effective from non-effective teachers. Another writer thinks that intelligence is important but maintains that we cannot prove that fact. Effective teachers, one states, are peppy and popular, with pleasing voices. One other example: a teacher should have magnetism, self-control, and enthusiasm. A complete listing would contain a finite number of attributes, but the number seems to be approaching infinity as a limit.[1]

What attributes would the reader assign to a successful teacher? The reader is in good company if he feels inadequate to conjure up such a list, judging from the above quotation.

How Well Trained Are In-Service Teachers? Since substandard teaching certificates are obtainable in most states, is it safe to assume that a large percentage of the elementary teachers in the field do not meet minimum state requirements for the position? Data reported in an April, 1963, *NEA Research Monograph* shed some light on this question. The figures given in Figure 17 appeared in this bulletin. Can the reader draw any conclusions relative to the question raised above from the data presented in Figure 17?

Actually, a relatively small percentage of teachers depend upon a substandard certificate to teach in the elementary school. In 1960,

[1]Reprinted from Fred T. Tyler, "Teachers' Personalities and Teaching Competencies," *School Review*, 68, No. 4 (Winter, 1960), 429, by permission of The University of Chicago Press, publisher. Copyright 1960 by The University of Chicago.

approximately three-fourths of the elementary teachers possessed a bachelor's degree, and nearly one-seventh possessed a master's degree. Even though a number of these degrees were earned in fields other than elementary education, many individuals in such a position qualify for a standard certificate because they complete the necessary

FIGURE 17

HIGHEST COLLEGE DEGREE BY YEARS OF PREPARATION FOR
ELEMENTARY TEACHERS, 1960-61*

Education	Percent of Teachers
No degree	23.8
BA degree, less than 5 years college	50.4
BA degree, 5 or more years college	11.8
MA degree, less than 6 years college	9.7
MA degree, 6 or more years college	4.2
Doctor's degree	0.1

*NEA Staff, "The Public School Teacher, 1960-61," *NEA Research Monograph* (April, 1963). Reprinted with permission.

course work for certification after graduation. Can this statement be substained by the data presented in Figure 17?

Increasing numbers of hiring officials prefer to employ candidates who possess an appropriate bachelor's degree for elementary school positions. Therefore, it seems safe to assume that today's classroom teachers not only are better prepared to teach than their predecessors, but they usually are able to qualify for a standard certificate.

How Intelligent Are Elementary School Teachers? Individuals who choose to teach in the elementary school are frequently stereotyped as shallow thinkers. An eminent American writer once observed that anyone who could enthusiastically teach a group of youngsters how to attach the letter "A" to the letter "B" not once, but 30 or 40 times in the course of a teaching career, certainly appeared to lack some of the more complex mental faculties. The facts contradict his observation. An often-quoted study which was completed in 1953 revealed that over 90 per cent of the in-service teachers ranked in the top 20 per cent of the population in intelligence! These figures indicate that the children of our society are in capable hands.

Are Elementary Teachers A Contented Group? It is quite difficult to obtain appropriate data for this question, because most studies do not distinguish between the specific types of teaching positions. One study concluded that morale was found to be higher among elementary school teachers than among teachers in secondary schools. Little meaning can be attached to this conclusion, however, as baseline figures are not available. Another study which surveyed the attitudes of over 5,000 teachers toward teaching reported that more than three-fourths of the women and nearly two-fifths of the men in the sampling group indicated that they probably would select teaching if they were unexpectedly given a chance to relive their lives. These figures serve as mute testimony to the fact that the rewards of teaching are greater for many individuals than the problems they encounter in the course of a teaching career.

A number of researchers who recognized a need for additional data on teacher behavior attempted to investigate factors that affect the morale of teachers. Their efforts were primarily aimed at determining the relationship between morale and a variety of relevant variables (like personnel policy in the school, administrative behavior, etc.). The inconclusive results reported thus far serve notice that the research methodology employed in these studies may not be appropriate for studying teacher morale. More sophisticated research methods appear to be needed to study this problem.

THE PRINCIPAL

Why should the principal's position be studied as a part of an introductory course? One reason stems from the fact that many undergraduates and in-service teachers do not clearly understand the principal's role in the elementary school. A second reason stems from data reported in studies of human relations in industry. These findings suggest that relationships with an immediate superior directly influence a staff member's attitude toward his work environment. It is for these reasons that the principal's position is analyzed at this time.

What Is the Principal's Role In the Elementary School? Most college texts on elementary school administration indicate that the principal's role is primarily one of educational leadership. This role may be rather difficult to detect if the daily functions of the typical principal are recorded and then analyzed. His day may be devoted to personnel problems in the school, to improving relations with parents, to business and management matters, to special services provided by the school, to supervising instruction, or to any one of several hundred responsibilities that happen to fall within the realm of his office. (One writer recently listed 474 specific responsibilities and duties that are assumed by principals.)

One elementary principal had this to say about his position: "The trouble with my work is that it consists of the interruptions that have nothing to do with my job."[2] His observation pinpoints one of the key frustrations of the elementary principal. Clerical and administrative demands cause the typical principal to sacrifice time devoted to instructional leadership. If a principal allows the clerical and administrative duties to pattern his position, he fails to carry out his leadership responsibility in the school. Then, according to the college texts, he does not fulfill his primary reason for being.

Should the principal function as an instructional leader or as an expediter of clerical and administrative tasks in the elementary school? This question strikes at the heart of a problem every elementary school principal must resolve. His solution determines his role in the school.

How Can an Individual Become an Elementary Principal? Many educators contend that the competence of administrators markedly influences the quality of elementary education. Therefore, it seems logical to assume that elementary principals are well-qualified, highly competent individuals. This is true in many geographical areas of our country. Requirements for principals in these areas include a history of successful teaching in the elementary school, specified graduate training for the position, and some measure of personal stability.

Unfortunately, a number of school districts disregard these practices. Some school districts employ principals who have not been trained in either elementary school teaching or administration. Some districts "reward" individuals who have taught in the elementary school for many years with a principalship—even though these individuals are not trained for the position. Some even take it for granted that an individual can function effectively as a principal while teaching a class full time. In each case, school district personnel disregard the advice of many well-informed educators.

[2]Harold G. Shane, in Chester V. Harris, ed., *Encyclopedia of Educational Research* (3rd ed.; New York: The Macmillan Company, 1960), p. 422.

Even though requirements for the elementary principalship increase yearly, numerous instances of superficial pedagogical thought are apparent when principals are selected.

Is the Elementary Principalship a Respected Position? Job status appears to be related to the requirements established for the principal's position. If any Tom, Dick, or Harry is able to qualify for the principalship, the position lacks status in the school and the community. On the other hand, if well-qualified, intellectually able individuals are attracted to the principalship, the status of the position soars.

About ten years ago, one of the writers taught with an individual who also served as the school's principal. He held this position because he had taught in the district longer than anyone else. Staff members compared his intellect to New England topsoil—thin, but well cultivated. This individual was the victim of much of the staff's humor because of his frequent faux pas in executing his administrative responsibilities. Unfortunately, he was a failure as an instructional leader in the school. In contrast to this individual, the writers worked with two outstanding elementary principals in two other school situations. Each of these individuals commanded staff and community respect. Each functioned as an instructional leader in the school.

The classroom teacher and the elementary principal—two important members of the elementary team—were analyzed in the above paragraphs. Data presented certainly do not begin to touch upon all that is known about these positions. If the reader desires additional information, he can consult the following sources in his local library:

Teacher

1. Department of Classroom Teachers, *Conditions of Work for Quality Teaching* (Washington, D.C.: National Education Association, 1959).
2. David G. Ryans, *Characterisitcs of Teachers* (Washington, D.C.: American Council on Education, 1960).
3. L. J. Stiles, *The Teacher's Role in American Society,* Fourteenth Yearbook of the John Dewey Society (New York: Harper and Brothers, 1957).
4. Willavene Wolf and William C. Wolf, Jr., "Teacher Drop-outs: A Professional Lament," in Anthony C. Riccio and F. R.

Cyphert, eds., *Teaching in America: Selected Readings* (Colombus, Ohio: Charles E. Merrill Books, Inc., 1962).

Principal

1. Gertrude G. Howard, Chairman, *The Elementary School Principalship—A Research Study*, Thirty-Seventh Yearbook of the Department of Elementary School Principals, NEA (Washington, D.C.: The Association, 1958).
2. Project on Instruction Staff, *The Principals Look at the Schools* (Washington, D.C.: National Education Association, 1962).

CONFLICT AND THE ELEMENTARY TEAM

Whenever individuals interact within a power structure, conflict can be expected. The elementary school team is no exception to this implied rule. Since problem situations point up team interaction quite vividly, a series of team conflicts are presented. How would the reader behave as a classroom teacher in each of these situations?

SITUATION ONE

Miss Ritter arranged her children into four reading groups to try out an exploratory pattern developed by the principal, Harry Meyers. Harry believed that four groups enabled the teacher to deal with children's varying abilities most effectively. Ellen Kline, a visiting elementary supervisor, suggested to Miss Ritter that four reading groups are too difficult to handle. She pointed out that face-to-face instruction is considerably reduced when a teacher divides her time among four groups. She preferred two or at the most three reading groups for this reason. How should Miss Ritter react to these varying viewpoints on grouping children for instruction in reading?

SITUATION TWO

Special teachers provide instruction in art, music, and physical education in Harry Meyers' school. Harry arranges a detailed weekly schedule early in the school year, so that all children in the school can profit from these special teachers. As might be expected when special areas are closely scheduled, time infringements occur. Gerhard Gantry, the art teacher, frequently becomes so engrossed in his classroom activities that he fails to note the passage of time. Consequently, he is usually responsible for the failure of the third grade to get to the gym on time for physical education. When he extends his time allocation for the third graders, he also infringes upon the time designated for Miss Ritter's fourth graders. What can Miss Ritter do to sensitize Gerhard to the problem situation he inadvertently creates?

SITUATION THREE

Floyd E. Franklin, the school custodian, has seizures every time the art teacher works with clay. Children invariably spot the floor with clay fragments and glazing materials. After these materials settle on the floor, they are most difficult to remove. After an especially exasperating cleaning session in the art room, Floyd reached the end of his patience. Miss Ritter, the fourth-grade teacher, was the first person Floyd selected to tell his tale of woe. How should Miss Ritter react to Floyd's plight?

SITUATION FOUR

Each year Miss Renault, the third-grade teacher, teaches a unit on pioneer life in America. She exposes children to candle-making, soap-making, building furniture and implements, and so forth by first-hand experiences in the classroom. These projects require sawing, hammering, and other noisy activity, plus considerable pupil movement. The learning experiences are wonderful, she believes, in spite of the associated commotion and odors.

Other teachers in the vicinity of her classroom recognize the value of such concrete experiences, but they are unable to disregard the commotion and odors as easily as Miss Renault. These teachers feel that the third-grade projects disrupt instructional activity in their own classrooms. How should Miss Ritter react to the pioneer study being conducted by her neighboring teacher?

SITUATION FIVE

Emily Danner, the second-grade teacher, has established quite a reputation among the staff in Miss Ritter's school. Emily is not only a gossip and an instigator of school problems, but she can usually be found in the middle of any hassles that occur in the school. Recently, Emily became involved with the fifth- and sixth-grade teachers in a dispute over playground space. She argued that the older boys and girls are too rough on the playground before school and during the lunch recess. Therefore, she asked the principal to section off playground space for each grade level as one means of protecting the younger children. The upper-grade teachers balked at this plan, because they felt it was an unreasonable request. Emily was furious! She informed Miss Ritter of her position on the matter quite vividly one day in the teacher's lounge. How should Miss Ritter react to Emily Danner's condemnation of the fifth- and sixth-grade teachers' ideas?

SITUATION SIX

The multipurpose room in Miss Ritter's school is used primarily as a school library and as a place to view films. The room can be scheduled in advance by signing a reservation sheet in the principal's office. Teachers in the building have learned from experience that the room must be reserved well in advance, because Morton Brahms, the sixth-grade teacher, schedules the room for days at a time. Morton encourages his sixth graders to use varied source materials extensively, so he reserves the library for their study as often as possible.

When Miss Ritter attempted to schedule the room for a film she planned to show in conjunction with a social studies unit, she discovered that Morton had already reserved the room. Not only had he scheduled the room for the time Miss Ritter desired, he had reserved it for the entire week. What courses of action appear to be open to Miss Ritter in this situation?

SITUATION SEVEN

Sally Blank, the speech teacher for the district, is able to visit Miss Ritter's school each Tuesday and Friday from 1:00 until 2:30 P.M. At that time, she attempts to work with children in the school who evidence speech difficulties. She meets these children in small groups or individually in the school's infirmary. A number of children have worked with Mrs. Blank for several months.

Several teachers have expressed the opinion that the children working with Mrs. Blank show little improvement in their speech. Therefore, these teachers argue that the speech lessons may not be as important as the classroom instruction missed by children who take part in Mrs. Blank's program. This topic engaged teachers in heated debate quite frequently during coffee breaks in the faculty lounge. What seems to be a sensible position for Miss Ritter to take on the matter?

275

TOMORROW'S ELEMENTARY SCHOOL TEAM

Contemporary practices in the elementary school are a composite of pioneering ventures of previous decades. Who would have predicted fifty years ago that the majority of elementary school teachers in 1965 would be college graduates? How many individuals in 1870 envisioned an administrative unit called the elementary school with a principal and diversified teaching staff? Or who could have imagined speech and hearing therapists, guidance counselors, school psychologists, and dieticians serving as members of an elementary school team forty or fifty years ago? These developments were not suddenly thrust upon education. Rather, they were part of the gradual evolution of the elementary school in our society.

It is not unreasonable to believe that the evolutionary process will continue between the present and the turn of the next century. If history repeats itself, tomorrow's elementary school team may be an entirely different entity. What new developments in today's pattern may ultimately influence the evolution of tomorrow's team? Clear-cut answers to this question are not available. However, perceptive educators do recognize several familiar but currently unpopular and several pilot practices that may serve as a basis for predicting tomorrow's patterns. A number of developments that may influence the future elementary school team have been mentioned in previous chapters. A few of these ideas plus one new one are amplified in the following paragraphs. As you study each idea, think about the impact it is likely to have upon the team composition.

A Departmentalized Elementary School Team

In North Reading, Massachusetts, the intermediate grades are organized by departments, and all teachers are subject specialists. The rationale for this arrangement is summed up as follows:

> During the 1960-61 school year, a trial of the departmental organization in two schools showed results so encouraging that this year, all four of North Reading's elementary schools are organized in this manner. According to Gregory C. Coffin, formerly superintendent in North Reading and now in Darien, Conn., the method has one tremendous advantage from which many other benefits accrue. As he puts it, "There used to be a time when pupils in elementary science pressed leaves between sheets of waxed paper. They don't do that any more. They watch Cape Canaveral on

television, and they want to know why rockets have to be so big, and what makes them go. In a departmentalized setup, with each teacher a subject specialist, the science teacher knows the answer when such questions are posed. In fact, since she is teaching four or five science classes daily, she not only knows the answers; she is prepared to lecture on the subject.

"Teachers who are subject specialists are encouraged to concentrate on self-training in that subject, too," he says. "They do a more thorough job of instruction. They have the interest and knowledge to lead the children more deeply into a subject. In other words, the specialist is not a jack of all trades. She is a master of one.

"Since any administrator will tell you that he has teachers who are crackerjacks in one or two subject areas," says Coin, "why not utilize their talents? Some teachers love science, for example. They spend their spare time reading all about science. They're experts. So why waste their time and talent by forcing them to teach a subject in which they have no interest?"[3]

Departmentalization, as an administrative structure, is not a new idea. Rather, it has flourished and floundered in quasi-cyclical fashion during the past hundred and fifty years. The North Reading plan represents a resurgence of interest in departmentalization around the country. Do you think the plan described will have much impact upon the elementary team?

SCHOOL CAMPING

Reference was made in Chapter Six to school camping as a potential influence upon tomorrow's elementary school curriculum. While this potential is not apt to become a reality in the perceivable future, there are pilot probes currently under way. For example:

Some schools today, particularly schools in Texas, California, and Michigan, are acting to take certain areas of education out-of-doors. For many years the sixth grades of the Laboratory School at the University of Chicago have, in the spring of the year, spent a week or two in the country, working, playing, and studying together in an informal atmosphere. This kind of camping is developing and should be expanded to include all children eventually. Since the existing facilities for camping lie dormant during most of the year, it

[3]"Are Your Elementary Grades Properly Organized?" *School Management*, 5 (December, 1961), 61. Reprinted with permission from *School Management*, Copyright 1961, School Management Magazines, Inc.

seems reasonable to assume that a wider utilization of the existing facilities by schools, together with a closer relationship between schools and camps, between teachers and counselors, will make it possible for all children to have a better camping experience and make the camping a valuable experience for all concerned.[4]

If the camping idea catches on, well-qualified persons will be needed to staff the camps. Can you envision the varied roles such a person might assume as a member of the elementary team?

TEACHER AIDES

M. J. Greenshields, in an attempt to alleviate some of the growing pains of education, recommended in 1942 the use of helpers in checking seatwork, supervising study and play periods, assisting in projects, doing some drill, and working in many other ways to assist the teacher who had large numbers of pupils assigned to her room. These helpers usually are housewives, college students, retired persons, or high school students. A number of school systems have implemented Greenshields' recommendation since 1942 (reference was made to the Bay City, Michigan, experiment in Part Two of this book).

John Deason summed up written views on this subject in an article entitled "What They Say About Teacher-Aides," which appeared in *The School Executive*. He reviewed several score articles that were published in the professional literature, and derived appropriate conclusions about the use of teacher aides from them. He summed up supportive arguments for the use of teacher aides as follows:

1. The plan is an excellent temporary measure in time of crisis;
2. It provides for enriching the curriculum through the efforts of outside talent;
3. An atmosphere which encourages wholesome personality development is created;
4. There is greater involvement of lay citizens in worthwhile school activities;
5. There seems to be slightly higher achievement on the part of students in classes with aides.

[4]Reprinted from Retha Jane Mason, "Camping—An Extension of Elementary-School Education," *The Elementary School Journal*, 58 (February, 1958), 278, by permission of The University of Chicago Press, publisher. Copyright 1958 by The University of Chicago.

Critical views assumed these forms:

1. Justifying larger classes by using teacher aides constitutes a threat to the welfare of children;
2. There is danger of a return to rote learning and the possibility of a departure from facilitating broad learnings;
3. Not all teachers, even good ones, can work with aides.[5]

Deason predicted that the literature on the subject would increase substantially in the near future, as there would be much more experimentation on providing assistance to classroom teachers.

What form do you think this experimentation might assume? How do you react generally to a scheme that uses nonprofessional aides to justify the continuance of high teacher-pupil ratios in the elementary school? Are you of the opinion that such a plan will strengthen the elementary team?

THE TEACHING INTERN

The state of Arkansas, working in cooperation with the Ford Foundation, initiated a new kind of teacher education curriculum in 1953. The proposed plan substituted for four years of combined general and professional education four years of the former and a fifth year of the latter. The fifth year would combine formal study of education with extensive supervised internship experiences in cooperating public schools.[6] The plan is one of a number of undertakings that employ the concept of a teaching intern.

The duties of a teaching intern may vary from those of typical student teachers to assumption of the actual responsibility for instruction in the classroom. Interns usually receive some remuneration for their services — often in the form of a university stipend or a subsistence wage from the school system — because they frequently become an integral part of their school's team. Interns are supervised by school district and university officials throughout their experience.

Experimentation with the internship concept seems to be gaining momentum in the sixties. Many liberal arts colleges have established pilot programs of this sort in cooperation with neighboring school systems. A number of large multipurpose universities have also ini-

[5]John Deason, "What They Say About Teacher Aides," *The School Executive*, 77 (December, 1957), 59-60.

[6]Richard Colvard, "The College and the 'Arkansas Purchase' Controversy," in M. Miles, ed., *Innovation in Education* (New York: Teachers College, Columbia University, 1964), p. 118.

tiated similar ventures. However, the essence of the role is still being determined.

If you had an opportunity to transfer into an internship program that required five years for certification instead of four, would you take advantage of it?

If one generalized from the ideas presented above, he might conclude that tomorrow's elementary school team will consist of subject matter specialists who are assisted by aides and interns in the classrooms and camps maintained by a school system. Such an outcome would be vehemently criticized by a vast majority of today's professional educators as impractical, if not impossible. What do you think the salient features of their criticism might be? Would you be inclined to defend the essence of the generalization pertaining to the team of the future?

QUESTIONS FOR DISCUSSION

1. Innovation in education has often taken the form of an experimental school. Lancaster, Montessori, Dewey, and Hansen founded schools to demonstrate their educational theories. The essence of the instructional team is markedly influenced by the founder's theoretical beliefs.
a. What factors probably contribute to the initiation of a new educational theory?
b. How does an innovator staff a school that may be a radical departure from current practice?
c. What problems might an innovator encounter in creating such a school? Consider certification, legislated curriculum requirements, and public opinion as a part of your response.

2. Teaching interns at Harvard University enroll in the Harvard-Newton Summer Program, which provides courses in apprentice teaching and study of the teaching of language arts. The interns spend half of the following academic year as full-time graduate students and teach during the other half of the year, while carrying a minimum course schedule. Two interns are employed as a pair to replace one beginning teacher. One intern teaches the first half-year, followed in the next term by the second intern. Interns are paid a salary of $2,100 during the teaching semester. Completion of the plan requires one full calendar year.

a. How might the Harvard plan be compared with other teacher education plans? How does it compare with your program?
b. Do you think parents might become concerned when they learn that an intern, who has studied the discipline of education for one summer session, is about to assume the responsibility for teaching their children?

ADDITIONAL REFERENCES

Educational Leadership. The theme of the December, 1961, issue is "What is Teaching?"; the theme of the November, 1962, issue is "Continuing Growth for the Teacher"; the theme of the February, 1964, issue is "The Staff Works To Improve"; the theme of the December, 1964, issue is "Schools Are People Changing."

Chapter Twelve

PROFESSIONALISM AND
THE ELEMENTARY SCHOOL TEAM

An opportunity was afforded the reader in the previous chapter to analyze the team held responsible for providing elementary school-aged children with the best possible education. This chapter is structured to explore the status of two team positions — those of the teacher and the administrator. Are individuals who hold these positions engaged in a profession, a craft, or a job? Myron Lieberman has noted that the vast bulk of professional writing assumes that education is already a profession.[1] This assumption, he wrote, is seldom questioned or seriously criticized by educators. He set forth his ideas on the status of educators in a more recent publication which includes a chapter entitled "The Myth of a Teaching Profession."[2] Professor Lieberman's views have contributed to considerable controversy with regard to the status of educators and the nature of educational organizations in America.

At present, approximately 2,000,000 individuals are referred to as educators (i.e., teachers, administrators, and specialists) in the United states. Of this number, approximately 800,000 are affiliated with the National Education Association and 80,000 with the American Federation of Teachers at the national level. These figures raise a soul-searching question, namely, can less than 50 per cent of the educators be counted upon to advance their professional position in America?

[1]Myron Lieberman, *Education as a Profession* (Englewood Cliffs, N.J.: Prentice-Hall, Inc., 1956), p. vii.

[2]Myron Lieberman, *The Future of Public Education* (Chicago: The University of Chicago Press, 1960), Chapter 5.

Or, to put it another way, do large numbers of educators fail to participate actively in undertakings designed to upgrade the educator in our society?

A surface analysis of the data presented in the above paragraph might lead the reader to conclude that Lieberman's position — that the teaching profession, as we know it, is a myth — has some validity. Few would deny that the apathy of a significant segment of today's educators is a crucial contemporary problem. However, the data also indicate that nearly half of the educators in our country have joined together in an attempt to improve the lot of teachers, administrators, and other educational specialists.

The following sections of this chapter are structured to acquaint the reader with information that contributes to a better understanding of the educator's status in our society.

WHY MIGHT ELEMENTARY TEAM MEMBERS DESIRE PROFESSIONAL STATUS?

Generally speaking, educators are not well paid for their service to society, they often work in drab environments, and they frequently complain that available instructional materials are not adequate to provide for children effectively. Nevertheless, these job limitations do not prevent innumerable individuals from choosing education as their life's work. Many who choose education as a career seem to be motivated by its service aspect. These individuals appear to derive satisfaction from the stamp of approval that society places upon their work.

Opinion pollsters who have researched the question of teacher prestige in our society have reported that teachers enjoy considerable prestige in America. As a matter of fact, their surveys reveal that the level of prestige is actually increasing. So long as teachers receive such recognition, they probably will be satisfied with the salary offered for their service.

Since job satisfaction and prestige play an important role in attracting individuals into education, it does not seem unreasonable to believe that educators would prefer to identify with such groups as medical doctors, lawyers, and dentists than with truck drivers, sales clerks, and plumbers. The former positions enjoy considerable prestige in our society. It is probably for this reason that educators refer to themselves as professionals in their publications.

Professional Activities. The National Education Association is one of several associations which have undertaken the tremendous task of organizing and representing America's teachers. The NEA headquarters building in Washington, D.C., and an Executive Committee meeting of one of the organizations affiliated with the NEA are depicted in the pictures. Have you any views on how this or any association might effectively serve educators at the local, state, and national levels?

284

Courtesy Carl Purcell, NEA

Many individuals with a liberal arts orientation view "education-ists" as craftsmen. Some have meticulously spelled out their position in speeches and publications in recent years (see Chapter One). Obviously, the status of American educators has not been enhanced by these viewpoints.

The educator's role in our society is currently a highly contro-versial topic. The controversy revolves around whether educators should be classified as professionals, craftsmen, or job-holders. This problem seems to be approachable. For example, by first examining the characteristics of a profession, and then evaluating education within the framework of these criteria, it is not unreasonable to believe that some salient aspects of the controversy can be resolved. Such an examination is carried out in the following manner.

PROFESSIONAL CRITERIA

What makes a profession a profession? Paul Woodring believed the following to be most appropriate when distinguishing between professions and other vocations:

1. A profession requires a deep commitment on the part of its members — a motivation that goes far beyond the mere desire for pecuniary gain.
2. A profession, unlike a skilled trade, clerical occupation, or business, rests upon an organized body of scholarly or scientific knowledge.
3. A profession requires careful selection of its members and an extended period of advanced education of a kind best provided in a college or university.[3]

Other writers include different factors in their description of a profes-sion. The authors of this text compiled a list of 25 distinct characteris-tics as a result of a survey of six representative publications on the topic. This survey barely touched the surface of the available litera-ture on professionalism.

A number of the listed characteristics seemed to be equally appropriate for describing a craftsman or a job-holder. For example, one writer included self-improvement on his list of characteristics of a profession. This seems equally appropriate for describing a cabinet-maker, real estate salesman, or a golf caddy. Individuals who hold

[3]Paul Woodring, "Teaching: A Unique Profession," *California Teachers Association Journal*, 56 (March, 1960), 10. Reprinted with permission.

these positions are seldom considered to be professionals. Consequently, the list of 25 professional characteristics can probably be greatly condensed.

Which of the following characteristics could justifiably be added to Woodring's criteria for distinguishing a profession from other vocations?

1. A clear-cut code of ethics
2. Licensing standards
3. Job security
4. Personal responsibility for performance
5. Autonomy for both the group and its practitioners
6. Close supervision of the practitioners

One or two of these characteristics are rather controversial. Therefore, it is conceivable that an impressive case can be presented both for and against the inclusion of these statements as a part of a description of a profession.

The reader is encouraged to study carefully Woodring's list of distinguishing characteristics of a profession and to extend it in the light of new knowledge that he may have acquired. A clear-cut view of a professional criterion can be the result of his efforts.

PROFESSIONAL STATUS

Once distinguishing characteristics of a profession are clearly prescribed, it is possible to focus upon the professional practitioner. Why do medical doctors and lawyers enjoy more status in our society than plumbers and truck drivers? T. M. Stinnett believes that professional status is born within each member of a professional group as a result of a constellation of attributes. That is, professionals owe their status to the following:

> . . . knowledge of extraordinary competence in consequence of sustained and scholarly preparation; an inner sense of dedication to an important service to society; a serenity of spirit arising from the joy of helping others; a sense of security which is the logical concomitant of possessing competences and knowledges which others do not possess.[4]

The reader can easily subject Stinnett's attributes to a test to determine whether they adequately account for the current status of

[4]T. M. Stinnett, "Professional Status: A Concomitant," *Teachers College Record*, 59 (October, 1957), 53. Reprinted with permission.

professional practitioners in America. Do these attributes apply only to professionals, or do they also describe cabinetmakers, plumbers, and truck drivers? A criterion of this nature must reveal concrete reasons why doctors and lawyers enjoy more social status than other vocational groups. If the criterion does not serve in this manner, then other variables need to be investigated.

The following publications will assist those who desire to pursue the problem further:

1. Articles by D. Ezell Stites, William F. Russell, W. Earl Armstrong, G. Howard Goold, and T. M. Stinnett in the section entitled "A Look at the Teaching Profession," *The School Executive*, 74 (November, 1954), 67-80.
2. Harry S. Broudy, "Teaching—Craft or Profession?" *The Educational Forum*, 20 (January, 1956), 175-184.
3. Morris L. Cogan, "Toward a Definition of Profession," *Harvard Education Review*, 23 (Winter, 1953), 33-50.
4. Albert J. Huggett and T. M. Stinnett, *Professional Problems of Teachers* (New York: The Macmillan Company, 1961).
5. B. G. Leighbody, "What Makes a Professional, Professional?" *The Phi Delta Kappan*, 34 (April, 1953), 295.
6. Myron Lieberman, *Education as a Profession* (Englewood Cliffs, N.J.: Prentice-Hall, Inc., 1956).
7. Catlin E. Tyler, "Is Teaching a Profession, Craft, or Job?" *Virginia Journal of Education*, 53 (October, 1959), 11-15.

A clear-cut account of status factors that distinguish professionals from other members of vocations can serve as a point of departure for educators who desire to identify with professionals. Educators are in a much better position to plan for the future when they possess this kind of information.

ARE ELEMENTARY TEAM MEMBERS PROFESSIONALS?

The positions of two team members—the teacher and the administrator—are the foci of attention in this chapter. In this section, these team positions are viewed within the framework of generally agreed-upon professional criteria to ascertain whether they are worthy of professional status. The analysis focuses upon Joan Ritter, a teacher, and Harry Meyers, a principal. Joan's and Harry's initial interest in education serves as the point of departure for the analysis.

THE TEACHER

Membership in a high school Future Teachers of America chapter proved to be a valuable experience for Joan Ritter. The organization afforded her opportunities to visit classrooms, to hear authorities speak on educational matters, and to associate with students interested in pursuing a teaching career. FTA membership helped Joan to decide upon teaching as her life's work.

Joan entered the state university so that she could enroll in a teacher education program. At State, she declared a major in elementary education. The program in elementary education consisted of a series of required and elective courses in the College of Education. In order to remain eligible for the program, she needed to maintain acceptable university grades and normal mental and physical health. A teaching certificate is awarded students who successfully complete the requirements of the program.

This teacher education program was recently evaluated by NCATE (National Council for Accreditation of Teacher Education), an independent accrediting agent sponsored by the National Education Association. NCATE is one of several accrediting bodies that evaluate teacher education programs offered by colleges and universities. While these organizations enable educators to police their own efforts to educate teachers in America, they do not have the authority to force institutions which maintain an inferior program to discontinue this type of operation.

After graduation, Joan contracted to teach in a township elementary school near her home community. She rationalized that the low cost of living in the area compensated for her low beginning salary. Joan soon discovered that the low salaries paid by the district did not attract many qualified teachers. Nearly two-thirds of her staff associates held a substandard teaching certificate which required yearly renewal. Individuals who qualified for a standard teaching certificate were the exception rather than the rule in the district.

Joan affiliated with state and national education associations in the early part of her first year of teaching. These organizations kept her up to date on teaching developments via publications, conferences, institutes, and other meetings. Through these organizations, Joan also had a voice in the formulation of state and national legislation which affected education. Joan was amazed when she discovered that many of her teaching associates did not affiliate with any educational organizations.

Joan resigned her teaching position in the township after two years in order to move closer to an urban area. She was able to obtain a teaching position in a suburban school system adjacent to a sizable city. Joan soon discovered that the new school situation was quite different from her initial experience. Nearly all of her staff associates held standard teaching certificates, they actively engaged in functions of a variety of educational associations, and many of them pursued advanced degrees on a part-time basis at a nearby university. It did not seem possible to Joan that two school districts could be so different.

THE PRINCIPAL

Harry Meyers' motivation to become a teacher and his undergraduate preparation parallel those of Joan Ritter. After teaching fourth-, fifth-, and sixth-grade children for three years in a small community, he moved to a teaching position in a university community. While he served as a fifth-grade teacher in this situation, he took course work at the university on a part-time basis. Upon completion of the requirements for a master's degree in elementary school administration, he submitted his application for a principalship in the district. Since he qualified for a state principal's certificate and possessed an extensive background of classroom teaching experience in the elementary school, he was well equipped to fill any vacancy that might occur. Harry did not wait long before he was appointed to a principalship in the district.

Harry readily adapted to the duties normally carried out by a principal. He also got a better perspective on his position through attendance at meetings of elementary school principals. Participation in these meetings sensitized him to the fact that many inequalities exist among individuals holding elementary principals' positions. While many individuals Harry met were highly trained and capable of performing as excellent school leaders, many others could not be similarly characterized. These individuals either were unable to qualify for a principal's certificate because they lacked the necessary course work, or they had never taught in an elementary classroom. Harry had difficulty in understanding why there should be so much variance in the training and professional characteristics of elementary principals.

A FRAMEWORK FOR ANALYSIS

The reader has previously been made aware of elements that constitute a professional definition. At that time, he was encouraged to study various views of professionalism as one means of clarifying the concept to his satisfaction. Among the generally agreed-upon professional criteria which he probably uncovered are the following: (1) service, (2) recruitment, (3) admission and certification standards, (4) accreditation of training programs, (5) organization, (6) research, (7) autonomy, and (8) a code of ethics. These elements will serve as the frame of reference for determining whether the teacher and the principal on the elementary team merit professional recognition.

The previous descriptions of Joan Ritter's and Harry Meyers' orientation to education and their educational experiences function as a source of data for the following analysis.

1. Service: Teachers perform a vital service to society. Few individuals are apt to challenge this statement.
2. Recruitment: Through Future Teachers of America chapters in high schools and through extensive advertising promotion, educators strive to make teaching appealing to promising young men and women. At the college and university level, numerous educational organizations serve the needs of students who major in education. Educators have accepted the responsibility for attracting capable individuals.
3. Admission and Certification Standards: Satisfactory grades and normal mental and physical health were the requirements prescribed by the college of education which Joan Ritter attended. Few education programs specify more rigid requirements than these for admission and good standing. It is conceivable, then, that any student who is in good standing in a college or university is eligible for the teacher education program.

    Students who complete an education program in an institution of higher learning usually qualify for a state teaching certificate. One might infer from this statement that all in-service teachers possess a valid certificate to teach. Unfortunately, this is not the case. Many in-service elementary school teachers have not completed a college program, or their college experience was not related to elementary education. These individuals do not meet the requirements for a standard teaching certificate. Thus, many unqualified individuals are currently teaching children in American elementary schools.

4. Accreditation: It was pointed out in the previous description that several accrediting bodies do exist to evaluate teacher education programs in institutions of higher learning. At present, these groups do not have the power to curtail or eliminate inferior programs that are offered by a college or university. Their function has been more or less advisory to date.

5. Organization: The introductory subsection of this chapter contained data indicating that slightly less than half of the in-service educators are affiliated with a national association. State and local associations on the average attract a higher percentage of the active educators. These organizations have historically performed lobbying services at the state and national levels, disseminated pertinent literature, sponsored a variety of meetings, and engaged in collective bargaining for educators. Recently, one of the major associations has taken a major step toward implementing ideas held on teacher education and teaching standards. While these state and national associations currently contribute significantly to the development of education, they do not influence the course of education as markedly as the American Medical Association influences medicine or as bar associations influence law.

6. Research: It has been estimated that approximately one-half of 1 per cent of the money spent on education each year is budgeted for research purposes. When this figure is compared with the 3 to 8 per cent of gross income that is allocated for research by many public and private enterprises engaged in commerce and industry, it is not a very impressive figure. The actual sum of money is impressive, however, if one considers that approximately fifteen to eighteen billion dollars are spent for educational purposes yearly in America.

7. Autonomy: The 50 states each assume the responsibility for education within their geographical boundaries. State boards of education usually are appointed to execute the mandate of education within a state. This board in turn delegates responsibility to numerous local boards of education. Educators seldom are elected or appointed to positions on these boards. Among the responsibilities discharged by local and state boards are the following: (1) appointing local and state superintendents, other administrators and specialists, and classroom teachers; (2) allocating funds for the operation and maintenance of school

systems; (3) approving the pedagogical direction for school systems; and (4) influencing legislation that pertains to education. This paragraph emphasizes one of the major problems confronting educators today: that is, educators lack the machinery to guide their own destiny.

8. A Code of Ethics: Several statements of a code of ethics for educators exist. Since these statements have not been widely accepted or enforced, to all intents and purposes educators go about their daily business without the guidance of a clearly defined code.

Now, do educators merit professional status, or are their functions more closely related to those of craftsmen and job-holders? Relevant factors that constitute professionalism were reviewed in the above paragraphs. Positions held by Joan Ritter and Harry Meyers were then analyzed in the light of these factors. The reader, after considering all the variables presented above, appears to be in an excellent position to take a stand on the status of Joan and Harry. Furthermore, it is not unreasonable to believe that the stand taken on these educators is also applicable to educators in general. Where do educators stand in your eyes?

TOWARD PROFESSIONALISM

Since most educators accept the thesis that education ought to be a profession, it is important to know what is being done to further this viewpoint. T. M. Stinnett, a past Executive Secretary of the National Commission on Teacher Education and Professional Standards, stated that teachers are now realistically facing up to the proposition that they will have unqualified professional status only to the extent that they create it themselves. This means, he pointed out, self-determination and self-regulation of the profession by its members.[5] Two distinctly different ways of attaining such an end have emerged in recent years. These alternate courses of action are examined in the following paragraphs.

Some educators have utilized procedures traditionally associated with the American labor union to bring about an educational profession. The American Federation of Teachers, affiliated with the AFL-CIO, has organized groups of teachers, served as their bargaining agent, and employed the strike when needed to further the ends of

[5]*Op. cit.*, p. 52.

teachers. The AFT was organized to improve working conditions for the classroom teacher as quickly and judiciously as possible. The necessity of an AFT affiliation with the powerful AFL-CIO is not clearly understood by the writers.

The AFT can point to a series of benefits won for teachers as a result of strikes or the threat of a strike in specific communities. A successful strike is described in the following newspaper clipping:

NEW YORK CITY GETS MONEY
TO INCREASE TEACHERS' PAY[6]

NEW YORK (AP)—The state's Republican governor and the city's Democratic mayor huddled for 3 1/2 hours here Thursday night and came up with a formula that will give city schools an additional $13 million and possibly permit final settlement of the dispute that led to a one-day teachers' strike.

The strike by the United Federation of Teachers (AFL-CIO) was called off Thursday following a court order.

Charles Cogen, president of the union, said that with the additional funds "we think we can go back and negotiate."

The formula by which the state gives aid to city schools has been a bone of contention between Gov. Nelson A. Rockefeller and Mayor Robert F. Wagner, with Wagner charging the state had "short-changed" the city, and Rockefeller calling Wagner a "buck-passer."

Caught in the middle, the board of education said it could not possibly offer the city's teachers more than a total of $28 million in raises for the next fiscal year.

The UFT, demanding $53 million—but in no case less than $33.8 million—called the strike.

The walkout crippled the city's 900 schools, closing some of them, and disrupting classes for their one million pupils.

The conference attended by Rockefeller and Wagner, along with city, state, school and teacher officials, was the first known meeting between the two men on the issue.

It was held in Rockefeller's Manhattan office and ended with a joint statement by the two men.

Their agreement enables the city to borrow the $48.6 million it needs for current school operations from the $62 million it is to receive next September.

After the city repays the $48.6 in September, it will have $13.4 million—less interest charges. It will then keep borrowing from year to year, under a plan of deferred payment.

---

[6]From the *Columbus Dispatch*, April 13, 1962, p. 4A. Reprinted with permission.

Without doubt, results obtained by this procedure are quite tangible. Nevertheless, vast numbers of educators do not choose to identify with this method of attaining professional status. It is probably for this reason that the AFT has not been a highly influential educational organization to date.

For every educator who has identified with the AFT cause, ten have identified with the principles of the National Education Association. The NEA has adhered to a principle of gradualism, in contrast to the AFT principle of action, as the most appropriate method of professionalizing education. Over the years, the NEA has attempted to improve the teacher's position by disseminating pertinent information, by lobbying in the state and national legislatures, and by prescribing conditions of work for quality teaching.

These efforts have been criticized by some educators as being too nondirective. The NEA, they argue, has not been nearly as vigorous in serving classroom teachers as other professional organizations have been in serving their constituents. Indeed, the NEA usually is unable to point to a specific salary increase or improved working conditions as a fruit of its labor. It is probably for this reason that the NEA has recently undertaken an aggressive "New Horizons" program as one means of professionalizing education, and it has resorted to sanctions as a punitive measure.

Additional information can be obtained from the following publications:

1. B. J. Chandler, "What It Takes to Professionalize Teaching," *School Executive,* 77 (December, 1957), 48-49.
2. Louis Fischer, "A Profession Without Members?" *The Journal of Teacher Education,* 12 (June, 1961), 139-142.
3. Burton W. Gorman, "The Teaching Profession Tomorrow," *School and Society,* 82 (October 29, 1955), 130-132.
4. Neal Gross, *Who Runs Our Schools?* (New York: John Wiley & Sons, Inc., 1958).
5. Vernon Hicks, "To What Degree Is This a Profession?" *Michigan Education Journal,* 38 (April, 1961), 378-379.
6. Myron Lieberman, "Teachers Strikes: An Analysis of the Issues," *Harvard Education Review,* 26 (Winter, 1956), 39-70.
7. Margaret Lindsey, ed., *New Horizons for the Teaching Profession* (Washington, D.C.: National Commission on Teacher Education and Professional Standards [NEA], 1961).
8. Benjamin Solomon, "A Profession Taken for Granted," *The School Review,* 69 (Fall, 1961), 286-299.

9. Willavene Wolf and William Wolf, "Professional Teamwork Contributes to Professional Education," *Peabody Journal of Education*, 39 (November, 1961), 138-143.

Where does the responsibility for leadership of American education lie? While educators prefer to believe that leadership is their responsibility, this view is not supported by all the facts. For example, the purse strings of education are controlled by noneducators, licensing standards are usually prescribed by noneducators, and in recent years curriculum changes have been championed by noneducators. Some writers contend that the major responsibility for leadership of education is rapidly passing out of the hands of educators.

Recent developments in education do not lend support to this contention. Organizations representing educators have become more aggressive in stating their respective cases for autonomy. Both the American Federation of Teachers, by using collective bargaining techniques, and the National Education Association, by championing a "New Horizons" program and by using sanctions, intend to exercise a stronger leadership role in matters of education. Even though the means vary, the aim of these organizations appears to be true professional status for pedagogical practitioners.

Several major victories must be won before one or both of these organizations can enjoy the fruits of their labor. First and foremost, neither organization can function effectively when vast numbers of educators prefer not to affiliate with a national organization. Therefore, an aggressive campaign to organize these practitioners needs to be undertaken. Second, little can be done to raise standards in education until educators become an autonomous group. Once this goal is attained, substandard teaching licenses can be eliminated. Third, influential accrediting bodies are needed to assess the quality of existing teacher training programs periodically. These bodies can markedly influence the caliber of education colleges in America. Victories of this nature can be realized—indeed, must be realized—if educators intend to influence the direction of education in our country.

QUESTIONS FOR DISCUSSION

1. Dennis Dean is in the process of completing his preservice experience before graduation from his state's university. Presently, he is a junior majoring in elementary education and has approximately one and one-half years remaining before he can become a member of

the professional teaching force. As a result of his professional experiences, he has raised several questions that are quite thought-provoking. How might an education professor respond to the questions posed by Mr. Dean?

a. What are some positive steps taken in the last ten years by the teaching profession to improve classroom instruction?

b. What is the relationship between professional education and classroom effectiveness?

c. How effective are local communities in bringing about professional teaching conditions?

2. Schoolteachers—once regarded as "underachievers" in the labor movement—are beginning to feel their oats in collective bargaining. According to a University of Chicago researcher, "The spring of 1965 has been the most turbulent period the nation has ever seen in the increasingly militant and aggressive drive of public school teachers for control over the conditions under which they will teach."

a. What do you think this aggressiveness might accomplish?

b. How active would you become in the "militant and aggressive drive" to improve conditions of employment?

ADDITIONAL REFERENCES

Becker, Harold S., "The Nature of a Profession," in Nelson B. Henry, ed., *Education for the Professions*, The Sixty-First Yearbook of the National Society for the Study of Education, Part II. Chicago: The University of Chicago Press, 1962. Pp. 27-46.

Callahan, Raymond E., *An Introduction to Education in American Society.* New York: Alfred A. Knopf, Inc., 1960. Chapter 18.

Lindsey, Margaret, ed., *New Horizons for the Teaching Profession.* Washington, D.C.: National Commission on Teacher Education and Professional Standards (NEA), 1961. 243 pp.

National Commission on Teacher Education and Professional Standards, *The Education of Teachers: New Perspectives*, Report of the Second Bowling Green Conference. Washington, D.C.: National Education Association, 1958. 399 pp.

National Commission on Teacher Education and Professional Standards, *A Position Paper on Teacher Education and Professional Standards.* Washington, D.C.: National Education Association, 1963. 33 pp.

SUMMARY: PART IV

Today, relatively few individuals assume sole responsibility for educating children in our society. Rather, as our society assumes more complex dimensions, so does the elementary school structure. This structure, in order to operate effectively, demands individuals with specialized training. Hence, a team of educators usually assumes the responsibility for educating children in today's elementary schools.

The typical elementary school demands individuals who can work together effectively to provide the best possible education for children. These individuals must not only be skilled in their own specialty, but they must also understand the nature of other team members' responsibilities in the school. Such understanding is conducive to cooperation and harmony within the team.

In Chapter Eleven, the ingredients of the team, how it evolved, an analysis of several team positions, conflict within the team, and tomorrow's elementary school team were treated. Chapter Twelve was structured to explore the status of two team positions—the teacher's and the administrator's. A framework for analyzing elements that constitute a professional definition was offered to assess the status of these two positions. The chapter was culminated by an account of directions that might affect the professional status of educators.

APPENDIX

Since a book of this nature would not be complete without a section pertaining to organizations and journals of interest to elementary educators, both of these areas are developed in this Appendix. An attempt has been made to compile representative lists of organizations and journals that are geared toward elementary education. The prime function of these lists is to inform the reader of the types and varieties of organizations and journals that are available in the United States.

Once the reader takes a teaching position, he will have many opportunities to identify with various educational organizations and to subscribe to a whole host of educational publications. One way to avoid on-the-job trial and error samplings of this sort is to become acquainted with these dimensions of education during a period of study at a college or university. The student who spends a few afternoons in the school's library can obtain valuable insight into the nature, scope, and quality of many of the educational publications listed. Conversations with fellow students and instructors can also shed additional light on the caliber of organizations that capture the student's interest. Time spent in this manner might ultimately benefit the student through in-service contacts and experiences at meetings of the chosen organizations and through new ideas and procedures that might be derived from selected publications.

ORGANIZATIONS OF INTEREST
TO ELEMENTARY EDUCATORS

1. American Association for Gifted Children, Inc.
   15 Gramercy Park
   New York 3, New York

2. American Council on Education
   1785 Massachusetts Avenue, N.W.
   Washington 6, D.C.
3. American Federation of Teachers
   28 E. Jackson Boulevard
   Chicago 4, Illinois
4. American Teachers Association
   Executive Secretary — H. Councill Trenholm
   Box 271
   Montgomery, Alabama
5. Association for Childhood Education International
   1200 15th Street, N.W.
   Washington 5, D.C.
6. Association of Educators of Gifted Children
   School of Education
   University of Pennsylvania
   Philadelphia 4, Pennsylvania
7. Associated Public School Systems
   525 W. 120th Street
   New York 27, New York
8. Association for Student Teaching
   Iowa State College
   Cedar Falls, Iowa
9. Association for Supervision and Curriculum Development (NEA)
   1201 16th Street, N.W.
   Washington 6, D.C.
10. Child Study Association of America, Inc.
    132 E. 74th Street
    New York 21, New York
11. Children's Library Association
    50 E. Huron Street
    Chicago 11, Illinois
12. Council for Basic Education, Inc.
    208 Union Trust Building
    Washington 5, D.C.
13. Council for Exceptional Children (NEA)
    1201 16th Street, N.W.
    Washington 6, D.C.
14. Council on Cooperation in Teacher Education of the American

Council on Education
1785 Massachusetts Avenue, N.W.
Washington 6, D.C.

15. Department of Classroom Teachers (NEA)
    1201 16th Street, N.W.
    Washington 6, D.C.

16. Department of Elementary School Principals (NEA)
    1201 16th Street, N.W.
    Washington 6, D.C.

17. Department of Kindergarten-Primary Education (NEA)
    1201 16th Street, N.W.
    Washington 6, D.C.

18. International Reading Association
    5835 Kimbark Avenue
    Chicago 37, Illinois

19. Kappa Delta Pi
    East Lafayette, Indiana

20. Kappa Phi Kappa
    McGuffey Hall
    Miami University
    Oxford, Ohio

21. National Association for Gifted Children (The)
    409 Clinton Springs
    Cincinnati 17, Ohio

22. National Association for Nursery Education
    155 E. Ohio Street, Room 200
    Chicago 11, Illinois

23. National Association for Retarded Children, Inc.
    99 University Place
    New York 3, New York

24. National Congress of Parents and Teachers
    700 N. Rush Street
    Chicago 11, Illinois

25. National Council for the Social Studies (NEA)
    1201 16th Street, N.W.
    Washington 6, D.C.

26. National Council of Teachers of Mathematics (NEA)
    1201 16th Street, N.W.
    Washington 6, D.C.

27. National Education Association of the United States
    1201 16th Street, N.W.
    Washington 6, D.C.
28. National Kindergarten Association
    8 W. 40th Street
    New York 18, New York
29. National Science Teachers' Association (NEA)
    1201 16th Street, N.W.
    Washington 6, D.C.
30. Phi Delta Kappa
    Eighth Street and Union Avenue
    Bloomington, Indiana
31. Phi Lambda Theta
    1129 Vermont Avenue, N.W.
    Washington 5, D.C.

JOURNALS OF INTEREST
TO ELEMENTARY EDUCATORS

1. *American Childhood*
    Milton Bradley Co.
    74 Park Street
    Springfield 2, Massachusetts
2. *Child Development*
    Society for Research in Child Development
    Purdue University
    Lafayette, Indiana
3. *Child Development Abstracts and Bibliography*
    Society for Research in Child Development
    Purdue University
    Lafayette, Indiana
4. *Child Family Digest*
    5320 Danneel Street
    New Orleans 15, Louisiana
5. *Child Life*
    W. S. Hawkes
    30 Federal Street
    Boston 10, Massachusetts
6. *Child Study*
    Child Study Association of America, Inc.

132 E. 74th Street
New York 21, New York
7. *Childhood Education*
Association for Childhood Education International
1200 15th Street, N.W.
Washington 5, D.C.
8. *Children*
Interprofessional Journal published by the Children's Bureau,
U.S. Department of Health, Education, and Welfare
Superintendent of Documents
Washington 25, D.C.
9. *Children's Activities*
Child Training Association
111 S. Wabash Avenue
Chicago 5, Illinois
10. *Children's Digest*
Parent's Magazine Publishers, Inc.
52 Vanderbilt Avenue
New York 17, New York
11. *Educational Leadership*
Association for Supervision and Curriculum Development
(NEA)
1201 16th Street, N.W.
Washington 6, D.C.
12. *Elementary English*
National Council of Teachers of English
704 S. 6th Street
Champaign, Illinois
13. *Elementary Leader (The)*
Ohio Department of Elementary School Principals
213 E. Broad Street
Columbus 15, Ohio
14. *Elementary School Journal*
The University of Chicago Press
5750 Ellis Avenue
Chicago 37, Illinois
15. *Exceptional Children*
Journal of the Council for Exceptional Children (NEA)
1201 16th Street, N.W.
Washington 6, D.C.

16. *Grade Teacher*
    The Educational Publishing Corp.
    Darien, Connecticut
17. *Instructor (The)*
    F. A. Owen Publishing Corp.
    Instructor Park
    Dansville, New York
18. *Journal of Exceptional Children*
    International Council for Exceptional Children
    Ypsilanti, Michigan
19. *Keeping Up With Early Education*
    Kindergarten-Primary Education Department (NEA)
    1201 16th Street, N.W.
    Washington 6, D.C.
20. *Look and Listen*
    33 W. 42nd Street
    New York 36, New York
21. *National Elementary Principal*
    Magazine of the Department of Elementary School Principals
    (NEA)
    1201 16th Street, N.W.
    Washington 6, D.C.
22. *National Parent-Teacher*
    The PTA Magazine
    Editorial and Subscription Offices
    700 N. Rush Street
    Chicago 11, Illinois
23. *News Bulletin for Classroom Teachers*
    Department of Classroom Teachers (NEA)
    1201 16th Street, N.W.
    Washington 6, D.C.
24. *Newstime*
    A scholastic magazine for middle grades (4-6)
    Scholastic Magazines
    33 W. 42nd Street
    New York 36, New York
25. *Parent's Magazine*
    52 Vanderbilt Avenue
    New York 17, New York
26. *Reading Teacher*

International Reading Association
5835 Kimbark Avenue
Chicago 37, Illinois
27. *Research Relating to Children*
Clearinghouse for Research in Child Life
Children's Bureau
U.S. Department of Health, Education, and Welfare
Washington 25, D.C.
28. *School Life*
U.S. Office of Education
Washington 25, D.C.
29. *Theory Into Practice*
196 Arps Hall
The Ohio State University
Columbus 10, Ohio
30. *Today's Child*
"2 to 5" World Inc.
1225 Broadway
New York 1, New York
31. *Understanding the Child*
Box 810
Chapel Hill, North Carolina

INDEX

PRINTED IN U.S.A.